TRIED & TRUE
OBJECT DEVELOPMENT

Managing Object Technology Series

Additional Volumes in Preparation

TRIED & TRUE
OBJECT DEVELOPMENT
Practical Approaches with UML

Ari Jaaksi
Juha-Markus Aalto
Ari Aalto
Kimmo Vättö

CAMBRIDGE
UNIVERSITY PRESS

SIGS
BOOKS

PUBLISHED BY THE PRESS SYNDICATE OF THE UNIVERSITY OF CAMBRIDGE
The Pitt Building, Trumpington Street, Cambridge CB2 1RP, United Kingdom

CAMBRIDGE UNIVERSITY PRESS
The Edinburgh Building, Cambridge CB2 2RU, UK
http: //www.cup.cam.ac.uk
40 West 20th Streeet, New York, NY 10011-4211, USA
http: //www.cup.org
10 Stamford Road, Oakleigh, Melbourne 3166, Australia

Published in association with SIGS Books

First published in 1999

Design and composition by Susan A. Ahlquist

Cover design by Yin Moy and Tom Jezek

Printed in the United States of America

A catalog record for this book is available from the British Library

Library of Congress Cataloging-in-Publication Data is on record with the publisher.

ISBN 0-521-64530-1 paperback

TABLE OF CONTENTS

Foreword

This is a great book about using object technology. Like all the new books in this area, it uses the Unified Modeling Language (UML), which is the standard notation for expressing object-oriented designs. For me, however, *Tried & True Object Development* really stands out from the recent flood of books on UML. Why? Because, this book is about the realities of object-oriented software engineering written from a position of authority. That authority is based on the authors' many years of experience developing complex software in Nokia, one of the world's most successful hi-tech corporations. The authors know the secrets of successful object-oriented development from the inside.

However, this book is much more than an experience report, it is truly about how to engineer software. Thus, unlike many other books, it is not written from the perspective of the single engineer working on a small new application. Instead it focuses on how real-world teams, large and small, can use UML and object-oriented methodology. It covers all the phases of software development from requirements through testing. It shows how the fundamental techniques for each of these phases can be molded into an incremental evolutionary life-cycle that can deal with project risk.

Real projects have to handle many problems that lie outside the tidy theories of object-oriented methodologies. This book faces up to those issues. For example, it covers how to make objects persistent using a relational database, and how object-oriented design interfaces with GUI design.

If you want to know how to apply the latest ideas in object technology to product development, then *Tried & True Object Development* is for you. It is a unique contribution and not just another UML methods book.

Derek Coleman
Hewlett-Packard Software Initiative
Palo Alto

About the Authors

DR. ARI JAAKSI heads the Nokia Wireless Software Solutions development unit in Boston, Massachusetts. During the preparation of this book, he was on leave from Nokia acting as a professor of computer science at the University of Tampere, Finland. Dr. Jaaksi has over ten years' experience developing commercial software systems including CAD/CAM, production management, and telecommunication systems. He is a frequent lecturer in conferences and seminars, provides training and consulting services, and is the author of several publications about object-oriented software development. Dr. Jaaksi is a member of IEEE and ACM.

JUHA-MARKUS AALTO, M.Sc. in software engineering, works as the Head of Quality and Processes of the Network Management Systems business unit at Nokia Telecommunications, Tampere, Finland. He has over ten years' of experience in software development, process improvement, and quality management. Mr. Aalto has work experience as a programmer in the domains of health care, software development tools, and telecommunications. He has also worked as the software engineering manager at Nokia Telecommunications. Mr. Aalto has given several lectures and courses, and consulted in object-oriented analysis and large-scale software development.

ARI AALTO, M.Sc., Lic. Tech. in software engineering, heads an R & D Department at Nokia Telecommunications, Tampere, Finland. Mr. Aalto has held various positions in software product and customer project development in several Finnish software companies. He worked as a programmer, project manager, technical consultant, and product manager from 1986–1993. He joined Nokia Network Management Systems R & D in 1993, and has since then been involved in the development of core functionality of the Nokia NMS product family. His area of specialization is data management, and he has consulted and given numerous seminars on object data management in the Finnish IT industry.

KIMMO VÄTTÖ, M.Sc., Ph.L in software engineering, is currently acting as a project manager in Data Warehousing product development in Düsseldorf, Germany. He has experience in building software systems for healthcare, finance, and telecommunications. He joined Nokia Network Management Systems R & D in 1993, and has since then been involved in the development of the Nokia NMS product family. He specializes in data management, an area in which he has provided training and consulting. He has given numerous lectures at conferences and seminars, and he is the author of several publications about object data management.

Preface

What This Book Is About

This book is about software development. It presents approaches and practices for the construction of software systems based on features, objects, components, and architectural patterns. This book presents the key phases of software development, as well as the artifacts produced during these phases. Above all, this book communicates our practical experiences in developing large software systems.

The approaches presented here were developed at Nokia. We authors were involved in the development of the presented practices, which are currently used within Nokia and in other organizations of different sizes.

The approaches are blended from several commercial object-oriented methods and our own process improvement, and they use the *Unified Modeling Language* (UML) to visualize their phase products and blueprints. We have tuned the processes for our own needs for the development of large interactive software products. In addition, we have scaled the practices down to be applicable for projects of a few persons.

This book concentrates on the key elements of software development—the elements that we have found most important. First, we present our industry proven process model, its phases and deliverables. To be useful in real-life software projects, the process framework must be understandable and clear. We discus how to utilize the process model in different kinds of software projects.

Second, we present our practices for the development of the user interface and the data management. These elements exist in the majority of software systems, and are often the most difficult parts; still, the majority of publications and process models seem to ignore them. We discuss what kind of practices, software tools, and architectural solutions support the development of these parts. Third, we present our practices for dealing with software architectures starting with the architecture of entire product families and going all the way down to the architecture of individual software components. For us, architecture is the most concrete and essential element of any software system. Fourth, we present how to scale our practices in both directions, up and down. We present how to organize the development of large software systems, develop closely related products as product lines, support large-scale reuse, and organize the incremental development of big products. In addition, we present a downscaled version of our process model suitable for small projects of just a few persons or for companies just starting object development.

This book does not introduce a new all-purpose software development paradigm or method. Instead, it provides practical guidelines and process models for the development of software systems. The book utilizes our experiences; how we at Nokia have used the theories of object-orientation in practice. This book concentrates on the development of industrial-sized interactive software systems. The emphasis is placed on phases, phase products, and guidelines that, based on our experiences, work in practice.

The Structure of This Book

This book has four chapters. The chapters are closely related and reveal different views of software development. However, the chapters can also be studied separately.

Chapter 1, *Developing Interactive Software Systems,* presents our method framework, its phases and phase products. It concentrates on the development of interactive systems with graphical user interfaces and distributed architectures. This chapter shows how to use the UML to visualize specifications produced during the process. In addition, it gives examples of how to arrange software development projects around the presented process model.

Chapter 2, *Object-Oriented Data Management,* presents our guidelines for the development of OO data management solutions. It provides patterns of how to implement persistence by using different database approaches. This chapter also discusses the strategies on selecting proper data management technologies.

Chapter 3, *Large-Scale Development,* presents our way of managing large software systems. It discusses different levels of architecture and evolutionary software processes. This chapter scales the process model up to manage product families, features, and large development teams.

Chapter 4, *Small-Scale Development,* goes to another extreme: It gives an example of a very simple process model suitable for companies just starting object development.

Ari Jaaksi is the author of Chapters 1 and 4 and the supportive parts of the book. Juha-Markus Aalto is the author of Chapter 3, and Ari Aalto and Kimmo Vättö are the authors of Chapter 2. However, we have worked in close cooperation with each other to review and enhance each part.

Who Should Read This Book

We wrote this book for heterogeneous groups of people. Individual software developers can study our method of constructing object-oriented software systems all the way from requirements and product ideas to the delivered systems. They may also benefit from our architectural patterns, especially when developing data management or user interface parts of systems. Project managers can study our way of arranging software development according to different life cycle models. Product managers and system analysts can learn from our experiences on screening product concepts, collecting and analyzing requirements, and forming features, products, and product lines. Those managers responsible for organizing software development organizations, outlining product architectures, or managing product development that lasts years may find our practices for the development of large software products beneficial. Finally, those parts of software development organizations that select and develop tools and methods can hopefully learn from our experiences and suggestions.

The reader should know the basics of software engineering and object-orientation. Concepts, such as object, class, inheritance, and late binding, should be familiar to the reader. Also, the reader should know the basics of an object-oriented programming language, such as C++ or Java. In addition to these requirements, experience in real-life software projects would benefit the reader.

Acknowledgments

Thanks are due to many people in preparing this book. Writing a book was definitely more laborious and time-consuming than we ever expected. We would like to express our gratitude to our families for their endless patience and support.

We thank our numerous colleagues at Nokia Telecommunications and University of Tampere. In addition, the book has profited greatly from the comments of Prof. Ilkka Haikala from Tampere University of Technology; Dr. Akmal B. Chaudhri from The City University of London, UK, and M.Sc. Markku Ruonavaara from Nokia.

Introduction

Software systems are becoming larger and more complex. Large groups of designers with different skill levels participate in the development of these systems. On one hand, the systems are becoming more critical and the requirements for their reliability and usefulness are growing. Thus, implementation of software systems is becoming more and more complicated and time-consuming. Because of this, major failures happen: software projects overshoot their schedules, systems do not function as required, or systems are not taken into use at all.

Because of the growing complexity and demanding requirements of software systems, software development cannot just depend on the exceptional but arbitrary achievements of talented designers. Instead, software development is becoming a more disciplined work, having both a scientific and an engineering basis. According to many researchers and practitioners, object-orientation together with the latest component-based paradigms is the most promising approach for systematic software development.

The Context of This Book

This book is about how to use objects and components in the development of large and complex software systems. It presents some new ideas but also introduces a synthesis of old ideas. These ideas and their combinations are currently in everyday use in various projects inside and outside Nokia. Thus, we have proof that the development of large software systems can be based on the presented approach. We have also experience with small start-up projects to add to these experiences, so the practices scale down as well as we will show.

This book presents practices that aim at the production of high-quality software systems. The writing of the actual code is only a part of the software developer's job. This book, therefore, presents a path for a software developer to develop a software system from requirements to a ready system. In addition, this book concentrates on some elements we have found especially demanding; for example, the specification and implementation of interactive applications, data management, and particularly the development of large systems.

When talking with our colleagues at Nokia, we call our process framework OMT++. The name originates from the most widely used object-oriented method, *Object Modeling Technique* (OMT), which was the starting point of our approach. However, not much is left from the original OMT. The name OMT++ itself illustrates the origin of our approach, the fact that we have modified and improved it for our own purposes, and that we use mainly it in the context of the C++ programming language. However, because we do not want to introduce a new, one-size-fits-all method, we would rather talk about "our process" instead of "OMT++."

Our process is a collection of practices, selected notations, and phase-product templates that assist software developers in their everyday work. It also forms the backbone of software project management and quality assurance. All the software development work is planned, managed, and performed according to its phases. One might call our process model a complete method, because it covers software development from the requirements to the tested systems and provides a means to monitor and manage this development. However, it is not a complete method in the sense that it would be fully documented and supported by some training organization, for example. After all, we are not interested in developing methods. Our main goal is to produce high-quality software products. We want to share a collection of practices that we have used to reach our goal.

One rigid approach is never enough. Even a single software company needs different process models for different types of projects. Large projects developing additional features on top of an established software product need different methods than do smaller projects developing the first versions of software entering new market segments. For the first project type, the key goals are probably to keep schedules and produce faultless outcome, whereas the latter project tries to enter the market as soon as possible, even with limited functionality and lower-quality standards.

Many elements of a method can be similar for different kinds of projects. The notation used is one of those elements. In this book, we use the *Unified Modeling Language* (UML) for the notation, because it provides all that is needed to support industrial software development. Actually, we need only a small subset of UML. One of the main problems of UML is that it is already too big and complicated. This problem seems to affect almost any "unified" approach.

Another widely accepted and almost unified approach that we use is the major phase structure of software development. According to it, we call the phases object-oriented analysis, design, programming, and testing. We make a clear distinction between analysis and design. Analysis deals with the concepts relevant to the end users. It analyses the requirements and produces the initial solution descriptions. After successful analysis, both the users and the developers should have a similar vision about the future system. Design deals with the concepts relevant to the programmers. Design specifies *how* the outlined and analyzed solution will be implemented. Design aims at programming, and the programming phase produces the software modules consisting of code. The programming phase makes the most detailed design decisions. Typically, testing the most elementary units of code, such as classes and functions, is considered to be programming. The testing phase integrates the modules together, builds the final software packages, and tests it against the requirements.

Art or Industry?

This book is about software development. However, it is not the only area of human activity where certain practices and commonly agreed-upon approaches are needed. As a comparison, let us examine a recording session in a recording studio as an analogy of software development.

Let us suppose that you are about to make a recording of one single musical tune. Although more and more music nowadays is recorded with computers, you will use real musicians. At first you want to record the tracks of a rhythm section: drums, bass, rhythm guitars, and keyboards. You have already made an arrangement of the tune beforehand, based on a composition that was available only on a cassette tape. This is typical, because many people play and sing their compositions on tape rather than write them down on a piece of paper. Based on that tape, you make the preliminary arrangements. In contrast to classical music or music played by larger bands, the details of the arrangements will be decided only while you are rehearsing the tune with the band.

At the beginning of the recording session, you listen to the original tape together with other musicians. After that, you briefly describe the basic ideas of your arrangement, including what kind of atmosphere and rhythmical feeling you have in mind. Then you give the arrangement to the musicians on a piece of paper, such as the one illustrated in Figure 1, and demonstrate your ideas on a piano.

FIGURE 1. A rough arrangement, or specification, of a tune.

The arrangement has many levels of information, although many details of the tune have not been written down at all. You have illustrated the structure of a song with markings such as INTRO, A, B, Solo, Chorus, and Bridge, as depicted in the upper right-hand corner of Figure 1. These markings provide a high-level view of the tune by illustrating the basic structure of verses, choruses, and other such elements. Some might call this structure the architecture of the tune.

In addition to the structural view, there is also a more detailed view of the arrangement. Chords, such as E7 and A7, illustrated in Figure 2, are the basic notation for the harmonics of a tune. The chords give musicians their harmonic limits. Within these limits they can choose individual notes and rhythmic details based on their musical intuition and our common agreements. This is typically all that a talented musician needs to produce music with others.

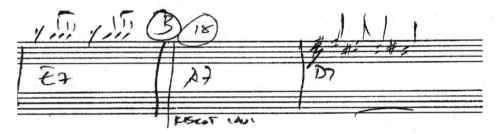

FIGURE 2. Some details of the arrangement.

In addition to the basic structure and harmonics of the tune, you have indicated some "hot spots" in the tune. It is of vital importance that every musician follows the arrangement during these hot spots. Such spots are typically needed, for example, when you move from a verse to a chorus and back. Also, certain riffs and other rhythmical patterns may need a more detailed description. These details are illustrated as notes, as depicted in the upper corners of Figure 2.

After you and other musicians have listened to the original composition and studied and discussed the arrangement, you start to practice for the recording. You play the tune several times and concentrate especially on the overall feeling, hot spots, and some tricky parts of the arrangement. After a while, you should try to play the tune on a tape and listen to it. After listening to the first take, you then typically make some minor changes and go for a final take.

After a few trials you and the other musicians manage to record the tune the way you wanted. The overall feeling is good, and there are no major errors. However, although the take is almost perfect, usually some minor things need corrections and overdubs. To make the corrections, you rewind the tape[1] and correct even a single note by rerecording it. After this, the recording of the rhythm section is done and the musicians deserve a break. After the break, you start to work on a different tune and after a couple of days, the horn section arrives and plays their parts. But that is another story.

This simple example of a recording session demonstrates the need for a method even when creating music. Much more than just an inspiration is needed, and not many people understand how much discipline and organized work is required to produce a piece of music. Without a method that includes a common working approach and notations, nobody would be able to create music with other musicians within a certain time frame. You must not forget the schedules, because recording studios can be extremely expensive to hire.

The recording pattern we have just explained is used all over the world. It has certain phases, such as making an arrangement, rehearsal for recording, doing the actual recording, and making corrections. It has also certain notations, as illustrated in Figures 1 and 2, which are known to all musicians. Without these elements, records would be hard to produce, and the larger the orchestra is and the more complicated the arrangement is, the more discipline is needed. Making a recording of a classical symphony, for example, requires much more detailed processes.

The process of software development is very similar to the process of music recording. Both tasks require the collaboration of people, must produce good quality products, and must be done within a certain time frame. In addition, adequate patterns for the construction the final products are required. For example, it is typical that the bass guitar follows the rhythmical pattern of the base drum in order to provide a nice groove. Also, if you use a horn section, you should arrange their part not to drown out the lead vocal. Similar patterns emerge in software development. You should design the data storage for efficiency and maintainability, distribute your application into executable processes without sacrificing the performance, and so forth. Such patterns increase the chances of quality outcome.

We claim that there are as much creative work involved in software development as in music. Nevertheless, both music and software development need a certain amount of discipline and rules that set the framework for the art itself. Only within frameworks that are flexible but tight enough can you produce something useful and creative. And although you need discipline, rules, and limits, no approach can render the skills and talents of a designer or musician useless. Software construction is a creative process, and sound methodology can empower and liberate the creative mind. However, a methodology cannot help individuals who lack the right skills, talents, and attitude.

---

[1]If you recorded directly on a hard disk, rewinding should be taken metaphorically.

CHAPTER 1

Developing Interactive Software Systems

Most modern software systems are interactive by nature. Systems communicate with a variety of external elements, such as end users, databases, printers, networks, and sensors. These entities communicate with the software systems by sending and receiving various types of events. Events emerge randomly and the systems must always be ready to handle them. The majority of software systems are thus event-driven. Communication is flexible; it is the interaction among these entities that typically is the most critical element of a system. Thus, software systems must handle events coming from various sources, and the main concern of software developers is developing applications that provide smooth communication with the outside world.

On the other hand, systems are just tools for end users. End users perform certain tasks with a system. The primary goal of the end user, for example, is to write a letter, to finalize the balance sheet of a company, or to send an e-mail. Thus, although events come from various sources and a system must respond to them, it is the end users who typically are in charge. The most important task of almost any system is to serve the end users. In this respect, the main concern of a software developer is to develop applications that provide the best possible support for the needs of end users.

1

Our process model aims at producing software systems the end user can use effectively. To implement such systems, we model software systems and their users as collaborative entities. The software development process consists of analysis, design, programming, and testing activities. This chapter discusses these activities and offers some examples.

Our Way of Developing Software

There are certain things that characterize our software development. First, we develop products. Requirements change during their lifetime and we must continuously enhance our products to meet the changing needs. This calls for modular architectures of high quality to minimize maintenance costs in the long run.

Second, we develop large systems in projects that consist of tens and even hundreds of developers. In such projects, certain practices must be harmonized to enable synchronization and communication. We need practical life-cycle models, project practices, and commonly agreed implementation guidelines that everybody can follow. We also need proper means of communication between developers, project managers, and customers.

Third, our systems must be developed in time. Other systems depend on our systems and we have a constant pressure to shorten the time to market. This calls for concurrent engineering. Developers must be able to develop components simultaneously with other developers in a rapid incremental fashion. We also need visibility so that delays can be detected as early as possible.

Such requirements for architecture, product quality, efficiency, communication, and time-to-market have forced us to pay attention to how we develop software. Arbitrary hacking does not scale up to meet our requirements.

Short History

In the early '90s, we started applying the object paradigm for the development of software system at Nokia Telecommunications. We based our approach on the method called *Object Modeling Technique* (OMT) [Rumbaugh et al. 91]. We began using the notations and practices of OMT according to our best understanding. However, we soon learned we could not simply read a method book and start following the presented practices. Nokia, among other organizations, was forced to modify and tune methods. Organizations and software systems vary too much for one off-the-shelf approach to be effective for all.

Our difficulties in using the OMT in the development of a large network management system forced us to refine and modify it. We took ideas from other major methods and developed practices of our own. We soon noticed that we did not need all the nuances and details of published approaches. We aimed at a practical way of developing software from the beginning.

At this time, the R & D organization was growing very rapidly. To manage the growth, we needed a clear process with phases and phase products to merge new resources to existing teams. The development practices had to be easy to learn and adapt to for newcomers; if it takes years to master a software development approach, it is useless.

We used OMT as the backbone of our approach. We used its notations and naming conventions, and even called our standard process model OMT++ [Aalto and Jaaksi 94]. OMT++ is still the name used internally at Nokia. Its basic structure is almost an unofficial de facto method for the development of interactive systems with user interfaces, especially at Nokia Telecommunications [Jaaksi 97]. Naturally, projects in an organization as big Nokia differ greatly. Some projects implementing embedded software systems utilize the Nokia-breed Octupus method [Maher et al. 96] in addition to OMT++. Other approaches are also being used to some extent.

We recently started using the notations of the *Unified Modeling Language* (UML) [UML 98]. Because we had already used OMT notations and had added use cases, subsystems, and components to our approach years before, learning to use UML was fairly simple. We are only pleased that others provide boxes, lines, and semantics.

The *Object-Oriented Software Engineering* (OOSE) method [Jacobson et al. 92], currently known as *Objectory* [UML 98] is one of our key sources. *Use cases*, which are the key elements of Objectory, are also an essential part of our practices. They are used to capture and analyze requirements and to prioritize development activities in incremental software projects. Thus, use cases provide a means for communication during the analysis phase and a means for specifying contents for project iterations. However, we carefully avoid using them for the specification of system architecture or division of labor between software developers, for example. We use other means, such as the concepts of applications, service blocks, and components, to handle such questions.

The idea of modeling the system and its communication with external agents with operation specifications is borrowed from the Fusion method [Coleman et al. 94], although we have slightly modified this method. We specify the functionality of software systems as *operation specifications*, which are produced during the analysis phase. These operation specifications illustrate the external behavior of software by using pre- and post-condition clauses, exceptions, and sequence diagrams of UML.

In addition, we have developed and enhanced some of our own practices, because we have not found satisfactory solutions from publications, from our business partners, or from the companies we have benchmarked or studied. Finally, we have documented the software development process and mapped the theories of object-orientation into practical ways of working.

Notation

Notation is a key tool for software developers. Notation enables visual appearance for abstract concepts. Software developers, as well as musicians, writers, or any other artists, must master the used notation. However, notation is often just a tool that enables people to communicate and document creative work. The work of Mozart wouldn't sound worse if musical notation were different, and the novels of Mark Twain wouldn't be of less value if written with Hebrew notation. The same applies with software development. Our software would not be any better or worse if we used the notation of OMT, UML, or Booch; however, we needed to pick one.

We use the Unified Modeling Language (UML). In particular, we use class, sequence, and implementation diagrams, including component and deployment diagrams. Natural language is also an essential modeling tool. Natural language is the way to capture requirements; it is typically used whenever there is a need to communicate with end users. Natural language is also used if there is a need to emphasize something related to diagrams.

We emphasize the clearness and readability of all figures and models. Class, component, and sequence diagrams should be drawn at a proper level of abstraction and they should only illustrate what is essential. If we need to choose between under-modeling and over-modeling, we always choose under-modeling and add textual commentary. Graphical notations are primarily for human beings, not for compilers or machines.

Overview of the Process

Our process consists of four main phases, namely *object-oriented analysis*, *object-oriented design*, *object-oriented programming*, and *testing*, as illustrated in Figure 1-1. Each phase views the developed system from the different levels of abstraction. Each phase builds on the previous phases, and each sets requirements for the following phases. Although the phases are listed sequentially, iterative approach is recommended, as we explain later.

FIGURE 1-1. The main phases of our process model.

The *analysis phase* consists of subphases called *requirements capture* and *requirements specification*. The requirements capture subphase collects and documents all requirements and use cases for the system to be developed. The *requirements specification subphase* analyses and models both the concepts, that is, the objects of the problem domain and the external functionality of the system. Thus, the analysis phase collects, analyses, and refines the requirements; produces the requirement statements, the use cases, the analysis class diagram and operation specifications, and specifies the user interfaces.

The *design phase* consists of *architectural design* and *detailed design*. The phase uses the artifacts of the analysis phase and produces technical specifications, which can be implemented by programming. Design specifies how classes form structures, what their public interfaces are, and how their instances collaborate. During the architectural design phase, the collaborative objects are typically entire executables, components, libraries, and devices, while in the detailed design phase the objects of interest are typically C++ or Java classes. Architectural design specifies the executable processes, libraries, data storage, devices, and other such components of the system. Detailed design produces an inside view to these architectural elements in the form of design class diagrams and sequence diagrams.

The details of the *programming phase* depend on the selected programming language and environment. With C++, for example, the programming phase may consist of writing the declaration files first and then writing the code itself, while in JAVA, for example, there is no such separation. The programming phase includes coding as well as compiling, linking, and debugging.

The *testing phase* tests the system to find errors in design and programming and to verify that the system meets the requirements. The testing phase also includes the final *integration* of the components. Part of the testing takes place during the previous phases. However, testing is typically the last major activity performed in a software project.

Two Paths: Static and Functional

Analysis, design, programming, and testing are separate phases. They can be arranged either in a waterfall or iterative manner. Each phase consists of activities that aim at modeling either the static or functional properties of the system. We identify two parallel paths in our process, as illustrated in Figure 1-2. Along the *static path*, we model how entities such as classes and components form structures and hierarchies. Along the *functional path*, we watch how these entities collaborate in a running software system.

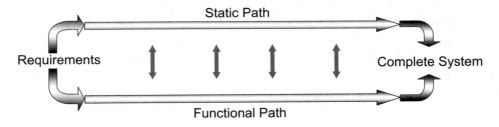

FIGURE 1-2. The two paths of our process.

All phases are based on these two perspectives, static and functional, although we do not emphasize their existence during requirements capture and testing. During the analysis phase, the static entities are the system itself: concepts the system deals with, external devices, and end users. During the architectural design phase, the static entities are components: executable processes, class libraries, and devices. Later, during detailed design, the programmable classes are the static entities of interest. During the programming phase, the static classes are finalized and implemented in C++, Java, or another such language. In each listed phase, the functional path concentrates on how instances of the static entities collaborate to provide the functionality of the system. Thus, for example, during the detailed design phase the functional path concentrates on how instances of programmed classes collaborate.

Figure 1-3 illustrates the main phases of our approach. Although we use two separate paths, the paths are closely related. From the notation point of view, the static path uses class, component, and deployment diagrams of UML to illustrate the static properties of the system. The functional path uses sequence diagrams to illustrate the functional and dynamic behavior of the system. These two paths complement each other and they both aim at a complete tested system.

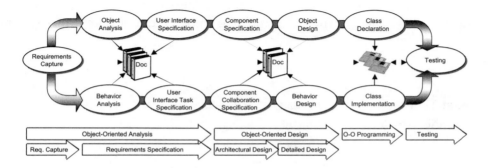

FIGURE 1-3. The main phases and the two paths of our process.

Analysis

Analysis is the first phase of a software development project. It collects requirements and analyze the problem at hand. The analysis phase then constructs a high-level solution to the problem from the users' point of view. It answers two fundamental questions: "What is the problem?" and "What kind of a solution solves the problem?" Thus, the analysis phase aims at presenting a software system that solves a set of end users' problems.

Analysis uses the concepts that are meaningful to the end user. First, it collects the requirements from the end users. The requirements are discussed and validated together with the end users and other parties. After this the software system is outlined to meet the requirements. This outlining produces the initial solution to the problems: A specification of the software as seen by the end users.

Domain Analysis

If an organization plans to develop more than one application for the same domain, it may need some kind of *domain model*. We use the class diagram notations of UML in the construction of domain models. Such models do not aim at the development of any particular system or application. They are developed before any software development project takes place and then are maintained concurrently with the projects, as illustrated in Figure 1-4. Domain modeling is an activity from which multiple software development projects are expected to benefit.

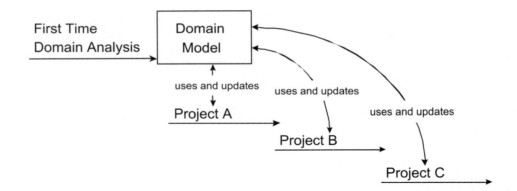

**FIGURE 1-4. Using and maintaining the domain model within
various software projects.**

Domain analysis produces the domain model that presents a general interpretation of the problem domain. The domain model defines the concepts of the domain and the terminology used, as the software development organization understands them. Thus, the domain model could model, for example, such domains as banking, car rental, telecommunication networks, or others without any software system as a target. Such a model provides a good foundation for the analysis class diagrams of future applications.

Collecting and Analyzing Requirements

Each software project captures requirements. Capturing requirements aims at eliciting and representing ideas and requirements for a new system or a system enhancement.

Before a software development project starts, a great deal of information typically is available. Such information, including customer requirements, requirements from the software developers or marketing people, market studies, future plans, domain models, meeting minutes, and simply good, fresh ideas set expectations and loosely describe the future system. In addition, correction requests, customer reports, and complaints from previous projects and versions of the system may be available. In most cases, ideas, concepts, and requirements are vague and need a lot of work to be trusted as a starting point of development activities. Above all, the requirements need to be documented. Only documented requirements are traceable.

The requirements-capture phase collects raw requirements from various sources, as we mentioned. It documents them explicitly as *requirement statements*. In this phase, the preliminary analysis of the requirements occurs. Instead of simply documenting raw requirements as the customers have communicated them, the software development organization must understand the real nature and meaning of each requirement. Requirements are merged, divided into parts, and rephrased to make them explicit, accurate, and measurable.

Requirement collection is not an easy task; it requires a lot of work, including interviewing, searching, holding discussions, and conducting market studies. Yet the documented requirements must be *easy* to read and study. Based on our experience, it is a good habit to document the collected requirements in a simple list and divide the list into two main groups, named *functional requirements* and *nonfunctional requirements*.

Functional requirements tell what the system does. They explain how the system functions when observed from outside and how the system collaborates with external elements. In addition, the functional requirements specify how the end user works with the system.

Nonfunctional requirements are mainly technical. They tell how closely the functional requirements must be met regarding attributes such as responsiveness, capacity, and usability. Nonfunctional requirements typically create frameworks for functional requirements by setting constraints and limits for the implementation.

Requirements must be documented in a form that allows the testing of the final system against them. At the end of the software development project, developers and users must be able to tell whether an individual requirement has been met. This testability is one of the most important characteristics of a requirement statement. Vague and implicit statements, such as "The system must be fast and easy to use," are not merely useless but may even be dangerous. Everybody agrees to such statements but also understands them differently. Thus, in the beginning of the project a common understanding seems to emerge about the requirements. However, if end users and developers have different interpretations of the imprecise requirement statement, the problems will emerge later—often far too late.

Let us now take an example to make the presented theories more concrete. The following example will be used throughout this chapter. In this example, you have an excellent product idea. You want to develop a *Short Message System* (SMS), which is to be an application that allows the user of a mobile phone to efficiently send text messages to other mobile phone users.

To communicate your idea, you create a slide set, such as the one illustrated in Figure 1-5. You use the slide set first in internal meetings while discussing it with your colleagues. Then you improve it based on these internal discussions and present the set to selected, key customers. In this way, you try to get feedback about the feasibility of the SMS concept and also sell the idea that you believe in. Such a slide set seems to be the starting point of almost any new feature or application. Thus, it is clearly a part of system development.

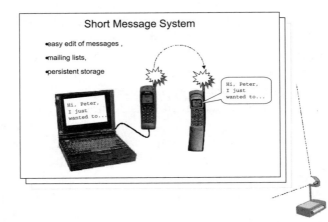

FIGURE 1-5. Sending a short message with a mobile phone and a laptop.

With your SMS application, the users of a mobile phone can type a short message with their computer and enter the phone numbers of the recipients to whom they want to send the message. The system sends the message by using the mobile phone attached to the computer. The recipients can then read the message directly from the screens of their mobile phones. Thus, your software should enable editing of the message text, selecting the recipients, and sending the message with the attached equipment.

The basic messaging functionality is provided, for example, in GSM[1] mobile networks. The users of a GSM mobile phone already can send and receive short messages by using the handset alone. They do not necessarily need your software. So, what is the added value that your planned software provides? SMS provides at least three advantages over a plain handset:

- It is much easier to edit messages with a proper screen and keyboard.
- Mailing lists enable the user to send the same message to multiple recipients at once.
- The messages, recipients, and groups enjoy persistent storage in disks.

You start to collect requirements based on these added-value features and the basic idea illustrated as a slide set in Figure 1-5. You discuss the idea with potential end users, the personnel of your company, potential resellers, and so forth. After an intensive collection phase you finally manage to write down the requirement statements for your application, as listed in Figure 1-6. We suggest that you also record the original source of each requirement, because it will help you to answer all the "why" questions in the future.

Functional Requirements:
  1. The end user can send short text messages from a PC through an attached mobile phone.
  2. The user can store and load phone numbers based on recipients names.
  3. The user can construct "mailing lists" of multiple recipients.
  4. The user can store and reuse the most common sayings as phrases.
  5. The user can save sent messages and view or reuse them later.

Nonfunctional Requirements:
  1. The system must run on Windows and Macintosh platforms.
  2. The system must allow multiple simultaneous accesses to the stored phone numbers and groups.
  3. All data must be stored into flat ASCII files.

FIGURE 1-6. The requirement statements for a SMS system.

Use Cases

The product concept and the documented requirement statements are just the beginning of a software development project. Both must be analyzed further. On one hand, end users and software developers must be able to discuss the requirements and form a common understanding of what kind of system will be developed. On the other hand, software developers need a deeper and more detailed understanding of the functionality of the system. For these purposes, we have successfully employed *use cases*[2] as an integral part of our process model.

In our model, use cases are simply textual presentations of the usage of the future systems. They provide selected examples of how the end user will use the system. Use cases are "short stories" that explain how the users of the system and the system itself will work together to achieve something beneficial.

Use cases minimize harmful misunderstandings of product concepts and requirements. Whereas a functional requirement specifies *what* the system should do, a use case describes *how* the system should do what it does together with the end user or any other external entity. For example, if a functional requirement specifies that "The system must print a report," a use case analyses this requirement by defining that, "First the user selects the information to be included into the report. Then he selects the report type . . . ," as illustrated in Figure 1-7. Thus, each use case provides an example of how the system meets a set of requirements.

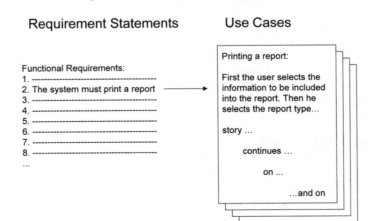

FIGURE 1-7. Use cases analyze functional requirements.

We have been forced to keep practical limitations of software projects in mind when applying method fragments, such as use cases. In theory, it would be fascinating to model all the functionality of a system as use cases. Unfortunately, there is not enough time in real-world projects, and we analyze only the most important functional requirements as use cases. In most cases, the issues presented in the promotion or marketing material of the software are the most essential features. At least these essential features should be analyzed with the help of use cases.

The use cases describe the flow of events between the user, the system, and external devices and other systems. The use case model uses *actors* to represent roles that the users can play and *use cases* to represent how the actors cooperate with the system under development. An actor is typically an end user in a specified role. In addition, an actor can also be, for example, another system asking for services. Use cases specify the functionality of the system from the user's perspective and do not describe the internal implementation of the system at hand. Each use case is a complete course of events with the system, and each complete use case must be beneficial to the end user as such.

Use cases explain the actions of the actors and the responses of the system. Use cases illustrate the typical use scenarios of the system, and these scenarios will guide the design and final implementation of the software. The user must be able to use the system according to the documented use cases. Thus, the customers or their representatives must accept the use cases describing the system, and the implemented system must allow the end user and other external entities to perform according to the accepted use cases. The system should be tested finally against the use cases to verify the equivalence between the use cases and the final system.

Use cases are concrete examples of how an actor uses the system to get some concrete benefits. The use case is a tool for collecting and analyzing different ways of using the system, and it provides a means of communication during the requirements capture and analysis phases. Use cases are functional in nature and do not discuss the architecture or implementation of the systems at hand. Therefore, use cases should not be used for the specification of software architecture. For that purpose, we use other means, such as the concepts of applications, service blocks, and components. However, use cases are an important source for architectural design.

Discuss use cases with customers. To assist the discussion, write use cases so that the customers can understand them and make comments. Typically, the designer of the software system writes the first versions of the use cases together with marketing. The use cases are then fine-tuned together with some selected key customers. After the use cases and other requirements have been documented and agreed on with the customers, they form the basis for the following phases of system development. In each step, phase products must be checked against the use cases and requirements. Finally, the use cases form the basic test case set for system testing.

The Form of Use Cases

Typically, we do not use any graphical notation, such as sequence or activity diagrams, to illustrate use cases. Instead, we use natural language written according to a predefined use case template. It is important that everybody, including customers, managers, designers, and testers, can read and understand the use cases. Natural language makes it possible for everybody to understand use cases and contribute in their creation. The predefined structure of our template forces the writer to include the most important elements in each use case. It also keeps the composition of use cases consistent and therefore improves the readability of the use cases.

Let us now continue with the Short Message System (SMS) example. In Figure 1-6, you documented a functional requirement: "The end user can send short text messages from a PC through an attached mobile phone." You must now specify how this sending takes place by writing a use case entitled "Sending a Short Message."

You speak with potential users to find out how they would like to use the software and you write the use case based on these discussions. Then you ask some selected end users to read and verify your use case. Based on this work, you finally document the way of sending short messages with your application, as illustrated in Figure 1-8.

The Description part includes the actual use case—the story itself. The story is "a typical way of using the system" and does not describe variations or exceptions. Instead, it provides one single path of execution, and separate exception clauses document erroneous situations or exceptional ways of working with the system. This method keeps the story simple and clear. Exceptions are added to the description part as *pointers*, which are explained later in their own sections, according to our use case template.

Use Case:	Sending a Short Message
Actor:	A regular mobile phone user
Usability Requirements:	The user can detect if the message has been sent successfully.
Preconditions:	User has the rights to use the system. There are recipients, groups, and phrases saved into the system.
Description:	The user writes a short message (Exception: Load a message) and adds his signature to the end of the message. He selects two different recipients plus two groups of recipients (Exception: No numbers are available). After that he saves the message for himself. Then he sends the short message to the selected recipients and groups. Finally, the application announces that the network has received the short message.
Exceptions:	Load a message: then the user loads a presaved message to work with. No numbers are available: then the user first enters the recipient's information into the system.
Postconditions:	The SMS is stored and sent.

FIGURE 1-8. The key use case of the SMS written according to our use case template.

Preconditions and *postconditions* provide a context for the use case at hand. They can also connect a use case with other use cases. For example, a precondition can determine that some other use case must be performed before the use case in question.

We present the usability requirements as a part of use cases. In most cases, the usability requirements are related to the operations performed by the end user. For example, we may relate a usability requirement, "The user must receive and recognize feedback from a successful operation," to the operation of "Sending a short message." However, such requirement may be useless or even wrong in the context of some other functionality.

Software systems must be useful. Only useful systems are worth making usable. We emphasize that designers should always plan the system for good usability from the very beginning of system development. Too often, usability testing or even the user interface specification phase comes too late. It is the basic functionality of the system that really matters, not the details of the user interface. Therefore, the majority of the usability work must be already done during the use case work. Even a superb user interface cannot cure applications whose basic behavior does not meet the requirements of users' workflow.

Let us go back to the example application. During your requirement collection work, you find out that *group* is one of the key concepts of the application. A group is a kind of a mailing list. By selecting a group as a recipient, the user can send the same message to multiple recipients at once. Sending to multiple recipients is something that the end user cannot achieve by using the short messages with their mobile phones alone. Thus, the concept of a group is one of the added values of your application, and you decide to write a use case to clarify its usage. Figure 1-9 illustrates the use case of creating and maintaining groups with the application.

Use Case:	Creating and maintaining groups.
Actor:	A regular mobile phone user.
Preconditions:	User has the rights to use the system. There are recipients and groups saved into the system.
Description:	The user creates a new group of message recipients. She adds six recipients to the group (Exception: Needed recipients are not entered into the system). Then the user deletes some other group. After this, the user removes one recipient from the first group and adds two new ones into it. Finally, the user starts to write a message.
Exceptions:	Needed recipients are not entered into the system: then the user first enters the recipients' information.
Postconditions:	Groups are modified and modifications are saved.

FIGURE 1-9. The use case for managing groups.

We do not typically specify the elements of the user interface, such as windows, buttons, or menus, with use cases. Instead, use cases describe the functionality of the system at a higher level of abstraction, in terms of end users' workflows. They describe what the user and the system do and in which order. We specify the user interface later in the project just to support these activities. For example, the presented use cases include actions such as, "The user creates a new group . . ." or ". . . the application announces that the network has received the short message." However, the use cases do not mention whether there is a separate dialog box for the creation, or whether the application uses some voice signal to indicate successful operation.

There are some dangers in working with buttons and menus during the use case analysis. The user interface should support the end user's work. Software designers must therefore first understand the users' workflows. Introduction of buttons, text fields, and other such elements too early would easily obscure the focus. In worst cases, use cases would be constructed according to the requirements of the hasty and precipitate user interface specification. Based on our experience, it is better first to focus on modeling the interaction between the system and the end user without the details of the user interface.

Getting the Best Out of Use Cases

When we originally started to work with use cases, it soon became obvious that it is not enough to describe use cases simply as "a sequence of transactions between the user and a system." This kind of a definition was too loose and produced use cases of bad quality. Software designers wrote vague use cases, which typically did not define the sequence precisely but rather presented a set of functional alternatives that the system may have offered. In the other extreme, software designers wrote use cases that were too detailed. These use cases were too limited for communication purposes and too detailed for the early phases of the system development.

To tackle these problems, we developed guidelines for finding and writing use cases [Jaaksi 98b]. These guidelines alone are not sufficient for the effective use of use cases. Instead, to benefit from these "ten commandments" the software developer must be familiar with the basics of use case analysis and object-oriented system development. The guidelines only concentrate on the problems we have met while working with groups and individuals producing use cases. By following these rules, designers can create use cases that work better.

Ten Commandments of Use Cases

1. **Use cases specify the most important functional requirements.**
   In the very first phases of the system development, we collect functional and other requirements for the system. Use cases are a tool to analyze these requirements and the term use case is not used in any other context. If we have a requirement, "It must be possible to print reports with the system," there may be one or more use cases where this printing takes place.

2. **A use case describes something that the designer can be proud of and the customer is willing to pay for.**
   Broad use cases may be either too complex to understand or too vague to be useful, whereas narrow use cases may be either too detailed or meaningless as such. Therefore, an entity that the customer is willing to pay for and at the same time the designer is proud of is a good candidate for a single use case. In addition, each use case must describe something that is beneficial to the end user as such. Thus, "Producing a sales report" sounds like a good use case, while "Selecting a printer" is obviously too small a use case and is not beneficial alone to the end user.

3. **A use case depicts a typical way of using the system—but nothing more.**
   One single use case depicts just one possible way of using the system. A use case should not try to cover issues outside of its area and should not try to define all possible ways of performing a task. Instead, each use case defines the recommended way of performing a task that the customer needs to carry out. Another way of using the system is described in another use case or in the "Exception" section of the use case in question.

4. **A use case is a play.**
   One use case is like a classical play. Anybody who wants to take the role of an actor must be capable of performing as intended in the play just by reading the manuscript—that is, the use case. The system plays the role of another actor. The use case should not provide too much freedom to the actors so that the play ends up in chaos. For example, in the system-testing phase the system tester acts as an actor and

reads the use case manuscript. He expects the system to follow the manuscript, too.

5. **A use case has a beginning, a main body, and an ending.**
Each use case should be a complete story with a beginning, a main body, and an ending. Each use case defines clearly where it starts by giving the preconditions and listing the initial steps of the use case. Each use case has a main body, the actual functionality that the customer is willing to buy. Finally, a good use case has some kind of an ending that closes it. A use case without these characteristics is probably too narrow.

6. **A use case is like an essay written by an elementary school pupil.**
A good use case is like a story written by a nine-year-old kid. Such a story typically reads as follows: "I played ice hockey with our team. First I scored two goals. Then Bill got a two-minute penalty for slashing. Then he also scored one goal. Our team won 3-0. After the game my daddy drove me home." At a certain age, children tend to write down stories that describe an explicit flow of actions that take place one after another, which is exactly what use cases should do. It would be unusual for an elementary school kid to write: "Obviously, Bill has problems with his temper. I suggest he should contact his psychiatrist. Otherwise he may ruin the strategy and jeopardize our goals by taking too many penalties. On the other hand, our coach could discuss with Bill. . . ." As the opposite of school children, software designers seem to be tempted to write the second kind of story in their use cases. Their stories lack the description of the typical way of using the system. Instead, they start to speculate about the functional alternatives or implementation possibilities of the future system. Perhaps simple and explicit use cases are hard to write because it is difficult for the writer to make any clear statements. The writer wants to leave the door open for later refinements. However, the writer should make refinements by modifying and improving the use cases later in the project, and not by writing such vague use cases that no changes are needed.

7. **A use case fits in one page.**
The description of a use case should fit in one page. Longer use cases are hard to understand. They are either too detailed, or they try to

cover too much functionality. In the latter case, breaking up the use case into two or more use cases can solve the problem.

8. **A use case is loud and clear.**
   Each use case must make clear statements. Use cases should be so clear and explicit that the people who read them, such as customers and software designers, can form strong opinions. A good use case describes the usage of the future system so precisely that customers and designers can improve the system by arguing, fighting, and finally agreeing on the use case. If nobody disagrees about the first version of the use case, it is probably too vague and should be made more explicit.

9. **Customers and software designers can sign the use case.**
   Each use case should be so concrete and clear that the customers and the designers can sign it. Use cases act as contracts between the customers and the developers. Nobody should make any modifications to the use cases without everybody's approval.

10. **A use case can be used in system development and system testing.**
   Use cases are not used in isolation. Use cases should be specified so that they can be used in object and behavior analysis later in the project. Also, use cases are so explicit that they can be used as the basis of system test cases.

Feasibility Study

We perform early requirement collection and analysis under a so-called *feasibility study* process. This is an independent phase that takes place before we start to monitor the actual software development under our project management practices. Feasibility study clarifies the product concept by collecting requirements and constructing use cases. Based on these, the feasibility study suggests how to implement the system. Finally, it estimates how much work is required to implement the suggested solutions. Feasibility study is typically performed by a group of the best experts available and it sets directions for the whole software development project.

According to our process model, we study the feasibility of the planned product, feature, or enhancement concurrently with requirement capture.

These collected requirements are the basis of different solution alternatives, such as implementing the system from scratch, enhancing and modifying an existing system, or purchasing a system from a partner company. Based on these alternatives, we produce solution suggestions and effort estimations. The collected requirements, solution suggestions, and effort estimations form the basis for the next phases of system development and for project planning, as illustrated in Figure 1-10.

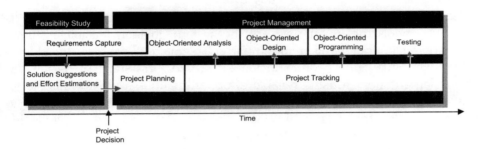

FIGURE 1-10. Feasibility study collects the requirements and forms the basis for software development and project planning.

The decision to start or abandon the development project is made based on the output of the feasibility study process. In addition, a feasibility study can act as an order for a subcontractor. A contract between a software development organization and its subcontractors can be based on feasibility study documents.

Feasibility study serves two purposes:

1. It collects requirements and screens solution suggestion for a development project.
2. It estimates development efforts based on the solution screenings. These estimates are the source for project decision and planning.

Feasibility study, therefore, should answer the following questions:

- What are the requirements for the system or enhancement?
- How does a system function to meet the requirements?
- Is it technically possible to implement a system to meet the requirements?
- What kind of different implementation solutions can be created?
- What is the most feasible solution, if any?

• How much work is required?
• Should the project be started?

As Figure 1-10 illustrates, the actual software project starts after the feasibility study phase is over. It is only after the feasibility study phase that we create a project plan and start to manage the project. Thus, the early phases of requirements capture are performed not under the project management process but under the feasibility study process.

Feasibility study includes the first steps of requirement specification because it models the functionality of the system. In fact, feasibility study is another name for our early requirement collection and analysis. In addition, the feasibility study phase often includes the very first steps of design, and even implementation. Making reliable effort estimations and studying the feasibility of the suggested implementation strategies often requires some design and programming trials. Thus, the feasibility study phase may actually include the first iteration cycle of the software development.

The presented feasibility study is actually just a technical feasibility study. It does not include, for example, market or cost-benefit analysis as a part of it. Such analysis is always required, though. A technically perfect product that meets a decent set of requirements is not worth implementing if there are no markets for it or if some other feature would be more profitable. You will need some analysis of the commercial potential of the software, and Chapter 3 of this book provides information about enhancing technical feasibility study to include such analysis.

Object Analysis

In most cases, clear use cases and explicit requirement statements are the best means to support communication between software designers and end users. We emphasize that requirement statements and use cases must be concrete. Such models do not require any technical skills, and customers, end users, and other experts of the domain can contribute to their creation. Therefore, each project produces concrete requirement statements and use cases that are discussed and agreed on with end users and customers.

We need to further analyze requirement statements and use cases. We do this by producing class diagrams and operation specifications, which are tools for software developers only and are not usually shown to end users. These tools help reveal missing and vague requirements. For software developers, they are a means to produce more detailed and accurate view of the problem and initial solution that has already been screened during feasibility study.

Object analysis is on the static path of our process model and produces an *analysis class diagram* that documents the static key concepts related to the system at hand and their relations. The main sources for the analysis class diagram are documented requirements and use cases. In addition, all other sources, such as domain models, documents of previous systems, standards, and conversations with the users provide data for the analysis class diagram.

The classes of the analysis class diagram are entities that have a meaning from the end user's point of view. Classes that are meaningful only from the programmer's point of view, such as data structures and UNIX processes, for example, do not exist in the analysis class diagram. These classes will be presented later in the design class diagram, which illustrates which kind of classes will be implemented. However, technical classes that are meaningful from the end users' point of view are part of the analysis class diagram. For example, a concept of a UNIX process would certainly be included in the analysis class diagram if the purpose of the application were to manage UNIX processes, for example. If the end users are system administrators and they want to manage UNIX processes, they are meaningful entities for them.

Typically, analysis class diagrams illustrate the classes of one application only. Requirements and use cases, which are the main sources of object analysis, are further analyzed from one application's point of view. The same entity of the real world may therefore be modeled differently in two separate analysis class diagrams. For example, we would model an entity called "a person" very differently if we were about to implement software for a medical instrument, such as a life-support system, compared to the software for a car dealer to manage his customers. The concept of blood pressure and genetic properties of persons would be irrelevant to the car dealer. On the other hand, the person's financial credibility is (we hope) not an object of interest in the development of a life-support system.

The classes of the analysis class diagrams do not typically include many methods. Based on our experience, there are no benefits in searching for the methods of the classes during analysis. Instead, the external behavior of the system is modeled as a black box. Trying to map these external operations of the system to the individual analysis classes does not produce anything useful that could be used later in the project. However, during the *design* phase the benefits of doing this is obvious, as we will explain.

According to our process, the analysis class diagram is always accompanied by a *data dictionary*, which briefly explains classes and relations of the diagram. Such a dictionary minimizes confusion related to the terms used in the analysis class diagram.

Let us now continue with the example application, the Short Message System (SMS). You study the documented requirement statements, use cases, and the descriptions of the product concept carefully. They are the main sources for the classes of the analysis class diagram. Based on your analysis, you draw the class diagram and the accompanied data dictionary, depicting the most important concepts and their relations, as illustrated in Figure 1-11.

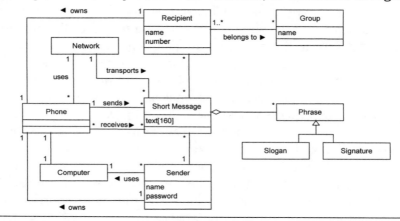

DATA DICTIONARY

CLASS	EXPLANATION
Phone	Sends and receives short messages.
Short Messages	A text message, max 160 characters.
Phrase	A predefined part of the short message text, such as a slogan or a signature.
Recipient	The one to whom the message is sent.
Group	A predefined group of recipients.
Sender	The user of this application.
Network	Network infrastructure consisting of services and network elements.
Computer	Attached to the sender's phone; runs this applications.

FIGURE 1-11. The analysis class diagram and the data dictionary of the SMS application.

Behavior Analysis

The analysis class diagram and the data dictionary illustrate key concepts of the domain and the information related to these concepts. These models are static and they do not analyze the functionality of the system. Therefore, the next step is to define the functionality in terms of user operations, which we define by using operation specifications along the functional path of our process model. We call this *behavior analysis*.

The first task in the behavior analysis phase is to identify the operations that the user carries out with the application. Use case analysis has already provided a set of selected usage scenarios. We now identify operations from these documented use cases and functional requirements. Each use case is divided into elementary operations—basic steps that the user takes with the application. These basic operations are first modeled without any user interface details.

We produce two types of artifacts during this phase: an *operation list* and *operation specifications*. The operation list is a collection of the names of the operations, such as, "Writing a message" or "Adding recipients to a group." The operations are extracted from the use cases and functional requirements. After we create the list, operation specifications take a closer look into each operation at a time. They analyze the communication between the system and external entities in the context of each such operation.

Use cases are the most important source of information when identifying the operations. However, use cases cover only the most important parts of the functionality of the system, because we model only the most useful and common usage sequences as use cases. Some fragments of functionality may not be a part of any documented use case, but they are mentioned in the functional requirements. Therefore, in addition to use cases, we find operations straight from the requirements, too. Whereas use cases demonstrate only a set of the most important usage scenarios, operations cover the whole functionality of the system, as illustrated in Figure 1-12.

The size is not the only difference between the use cases and the operations. For communicative purposes, the use cases are as concrete as possible, whereas for software development purposes, the operations are as generic as possible. This is how we use the concept of abstract use cases vs. concrete usage scenarios. We analyze the use cases, divide them into smaller elements, and abstract common behavior from them. We call these abstractions *operations*, not use cases[3]. Thus, in theory, use cases are typically concrete instances of several operations chained together.

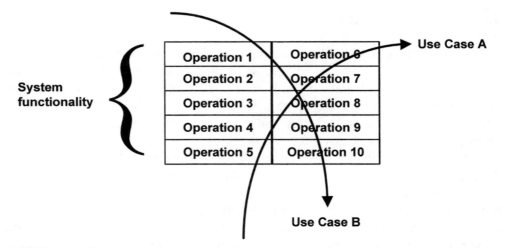

FIGURE 1-12. Use cases illustrate only the most important ways of using the system, whereas operations cover the whole functionality.

Use cases describe actors' typical workflows. The workflows may contain discussions with a colleague, browsing a manual, making a phone call, or performing other activities that are a part of the work but not covered by the software. Use cases may contain such parts. Operation specifications do not since they include only parts that will be implemented into the software system under development.

Let us now continue with the example application and analyze its behavior. Your SMS application supports a set of operations that originate from the use cases and functional requirements. You analyze these sources and produce an operations list, such as the one illustrated in Figure 1-13.

Operations of the Short Message System application:

1.	Writing a short message.	**7.**	Entering recipient's information.
2.	Adding a phrase.	**8.**	Creating a group.
3.	Selecting recipients and groups.	**9.**	Deleting a group.
4.	Saving a message.	**10.**	Adding recipients to a group.
5.	Sending a short message.	**11.**	Removing recipients from a group.
6.	Loading a message.	**12.**	Removing recipient's information.

FIGURE 1-13. The operations of the SMS application extracted from the use cases and functional requirements.

Operations that consist of communication between the application and external entities are further analyzed as operation specifications. They visualize operations as UML sequence diagrams accompanied with precondition and postcondition and exception clauses. Operation specifications model the system as a black box. They do not specify systems' internal implementation but only their external functionality.

As an example, Figure 1-14 illustrates the operation specification of "Sending a short message." According to it, the user first asks the application to send the message. Then, the application loops through each recipient and sends the message. Finally, the network delivers the messages asynchronously to the recipients' phones.

Operation: Sending a short message.

Preconditions: Message is written, the recipients are selected.

Sequence Diagram:

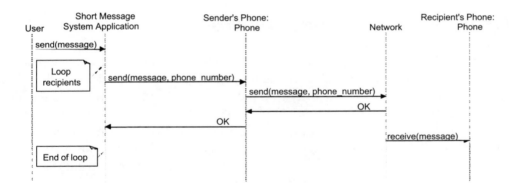

Exceptions: Sending fails: then show error message.
Recipient's phone does not receive the message: nothing can be done, the network attempts sending several times depending on its configuration

Postconditions: The message is sent to the selected recipients.

FIGURE 1-14. The operation specification of the operation #5 illustrates how the application communicates with external agents.

Operation specifications illustrate how the system collaborates with the external devices and users, but they do not specify the details of the user interface. Instead, the specification in Figure 1-14 only indicates that there must be some way to make the system send the message. How the sending is implemented in the user interface is not considered at this point but during the subsequent phases.

For us, a notation is mainly a means of communication between people. We try to keep the number of used notational elements as small as possible. We would rather use textual comments accompanied by figures than use exotic graphical symbols that some people may not understand. For example, Figure 1-14 illustrates a loop in the flow of events. We have decided to use the Note element of UML to depict its start and end points. For loops, we could have used a small * sign in front of the message name, and for some other places some other presentation option of UML [UML 98], [Fowler 97]. However, such elements may increase the complexity of the notation and raise the chance of fatal misinterpretations. Note-boxes are more self-descriptive.

User Interface Specification

Modern software development environments, user interface libraries, and user interface builders make the implementation of graphical windows and dialogs easy. Windowing systems, such as Microsoft Windows, Motif, and Java AWT with the Swing component set, provide full sets of user interface elements. Push buttons, text fields, bitmaps, and other facilities are provided for application developers. Tools such as Visual Basic, X-Designer, and Visual Age for Java make it easy to use these interface elements in the construction of windows and dialog boxes. Instead of coding, software developers draw the user interfaces.

Real life is more complex, though. The seeming simplicity of implementation may lead to haphazard construction of user interfaces. Instead of designing the best possible tools to help the user to work with the application, it is often too easy to fill windows with arbitrary sets of different apparatus and gears. Specifying user interfaces is more than just filling up the dialogs with buttons and text fields and implementing presentations for the objects of the application.

Above all, the user interface should support the end users and fit into their ways of working. The end users must be able to get their work done with the user interface. Thus, the purpose of the user interface specification is to design equipment that supports end users' tasks.

Collecting and Analyzing End Users' Operations

Our process model has already modeled end users' operations as operation specifications. These specifications model the functionality of the system as seen from outside (how the system collaborates with external entities). As the first step, we identify the operations that need end users' participation. We concentrate on each and every such operation one at a time and specify support for each. Support will be implemented with the help of the graphical elements of the user interface.

It is common for real-sized applications to have some 50–70 operations, such as those listed in Figure 1-13, to support. Such a large number of operations cannot be successfully managed as a single, flat list. Therefore, we typically first take some time to analyze the operations. We identify the operations that have something in common and group them together. For example, one group could include operations that have something to do with the saving and loading of information; one group could include operations that deal with the same classes in the analysis class diagram; groups may be formed based on the different actors of use cases, and so forth. Then, each group is further treated separately as a single unit, as illustrated in Figure 1-15. With a large number of operations, such analysis helps to form a big picture of the functionality of the application in question.

DEALING WITH THE ACTUAL MESSAGE
   1.   Writing a short message.
   2.   Adding a phrase.
   3.   Sending a short message.
   4.   Loading a message.
   5.   Saving a message.

DEALING WITH THE RECIPIENTS AND GROUPS
   6.   Selecting recipients and groups.
   7.   Creating a group.
   8.   Deleting a group.
   9.   Adding recipients to a group.
   10.   Removing recipients from a group.
   11.   Entering recipient's information.
   12.   Removing recipient's information.

FIGURE 1-15. Grouped operations.

Let us once again continue with the example application. You have now analyzed the operations presented in Figure 1-13 and grouped them into two groups, such as listed in Figure 1-15. Now identify the most important operations from the user's point of view. We call such operations *primary operations*. The analysis of importance is based on the use cases: The most common and time-consuming operations are typically the operations that the application is primarily implemented for. As an important usability goal, the performance of the primary operations should be as easy and as effective as possible.

In the Short Message System (SMS) application, you decide to select operations 1, 2, 3, and 6, which deal with the actual writing and sending of messages, to be the primary operations. According to the modern user interface paradigms, the most important and time-consuming operations should be performed in the main window of the application. Thus, the main window of the application should provide support for operations 1, 2, 3, and 6. In addition, you need several other dialog boxes to handle the rest of the operations, which are called *secondary operations*.

Specifying the Structure of the User Interface

GUIs are typically structured as windows, dialog boxes, HTML pages, and other such elements. During this phase of the process, we call these elements *dialogs*. Each dialog provides a selection of tools and components with which the user interacts. Depending on the windowing system in use, these are typically called *controls* or *widgets*.

Using the analogy of the architecture of buildings, dialogs are the rooms of a building, whereas buttons, text fields, and sliders correspond to the furniture in those rooms. The purpose of the building determines the floor plan. An office building requires a very different plan than does a summer cottage. Within the framework of the floor plan, individual pieces of furniture are placed in rooms based on the activities performed in each room. A bed belongs in a bedroom because people are supposed to sleep there, but you would not put a bed in a kitchen. People do not normally sleep in kitchens, and buildings are supposed to facilitate a normal way of living. Thus, the users' activities are the main concerns when designing the room structure and selecting furniture for each room. Of course, many other issues, among them aesthetic and legal issues, affect buildings as well.

The same goes for user interfaces. The "floor plan" and the "furniture" of the GUI should facilitate a normal way of using the application in question. The functionality of the user interface—support for the work at hand—is the main concern, although the visual appearance and style guides must also be taken into account. According to our practices, we first specify the dialog structure of the user interface and only after that start to think about buttons, menus, and other such elements. Similar to design of buildings, it is of vital importance that the floor plan—the dialog structure—fits its purpose. The structure must promote the smooth and effective performance of the end user's operations.

The dialog structure of the GUI needs to be visualized as early as possible. *Dialog diagrams* are the blueprints of this structure. The notation of dialog diagrams is UML's *state diagram notation*. Here, a state stands for a dialog box, window, or Web page, and an event causes a movement from one dialog to another.

Let us take another look at the Short Message System (SMS) example application. You have already analyzed the end users' operations illustrated in Figure 1-15. You ranked operations 1, 2, 3, and 6 to be the most important (primary) operations, and now you plan to implement a main window to support these operations. In addition, you plan to implement a dialog box for managing recipients and another box for managing groups. Finally, you need an additional dialog for saving and loading short messages. Based on these decisions, you draw the dialog diagram of SMS application, as illustrated in Figure 1-16. You have placed the operations listed in Figure 1-15 into the dialog boxes by using the "Do:" statement. Furthermore, you have illustrated the movements between dialogs with arrows. Thus the dialog diagram provides a visible image of the structure of the GUI. The diagram indicates the location in the user interface where each operation is performed and how the user navigates the network of dialog boxes.

Dialog diagrams are beneficial in various ways. First, they provide a visible view of the size and overall structure of the GUI. Second, they can assist preliminary usability checks. Software designers can estimate whether a dialog box is loaded with too many operations. Too many operations would probably make the final dialog messy and hard to understand. Designers also run use cases with the dialog diagram by using the operations allocated to individual dialog boxes. This exemplifies the use of the dialog structure in a context of use cases. Also, designers can reconsider the necessity of some dialogs is they are hardly ever used. Thirdly, as we will show, the dialog diagram will be one of the main sources when designing the architecture of interactive applications.

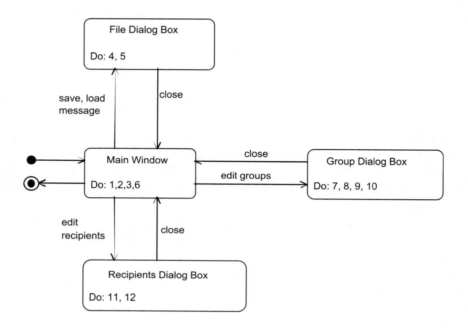

FIGURE 1-16. The dialogs of the SMS application illustrated as a dialog diagram.

Specifying the Layout of the Dialogs

The first version of the dialog structure of the application is now available in the form of the dialog diagram. The process can now continue by concentrating on one dialog at a time. Returning to the building metaphor, software designers work as interior decorators. They think about the purpose of each room (dialog) and the activities that take place within each room. Based on these observations, they select, design, and place the furniture in each room. In other words, they select or build the user interface components and elements and place them in the dialog under specification.

This phase produces the final layout and wording of the dialogs. You know the structure of dialog boxes, and now your goal is to create dialog boxes that support the end users' tasks as fully as possible. The dialog structure may well change during the specification process, because operations need to be moved from one dialog to another to create well-balanced dialog boxes. It is only now that you finally can see how much information will be needed in each particular dialog box.

While designing the layout of the user interface metaphors, you must take into account look-and-feel, style guides, and other such issues. This phase in the project is an ideal time to hire a graphic designer. The functionality and the dialog structure of the application is fixed. A graphic designer can now design attractive, well balanced dialogs to support the specified tasks.

While specifying the dialogs and windows, certain technical implementation issues must be considered. If the project is to build or use reusable user interface components, they must be identified during this phase. This identification allows developers, for example, to order required components from a separate component manufacturer team or steer their design towards the use of available user interface components.

Modern software development environments come with a selection of excellent GUI components. Also, various commercial and shareware sources offer reasonably prized ActiveX, Java Beans, and other GUI components. You should always check these sources before starting to specify the details of the user interface. Many elements of the user interface may already be available. For example, with our SMS example application, you should probably use a common, reusable file management dialog, such as the File Dialog Bean of IBM's Visual Age for Java, to implement the File dialog box. A similar dialog is also available in most GUI toolboxes.

This phase may also produce a user interface prototype. Prototypes can assist in obtaining feedback from the details of the user interface. Many handy tools, such as Visual Basic or Visio from Visio Corporation, are available to help develop good prototypes in short amounts of time. Thus, normally, no technical problems occur while developing prototypes. However, prototyping alone is not enough for the specification of the user interfaces. Arbitrary prototyping without systematic consideration of the end user's operations and user interface structure easily can cause failures in usability. Usability must be planned based on operations; it does not happen by accident.

One of the key problems with prototypes is that they can unnecessarily limit the solution. After the first prototype has been introduced, end users and designers start to think in terms of the prototype. They can imagine slightly modifying the details of the prototype, but they cannot rethink or question the very basics of the user interface anymore. Therefore, it is important that the fundamentals of the user interface are well thought out before the introduction of the first prototype. Software developers must carefully specify the user interface to support the operations of the end user—not the other way around!

Let us now continue with the SMS application example, concentrating first on the most important dialog: The main window of the application. According to the dialog diagram illustrated in Figure 1-16, you have specified that the main window will allow the end user to write short messages and send them to the selected recipients. You open your favorite GUI drawing tool and draw the main window as illustrated in Figure 1-17.

You do not want to overload windows and dialogs with any unnecessary elements; simple is always beautiful with GUIs. Therefore, your main window and other dialogs, illustrated in Figure 1-18, are not messy collections of buttons and labels but tight packages of required tools.

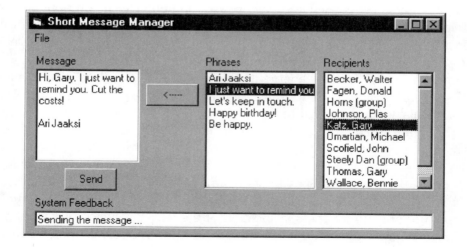

FIGURE 1-17. The main window of the SMS application.

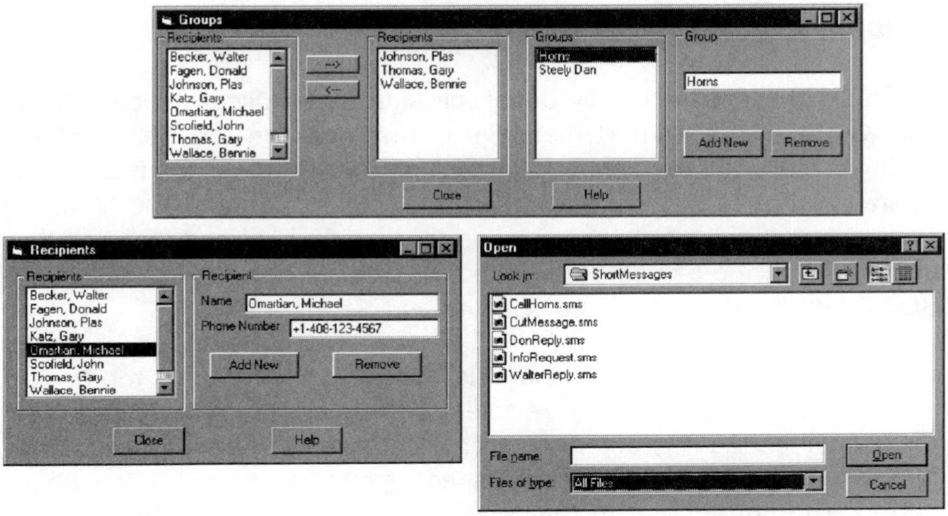

FIGURE 1-18. The other dialogs of the SMS application.

Writing the First Version of the User's Guide

In some projects software developers themselves write the user's guides, whereas in other projects they may utilize dedicated resources for constructing such documents. In either case, now is the right time to write the first versions of the user's guide.

If the software designers write the guides, they should now have all they need to write the first versions. They write the user's guide according to the use cases, such as those presented in Figures 1-8 and 1-9. The main idea is to fill the use cases with the concrete elements of the user interface, as illustrated in Figure 1-19. If a software developer finds it hard to describe how the use case is performed with the specified user interface, it follows that the end user will most probably have usability problems when using the application. Clear and simple explanations indicate simple and usable user interfaces and vice versa.

SENDING A SHORT MESSAGE

You start the application by double-clicking the application icon. After this you can write a short message in the Message text field. Before writing a message you can load a previously saved message from a file to start with (see Loading and Saving Messages). You can add phrases by selecting the desired phrase in the Phrases text list and pressing the arrow button. You can also save the message for later use by selecting Save from the File menu (see Loading and Saving Messages).

When the message is ready, you must select recipients from the Recipients list. If the name of your recipient is missing, you must add a new recipient (see Adding and Removing Recipients). Then you send the message to the selected recipients and groups by pressing the Send button. The bottom line of the window tells you how well the sending succeeds.

FIGURE 1-19. A first version of the user's guide.

Large projects may have dedicated resources writing the users' guides. In such cases software developers must provide enough information for the documentation personnel. Writers can create the first version of the users' guides based on this information. Then, after the final integration and testing the users' guides, they are polished to correspond to the final software. Such arrangements enable concurrent development of the applications and the guides, as illustrated in Figure 1-20.

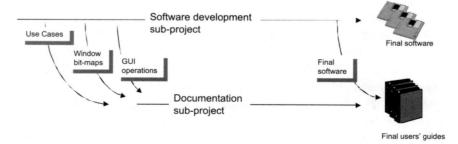

FIGURE 1-20. Parallel construction of software and users' guides.

Documenting Analysis

Documents contain the blueprints of software development. A group of people cannot develop software without proper documentation, and at least three purposes for the documents exist. First, documents provide a visible view to the system in each phase of system development. Documents are phase products that can be discussed, reviewed, and accepted within the organization and even with the customer during the software development project. Documents also provide visibility for project management and quality assurance. Second, the documents can be used to document the system and the requirements for a later study. By studying the documents, a designer who has not participated in system development, is able to understand not only the system as such but also the preconditions and requirements behind the system. Third, the documents form the basis for testing. The final product is tested against the documented requirements and design decisions.

Successful software development projects are often arranged around *features*. By features, we mean a new software system or system improvement that brings significant value to customer's operations. Thus, a feature can include completely new applications or changes to existing ones.[4] One purpose of a software project is to develop one or more features, and the analysis documents document the requirements, use cases, and other such elements related to those features under development.

The analysis documents are not maintained or updated after a software project. They are stored just as they are, and they are not maintained in future projects. Future projects that build new features will only study the stored documents and will produce their own, new analysis documents from scratch.

Based on our experience, there is typically no time or motivation within software projects to keep the analysis documents updated. Maintaining analysis documents from one project to another does not seem to be beneficial enough—not even if we built several versions of a software product during many years. Instead, the constructed software systems, together with their users guides, provide sufficient means for those who want to study the systems from their users' perspectives. Analysis documents produced during software projects are not later needed for this purpose. At their best, they simply reveal thoughts and ideas as they were in history, during previous projects.

We produce four types of documents during the analysis phase:[5]

1. **Preliminary memoranda and presentations about the product concept or feature.**
    *   All kinds of unofficial material including slide presentations, market studies, and other such documents.

2. **Feasibility Study Document.**
    *   An early requirements document.
    *   Includes the first version of the analysis document.
    *   Includes requirement statements, use cases, solution screenings, and effort estimates.
    *   May also include preliminary elements of other phase products, such as design diagrams and code.
    *   Basis for project decision and planning.

3. **Analysis Document.**
    *   The first document produced under the software development project.
    *   Includes requirement statements, use cases, an analysis class diagram with a data dictionary, and operation specifications.
    *   Requirement statements and use cases are copied from the Feasibility Study document and enhanced here.

4. **User Interface Specification Document.**
    *   Includes user interface operations, a dialog diagram, visualized dialogs, and the first version of the user's guide.
    *   May also include a user interface prototype.

Design

We make a clear distinction between analysis and design. *Analysis* produces problem descriptions, requirement statements, and the initial solution from the end user's point of view. *Design* uses these artifacts and specifies how the outlined solution will be implemented. During analysis the models, such as class and sequence diagrams, capture and exemplify the concepts and operations from the end user's perspective. During design, apparently similar graphs and models illustrate the technical implementation of the system in various levels of abstraction. However, also during analysis, the elements of the models illustrate the world of the users, whereas during design the elements illustrate the concepts of the programmers.

The outcome of design always depends on the operating system, the middleware, the programming language, and the programming environment used. For example, if designers use Java and Visual Age for Java, the result is a totally different design than if they use Microsoft's Visual Basic. If designers use UNIX, they may favor separate executable processes over threads; with Windows NT, they may want to work the other way round. Designers must master the operating system and the programming environment used, so which equipment they will use must be decided by, at the latest, the beginning of design. Good design uses tools, such as class and sequence diagrams, and the tools themselves can be used in a context of different technologies. However, the outcome and the semantic meaning of design, that is, the interpretation of the models, cannot be independent from the technology used.

Let us take a closer look at this issue, because we have seen many cases of people suggesting language independent design. Building software is like building bridges. During analysis a municipality, for example, studies the problem of people moving from one place to another over a river. As a solution, they suggest building a bridge. A group of designers starts to analyze what kind of a bridge is needed. For example, they may decide the bridge needs two lanes and sidewalks on both sides. Other considerations, such as environmental and economical issues, must also be taken into account. Thus, analysis is about defining the problem and finding a solution.

During design, engineers plan how to build the bridge. First, they decide the bridge will be made of steel for economical and aesthetic reasons. Next, the designers use various mathematical models and architectural blueprints to specify and illustrate the bridge. They would use the same type of models, formulas, and notations as they would if they planned a concrete bridge. However, nobody would suggest that the designers use the same design for both a concrete and a steel bridge; a bridge made of concrete according to the plans of a steel bridge would probably collapse. We claim the same goes for software. A C++ application that runs on UNIX should not be constructed according to the plans of a Visual Basic application designed for Windows 95. The architecture just cannot be copied as such.

Architectural Design

Architectural design is the first design activity in our process model. Architectural design aims at constructing the best possible component structure for the application under development. As with other phases in our process, we use two parallel paths in architectural design. The static path of architectural design produces the component and device structure, which forms the architecture of the system. The functional path illustrates how these components collaborate in a context of given operations.

Philippe B. Kruchten presents a 4+1 View model of architecture. We suggest a slightly modified version of the approach using three plus one views of the architecture [Kruchten 95].[6] The views are the *logical*, *run-time*, and *development* view, plus the *scenario* view. The first three views are taken along the static path of our process, whereas the scenario view uses the use cases and operations on the functional path.

The logical view illustrates the high level partitioning of the system into application products and applications. This view is used mainly for communicative and product management purposes, for example, when discussing with customers and allocating work for projects and product lines. If the system contains a single application, such as the SMS example, the logical view is not needed. The logical view of the architecture is typically sketched very early in the analysis phase and then finalized during architectural design.[7]

The process of designing technical software architecture uses the run-time and development views together with the scenario view. The run-time view specifies all the *executable components* of the system, while the development view specifies the components that are *developed independently*. The scenario view illustrates the *collaboration* of these components in different usage situations. Thus, these three views are used together.

In our terminology, architectural design deals with components. A component means either a functional piece of software that is used as a basic building block of larger software systems or a device or an external agent that software collaborates with. In most cases, a good component is about the "size of a human-being"; meaning, one component is developed and maintained by a single application developer within a project. Thus, the software architecture both divides the system into components and enables the distribution of development work to individual software designers. Examples of typical components are a client application, a server application, a database connection library, and an ActiveX text editor component.

The component and device structure of an application depends on many things. From perspective of the development view, a good component architecture:

- Uses components that are developed as independent miniproducts with their own requirements, versions, milestones in a project, and responsible persons.
- Uses components that are consist of unambiguous files controlled by the software configuration management function.
- Enables multiple software developers to develop components concurrently.
- Minimizes interfaces and communication between components.
- Is clear and understandable.

From the perspective of the run-time view, a good component architecture:

- Is scalable, enabling the use of different hardware and software configurations.
- Makes the system perform efficiently.
- Is robust and tolerates exceptional situations.
- Is clear and understandable.

The process of developing the component architecture is typically iterative. The process uses at least the run-time, development, and scenario view. In many cases, the process must come back to architectural design after detailed design phase to verify and fine-tune the architecture.

Component Specification with Run-Time and Development Views

At the start of architectural design, the project team must identify the elements of the software system in question. The team needs to visually illustrate the static architecture of the application using both the run-time and development view. Thus, this phase we call *component specification* produces the physical component architecture of the system.

Architectural design typically starts with the run-time view of the component architecture. It first specifies the executable components and computational devices that will exist within the running system, as well as all the devices with which the system will interface.

There are many different paradigms and approaches to divide applications into software components. For example, you may use a simple two-tiered, client-server architecture, or a more advanced, three-tiered model. In the former you may have client applications using a common server that provides data management services; in the latter applications are divided into three executable components, that is, thin user interface clients, middle layer, implementing the business rules and the reusable functionality of the entire application domain; and the data storage layer, implementing persistence storage for the information used. In addition to these approaches, you can just model the application as a network of collaborating components. In such architectural approaches, every component can be a client and a server depending on the situation. In any event, the requirements for the scalability, performance, and robustness limit the framework for the run-time architecture of the application under development.

Architectural design takes also takes into account all external devices with which the system collaborates. The devices are modeled as such, because their interfaces and behavior cannot be changed. These devices typically exist already in the analysis class diagram.

The design of a well balanced run-time architecture is a subject for an entire book in itself. To present some concrete examples, let us come back to the Short Message System (SMS) application. There is a requirement that states: "The system must allow multiple accesses to the stored phone numbers and groups." Based on this, you decide to use a simple, two-tiered run-time architecture.

In your architecture, you have two major run-time components. The *SMS client* uses a mobile phone to send messages and the *SMS server* stores and loads recipients and groups. You illustrate the architecture as a UML deployment diagram shown in Figure 1-21. The figure shows these two executable components that can run even in different machines.

The stereotype notation of UML provides a means to illustrate components or other elements belonging to a certain predefined category. In Figure 1-21 there are two component categories: *clients* and *servers*. In addition, the stereotype «RMI» illustrates that the components communicate through an out-process communication mechanism of type Java *Remote Method*

Invocation (RMI). RMI is a distribution mechanism that enables programmers to create distributed applications in Java environments. «A5» is obviously a proprietary communication protocol of the phone manufacturer.

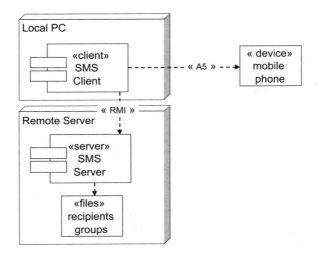

FIGURE 1-21. The run-time view of the component architecture.

A deployment diagram, presented in Figure 1-21, is not enough. In addition, you need to explain components in more detail. For this purpose, we use simple lists of components and their explanations, as illustrated in Figure 1-22. These explanations are only informative and help others to understand the roles of different elements within our applications.

COMPONENT	DESCRIPTION
SMS Client	The user interface application. Performs also the actual sending of a SMS by using the attached phone.
SMS Server	Provides services for saving and loading recipient and group information. Provides access for multiple clients. Can run in a same machine with the client, if used locally; for example, in a laptop computer.
recipients groups	Information about the recipients and groups stored in ASCII files.
mobile phone	A mobile phone implementing an A5 interface.

FIGURE 1-22. The description of the run-time components of an application.

You start to think about the development view concurrently with the specification of the run-time view. While the run-time view illustrates the executable components existing at run time, the development view presents the individual components that will be developed and managed independently. The components of the development view form also the concrete manageable items from which the software configuration management builds the executables.

High quality development architecture enables concurrent and independent development and management of individual components within a project. Typically, some components of the entire system are bought, some components are taken from other applications, and some components are developed from scratch. In all cases, the development view of the architecture highlights their independence as the units of work. Thus, the run-time and development views are different although closely related.

In the SMS example, you decide to construct the application from the components developed according to Figure 1-23. You purchase an editor component implemented as a Java Bean and reuse the file management library developed within your company. The editor will be an in-process component working within the same executable process with the SMS client component. The same apply with the SMS server and the File MGMT component. The components communicate through the interfaces called *Text*, *Recipients*, and *Data*.

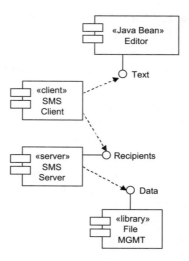

FIGURE 1-23. The development view of the SMS application.

The components of the development view need to be explained, as illustrated in Figure 1-24. These components are the concrete entities of the development activities. Each component is the responsibility of one person who takes care of the implementation, the purchase, or the enhancement of the component within the project. Software developers manage these components as independently as possible and project manages monitor the status of these components. These are also the software configuration items. The software configuration management function monitors their versions and status and build executable systems from them.

COMPONENT/ INTERFACE	DESCRIPTION
Editor	An editor component subcontracted from a small local company called Java Tools Ltd.
Text	An interface the SMS client uses for retrieving and setting the text in the text editor component.
SMS Client	The user interface component. Implemented in Java. Collaborates with the mobile phone.
SMS Server	Provides services for saving and loading recipient and group information. Implemented in Java.
Recipients	A Java RMI interface for clients to save and load recipients and groups.
File MGMT	A Java library component implemented within our company. Reads and saves textual data from/to ASCII files.
Data	A Java interface for saving and loading text strings.

FIGURE 1-24. The description of the development view components and interfaces.

During this phase we would also specify the database solutions for the application. Tables and fields of the database would be explained. In a sense, a database can be seen as a component.[8]

Component Collaboration Specification with Scenario View

The components of an application collaborate to provide services to external entities, such as users, other systems, and devices. We already specified the services as operations during the analysis phase. These operations are the starting point of *component collaboration specification*, which specifies how components co-operate to perform the operations of the application.

We model the collaboration with sequence diagrams. The diagrams provide the *scenario view* to the architecture. The scenario view deals with the functional aspects of the component architecture, and is therefore on the functional path of our process model.

Sequence diagrams can illustrate both the collaboration of the *executable* components of the run-time view and the *implementable* components of the development view. In the former case, the collaborative components are the processes and devices that will run independently in a functioning system. In the latter, the components are the entities that will be developed independently as Window programs (.EXEs), UNIX processes, libraries, ActiveX components, and so on. The sequence diagrams are used with precondition, postcondition, and exception clauses, similar to the operation specifications of the analysis phase. During design, we call them *scenarios*.

The scenarios, using the components of the development view, support the specification of *interfaces* between the components. Interfaces are agreements between components. A component "promises" to implement a certain interface. In addition, development view interfaces are also agreements between software developers. Each developer promises to either implement or use a certain interface, according to commonly agreed-upon rules of architectural specifications.

The scenarios, using the components of the run-time view, help the tuning and balancing of the run-time installation. These diagrams illustrate how executable components communicate in a running system. Such an illustration is necessary to analyze the performance and scalability of the system at hand. The scenarios show what kind of data, how much of it, and how often it is transferred from a component to another. With the run-time component scenarios, designers simulate different usage patterns and analyze the performance of the system against the requirements.

In simple architectures of less than, say, ten components, the scenarios of the development view, accompanied by external devices, often are enough. Such diagrams include also the collaboration of run-time components, because the run-time components are made of development components. Thus, the components of the run-time view are configurations of the components of the development view.

When drawing the scenarios and the sequence diagrams within them, some changes to the preliminary component architecture may be necessary. It is only now that we can see and understand how different end user's requests, for example, are served by collaborative components. Because the sequence diagrams provide a visible view of the component collaboration, they help in detecting problems in performance and robustness. Changing the initial run-time component architecture may solve such problems. However, the architecture of an application cannot be judged based on one single scenario only. All operations, including meaningful communication between the components, must be studied as scenarios and taken into account when finalizing the architecture.

Let us now go back to the example SMS application. You illustrate how components of the SMS application collaborate. For this purpose, you draw scenarios for the operations of the application. One of those scenarios is drawn in Figure 1-25. In the sequence diagram of the scenario, the collaborative components are: The user, SMS Client, Editor, and Phone. In practice, many operations are so trivial that there is no point in drawing any diagrams. Thus, you should draw only those sequence diagrams where there is some significant cooperation between the components.

Operation: Sending a short message
Preconditions: Message is written; recipients are selected.
Sequence Diagram:

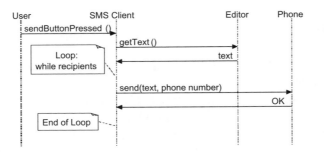

Exceptions: Sending fails: then show an error message.

Postconditions: The message is sent to the network.

FIGURE 1-25. A scenario illustrating the collaboration of components.

One scenario illustrates the communication of components in the context of only one of the operations listed in Figure 1-13. In a sense, we now open the "Short Message System Application" line in the analysis sequence diagram, illustrated in Figure 1-14, and concentrate on components *within* the line in question. As we already mentioned, during analysis we were interested in the services provided for the end user. Therefore, the system was just one black-box entity to be seen and used by the end user. Now, during the design phase, we specify how components provide their specified functionality by working together. Thus, now the system is a collection of collaborative components as seen by software developers.

Almost all real-sized systems consist of multiple, executable components—processes that communicate with each other. Concurrent processes are needed for several reasons, among them performance and robustness. For example, you can achieve better performance by allocating many simultaneous processes to work on different machines. You can achieve robustness, for example, by implementing guard processes that monitor performance of other processes. However, unnecessary process division is injurious. Functions within a single process are always faster to execute and easier to implement. Therefore, process division must be justified, and in many cases it can be accomplished only during detailed design. You can judge final process division by studying the design scenarios of both architectural and detailed design phases. Any benefits of crossing the process boundaries must be greater than the penalties.

Interfaces

Components communicate through *interfaces*. The components can be within the same process or in different processes. The communication through interfaces is thus either *in-process* or *out-process* communication. Although the interfaces of the run-time view diagrams are always out-process interfaces, the interfaces of the development view diagrams are of both types.

An interface is an agreement without implementation. In theory, any component can *implement* an interface, which means that the component works according to the agreement made by the interface. Another component, satisfied with the agreement, may then use the component through the interface. The user component is thus interested in the interface and its promises and not in the component actually implementing the promises of the agreement.

The scenarios of architectural design provide the methods, parameters, and return values for the interfaces. Sequence diagrams illustrate how a component calls another component and such calling goes through an interface. In most cases, an interface consists of function declarations only, and the actual data is hidden. The component that implements the interface provides code that implements the functions. The component that uses the interface simply calls the functions without worrying the implementation or the implementer at all.

Let us take an example. In a certain point in the scenarios of the SMS application, there is a part of a sequence diagram illustrated in Figure 1-26. According to the diagram, the SMS Client component calls the SMS Server component to get recipients and groups. This calling is done through the "recipients" interface because, according to the development view illustrated in Figure 1-23, that interface is the only way for the client to call the server in your application.

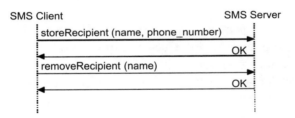

FIGURE 1-26. A part of the scenario illustrating the collaboration of components.

Based on the sequence diagram in Figure 1-26, you can now specify the Recipients interface illustrated in Figure 1-27. The interface includes the functions storeRecipient and removeRecipient, and the SMS Client will call these functions. SMS Server implements the interface, and SMS Client uses SMS Server through the Recipients interface.

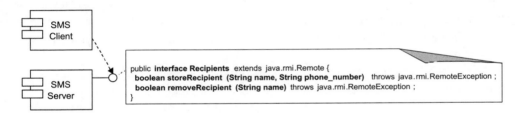

FIGURE 1-27. Collaboration of the components.

Technically, many ways to implement an interface are available. In the Windows environment, the (D)COM technology provides a usable option. It allows you to implement components that run either in a single process or in parallel processes, even in different machines. Tools, such as Visual Basic, Borland Delphi, Visual C++, and J++, support (D)COM interfaces. Thus the COM technology allows components implemented in different languages to collaborate in Windows environments. For Java environments, different ways of implementing interfaces exist. Within a single executable component, Java provides a concept of interface at the language level. Between two or more executable Java programs or applets, you can direct calls through an RMI interface. Thus, Java RMI is a technology that allows components implemented in Java to collaborate in machines of various types. Finally, Corba technology provides language and operating system independent interfaces. It enables components implemented in different languages and running in different machines to collaborate as long as Corba services are used.

Modern technologies, such as Corba and Java RMI, treat interfaces clearly as independent entities. An interface is a mini-product saved into its own file with its own identity and versioning. This practice is beneficial and supports robust and modular architecture. Such interfaces can be implemented by different components, and many components can implement the same interface. In this respect, all interfaces between components are similar to the Java interfaces between Java classes or abstract C++ classes between concrete classes. One Java class may implement multiple interfaces, and many Java classes can implement the same interface.

Whatever technology you choose, it is of vital importance to understand and use the concept of interface. An interface is an independent entity between the components of a system, and interfaces should never be mixed with the implementation code. However, the concept of interfaces does not require any particular technology. We use several very different technologies to build interfaces. We may implement an interface as abstract C++ classes if components run in a same C++ executable. Distributed applications can be implemented, for example, with carefully documented remote procedure calls.

Even if interfaces are built using remote procedure calls, pure C++, or some other technology that does not support interfaces so clearly, you should always treat an interface as a semantically independent entity. In practice, this means that interfaces have names, they are treated as mini-products with versioning, and they are not to be changed without a proper change control mechanism. Others using the interfaces and components through the interfaces must be able to trust their quality and stability. This promotes the independence of the components behind the interfaces and supports parallel development of the components by localizing the need of communication into the interfaces.

In practice, an interface can often be handled directly as a part of a component. The majority of interfaces emerge first as integral parts of components. Such interfaces are implemented by one component only, and the needs to provide additional implementations to this same interface emerge later, if ever. This means that an interface can typically be documented together with a component implementing it. However, this situation should not jeopardize the independent nature of an interface.

In some projects, we have first developed a limited basic component for certain purposes from scratch. Other components use that component through an interface, and only one component implements the interface. Then, later, we replace the component with a more advanced one or even with a commercial component that we have purchased. In many cases, when we have managed to design the interface properly, the users of the component have not even known about the change. Their implementations rely on the interface, not on the implementation.

Architecture of Interactive Components

In the previous sections, we have presented techniques to design the component architecture of an application. We have suggested that such architecture be built around interfaces to support concurrent and independent development of software components. The following sections will concentrate on how to implement such independent components. In addition to the entire architecture, the components themselves need to be designed also; and good architecture is required once again.

In an ideal case, an individual software designer develops a component as independently as possible. The component consists of Java or C++ classes, Visual Basic Forms and Class modules, or other such low level classes. Component architecture is about these entities, that is, it is about the structures of programmable classes.

Interactive Components

Components with a graphical user interface (GUI) are a part of almost every software system. Let us use such a component as an example of any component. We exemplify how to use the phase products of analysis and architectural design to support the design of object-oriented software components.

Good architecture of GUI components separates the user interface from the rest of the code. The approach of many modern programming environments and tools, such as Microsoft Visual C++, Visual Basic, Borland's Delphi, and even IBM's Visual Age for Java, does not necessarily support such an approach. Modern tools tend to build programs tightly around the user interface. In these tools, the GUI is the central part of the application component, and the rest of the application is typically built to directly support the GUI. Applications "hang" from the GUI, as illustrated in Figure 1-28. Practically all the code is written within the "Click" functions of Visual Basic, the "MouseDown" functions of Delphi, or the callback functions of Motif.

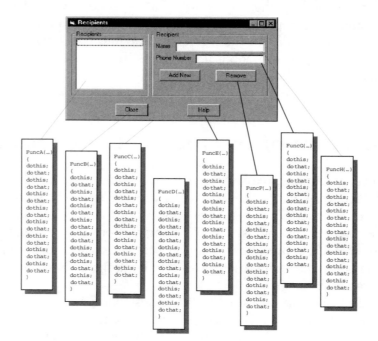

FIGURE 1-28. A typical architecture of many modern
application components.

Such a GUI-hanger approach is acceptable in small applications and prototypes. However, for most real-size programs, the GUI-hangar approach produces messy structures that are hard to maintain. The seeming simplicity of GUI-centered programming environments does not motivate designers to design robust and modular programs. User interface applications tend to grow arbitrarily around buttons, text fields, and menus. Even small changes in such user interfaces require significant reengineering of entire applications.

At the other extreme, some software designers misuse the object-oriented paradigm and the concept of class. Their C++ or Java classes are loose modules that include arbitrary sets of different functions. Classes do not have clear identity but are merely used as a means to divide functional code into parts. Such applications and components typically have only a few large classes. Also, all these classes typically refer to all other classes. If you need to add functions in such applications, you may well add the functions into whatever classes you choose. Because the classes do not have any semantic identity that originates from analysis, you cannot expect any particular functionality from a class. As an example, it is reasonable to expect that a Print() member function belongs to a Printer class. However, if the classes of the application are named as illustrated in Figure 1-29, such assumptions cannot be made.

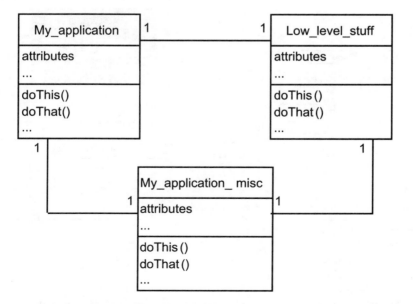

FIGURE 1-29. Splitting functional code into arbitrary classes.

Many problems are related to poor class structures, which are hard to read and understand. They get more difficult to maintain as software enlarges. Reuse is almost impossible to achieve because of the lack of proper modularity. To avoid these pitfalls, software designers need methods and tools to design high-quality, object-oriented class architectures within application components. The taken approach must also fit with the tools and programming languages at hand.

The Core of Object Paradigm

Object paradigm provides good solutions to the architectural problems within the components. According to object paradigm, you design applications starting from the classes found during object analysis. You try to keep the analysis classes and structures alive and well from analysis through design all the way to the programming phase, as illustrated in Figure 1-30. In the final code, you expect to find similar classes and similar class structures that were found during the analysis phase.

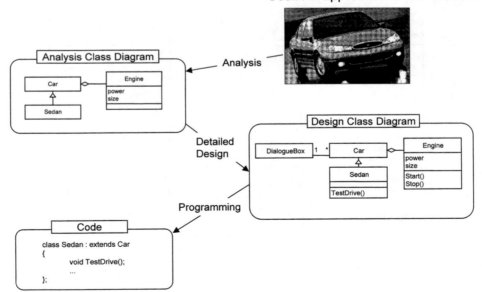

FIGURE 1-30. Object-oriented applications are built using the objects identified from the real world.

We claim that this is single the most important thing in object orientation. Programmed class structures and object collaboration patterns originate from reality, from the problem domain. Such applications are easier to understand, are more robust, and enable the reuse of the parts of an application. All other aspects of object paradigm are only a means to help the implementation of structures that resemble reality. After all, object paradigm originates from simulations, and Simula 67 was the first language that introduced the concept of classes. You should not forget where it all started.

Object-oriented languages, such as C++, Java, and Smalltalk, make the implementation of the reality-based structures and behavioral patterns possible. For example, the specialization relationship between "Car" and "Sedan" illustrated in Figure 1-30 is easy to implement with *inheritance* in C++ or with *extends* in Java. Notations, such as UML, help in illustrating these structures and patterns in different phases of software development. However, object orientation is merely a state of mind and a way to construct software structures. Notations and object-oriented programming languages are simply means to express and implement these properties.

We claim that we construct genuinely object-oriented applications. Using C++, late binding, abstract classes, UML, or any other such thing would not alone prove our claim. We base our claim on the fact that we use a continuous path from the analysis of the problem domain to the design of programmable classes. The following sections will show how we use the phase products of the analysis phase during design to produce high-quality, object-oriented architectures.

MVC++ Architecture

High-quality architecture is understandable and clear, and enables late modifications to software. For example, modifying the user interface should not cause too many modifications to the rest of the application. Many usable architectural approaches exist, such as the Model-View-Controller [Kranser and Pope 88], the Presentation-Abstract-Control [Coutaz 87], and the Document-View approach found in Microsoft's Visual C++. They all resemble each other. They divide applications into two or three main layers, namely the user interface layer, the domain specific functional layer, and some kind of a glue layer between these two.

In real software projects, vague guidelines, such as "separate GUI from the rest of the application" are not enough to steer architecture onto the right track. Software designers require practical and concrete how-to guidelines. We have created such a set of concrete guidelines to help designers in designing robust interactive components and applications and implement them by using Java, Visual C++, Motif or other such environments. We have successfully used the guidelines in large software projects, and they have improved both the speed of implementation and the quality of implemented applications. These guidelines help in making modular architectures without making their implementation unnecessarily complicated.

We use a modification of a famous Model-View-Controller paradigm and call our approach *MVC++* [Jaaksi 95]. Some significant differences exist between the original MVC [Kranser and Pope 88], [Gamma et al. 95] and our MVC++. First of all, MVC++ does not necessarily require any supportive infrastructure, such as base class libraries or frameworks. In addition, we have tuned it to work especially with Java and C++. Finally, we have minimized the communication between the parts and encapsulated the entire user interface including the receiving of users' actions into the view classes.

We have been forced to formulate such reference architecture. Our R & D units grow rapidly because we hire new, fresh employees. They start to work with software modules implemented by others now working in different positions. To maintain the quality of our software, we need basic guidelines. Guidelines keep the architectural vision clear, even when different designers work with the same application component. Also, such guidelines make it much easier to maintain the components in the long run, because all applications resemble each other by their internal structure. A common architectural pattern improves understandability, helping others to understand the architecture and functionality of applications.

MVC++ is one good example of a tested application architecture. Other similar patterns would also work well. Our main message is that, to be efficient and produce good quality software, a heterogeneous organization must follow some commonly agreed-upon architectural paradigms.

According to the MVC++ approach, three kinds of objects are in an executable program: *model*, *view*, and *controller* objects, as illustrated in Figure 1-31. Compared to the MVC approach used in the Java Swing component set and Rogue Wave's View.h++, for example, our MVC++ provides an architecture for entire application components, not for the user interface layer only.

- **The model layer** of an application corresponds to "the real world." It is a collection of classes representing the concepts of the problem domain. The model classes do not have any user interface elements. The first version of the model layer is directly derived from the analysis class diagram.

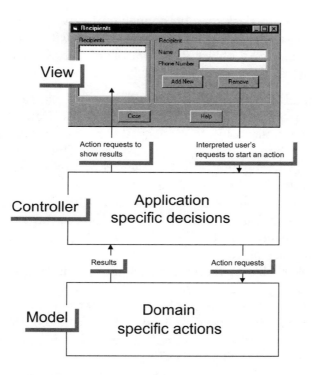

FIGURE 1-31. Parts of an MVC++ application.

- **The model layer** of an application corresponds to "the real world." It is a collection of classes representing the concepts of the problem domain. The model classes do not have any user interface elements. The first version of the model layer is directly derived from the analysis class diagram.
- **The view layer** is the outer software layer visible to the end user. The classes of the view layer form the user interface. Typically, there is one view class for each dialog box and window of the user interface. User interface components are typically implemented as classes that consists of text fields, buttons, graphics, scroll bars, and so on. These components are called view components, and they are object members of the actual view classes. The first version of the view layer is directly derived from the user interface specification.
- **The controller layer** controls the interaction between the model and the view. There is a single controller class for every view class. However, one controller class may have relations with multiple model classes, and

the same model class may be connected to many controller classes. In most cases, a view object can communicate with a model object only through a controller object. The controller layer evolves when the design phase finalizes the model and view layers.

The model objects represent the reflection of classes of the problem domain. The majority of the model classes originate from the analysis class diagram. The controller objects manage the model objects, and the model objects are not aware of the objects of the view. The view objects form the user interface, including the user interface components, call-back functions connected to buttons and other user interface elements, Java listeners, and so on. Although user actions, such as pressing a button or moving a slider, initiate functions of the view objects, the view objects do not decide how to respond to these actions. Instead, the view objects pass on the user's requests to relevant controller objects.

The controller objects then make all the application-specific decisions. They know how a particular application should work. Based on these decisions, the controller objects typically call the methods of the model objects, which finally serve the user's requests. Thus, the controller objects are adapters that integrate the model and the view objects in an application-specific way, as illustrated in Figure 1-32.

Each layer of an MVC++ component is made of several classes. View, controller, and model classes belong to different layers, as exemplified in Figure 1-33, which illustrates an artificial example of a MVC++ application. Such MVC++ structure originates directly from the phase products of the analysis phase. The dialog diagram produces the basic structure for the view and controller layers, while the model layer is based on the analysis class diagram, as illustrated in Figure 1-34.

Each executable component of an application is internally designed and implemented according to the MVC++ paradigm. Thus, MVC++ is an architectural solution for one executable component. For external communication, a component must have a means, such as RPC, Java RMI, (D)COM, or Corba IDL. For example, if the components use Java RMI, separate interface classes can specialize in the process-to-process communication, as illustrated in Figure 1-35. In Java, such classes in the server side would inherit UnicastRemoteObject and implement the specified interface. Also, in the client side, interprocess communication can be implemented within classes specialized for that purpose. The Proxy Design Pattern presented in the GOF book [Gamma et al. 95] can hide the details of interprocess communication from the rest of the application.

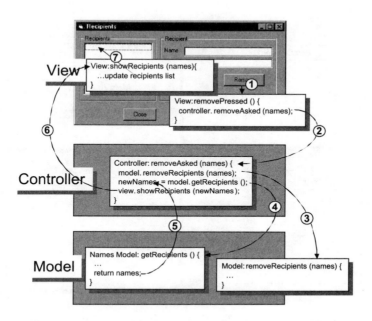

FIGURE 1-32. This is how an MVC++ application component works.

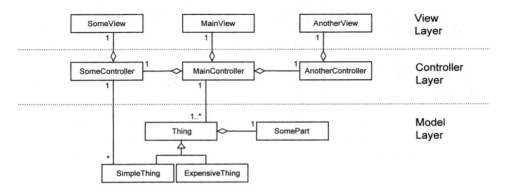

FIGURE 1-33. Each application has three main class layers.

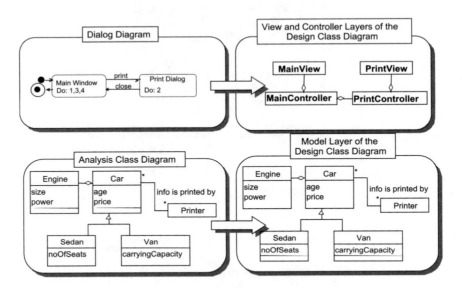

FIGURE 1-34. The MVC++ application layers originate
from the analysis phase.

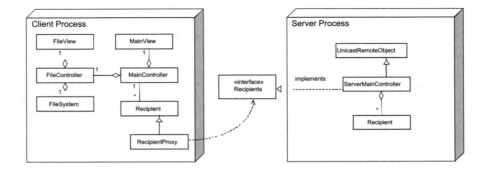

FIGURE 1-35. Components implemented according to the MVC++ paradigm.

Detailed Design

Detailed design concentrates on one component, that is, one executable process or library, at a time. Whereas architectural design specifies the components, devices, and their collaboration, detailed design specifies how classes within a component are programmed, what kind of structures they form, and how the instances of these classes collaborate. During the detailed design phase, each component is opened and its implementation is designed in terms of programmable classes.

The detailed design phase utilizes both the static and functional paths of our process model. Whereas the static path specifies classes and class structures, the functional path defines how instances of these classes collaborate to provide functionality specified in the analysis and architectural design phases. *Object design* is performed on the static path, whereas *behavior design* is performed on the functional path of our process model.

It is important to select a clear architecture for detailed design and stick to it. Having one commonly agreed-upon architecture enables the reuse of classes and class structures of one component in another. If the organization agrees on how to implement, for example, interprocess communication and the user interface, individual software developers can understand the design of others and use parts of it in their own solutions.

Actually, it is not that important which kind of application architecture is selected. The MVC++ architecture we mentioned has proven to be a good solution in C++ and Java environments. For Smalltalk, the original MVC would be better. For simple Visual Basic and Delphi applications, we combine view and controller layers into single user interface layer[9]. For Visual C++ applications, we can use the view layer as presented in MVC++. The document layer would work as a controller. In addition, programs that are not of document-editor type may require a domain-specific layer, separate from view and document. This layer corresponds to the model layer of MVC++. It should not use MFC classes, and so it can be reused in other environments.

The main idea is to separate the reusable domain classes of your application from the classes that implement application specific functionality or that provide interfaces to the external world. In addition to the separate user interface, we often implement a separate database layer or interprocess communication layer. Then we access this layer from the domain classes by using inheritance, association, or aggregation structures. Whatever we choose, the so-called domain classes are implemented independently so that the external world does not affect their implementation. As an example, your short message-domain class should remain the same no matter whether you have a Web based user interface, a command-line user interface, or no user interface at all. Such approach produces high-quality applications with understandable and clear structures. Also, such structures enable efficient reuse of both domain and interface classes.

Object Design

Object design specifies the classes that comprise the component in question. These classes will be coded during the programming phase in C++, Java, Visual Basic, or some other programming language. Thus, object design produces the design class diagrams of a single component to illustrate its class structure.

Like many others, we use the same notation for the analysis and design class diagrams. However, the design class diagrams semantically model different things. The design class diagram is not just an improvement of the analysis class diagram with some additional details. The design class diagram contains similar elements with the analysis class diagram and is derived from it. Whereas the analysis class diagram illustrates the concepts of the problem domain, the design class diagram depicts the classes that will be programmed. According to object paradigm, these two different groups of classes are closely related. However, what will be coded is not just an improvement of what has been analyzed from the real world. They are conceptually different things.

Object design builds on the analysis phase. It should also use commonly agreed-upon guidelines, such as the use of application frameworks and design patterns. We advocate the use of the MVC++ approach as a basis of object design. The MVC++ approach specifies the structure of applications by telling the designer how to design a layered class diagram that separates interfaces, application-specific functionality, and reusable domain-specific functionality in an object-oriented way.

The most low-level design decisions are done only during programming, and object design is done at the higher level of *abstraction*. The class diagram notation of UML provides good tools for design-level abstraction. However, one box in the diagram for every class in the code is not much of an abstraction. According to Alan Wills: "Many tools offer to translate your diagrams to C++: to me, that is missing the point. C++ is not that unreadable. Let's put the diagrams to better use [Wills 96]!"

We do not include all details, such as classes that implement data structures or each and every method and attribute of the design class diagrams. The readability of the diagrams is the most important aspect, because we do not generate code from them. Also, not every detailed modification of the code affects the design class diagrams. Thus, many details can only be found from the final code. For this purpose, graphical code visualization and browsing tools are handy.

Let us now continue with our SMS application example. Suppose that you alone are now responsible of the Client component, and your task is to design the implementation of that component. According to MVC++, you now draw the first version of the design class diagram for the Short Message Manager Client component, as shown in Figure 1-36. Each dialog box of the user interface forms a view class. For each view class, a controller class takes care of the application logic related to the dialog in question. Each controller class includes its view class as an object member. Thus, the connections between the view and the controller classes are established. In addition, you have copied the classes of the analysis class diagram presented in Figure 1-11 to the model part of the application. After these steps, Figure 1-36 illustrates the first version of the design class diagram constructed according to the MVC++ approach[10].

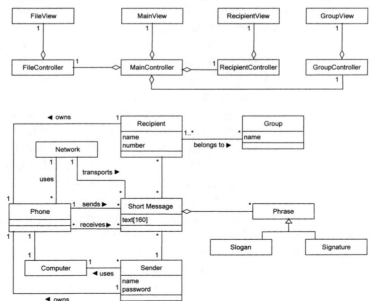

FIGURE 1-36. The first version of the SMS client component design class diagram.

The first version of the design class diagram is immature, and it needs a lot of refining and tuning. At this point, you do not guess what operations or connections there might be in the design class diagram. Neither do you guess which classes should be removed, added, or modified. The systematic use of scenarios including sequence diagrams will perform all such refining for the design class diagram. You analyze *every* operation in the operation list and draw sequence diagrams for each operation by using the design class diagram. By doing so, you refine connections between the classes and add operations, attributes, and new classes. We call this activity *behavior design.*

Behavior Design

Behavior design specifies the collaborations of the objects within an application component. We use scenarios to visualize the collaborations. Our scenarios include sequence diagrams and precondition, postcondition, and exception clauses. Behavior design uses scenarios to refine the design class diagram to its final form, produces declarations of member functions, and establishes connections for the classes.

The functional path of our process model uses sequence diagrams systematically. Operation specification during the analysis phase illustrated *how the system communicates with external entities.* During architectural design, sequence diagrams illustrated *how components communicate within the system.* During detailed design, sequence diagrams illustrate *how objects collaborate within a component.* And finally, sequence diagrams will *assist programming.* In a sense, the system seen as a black box during analysis is opened down to the object level, as illustrated in Figure 1-37. Operations are focused from analysis all the way to the C++ or Java object level.

We draw design scenarios including sequence diagrams for the operation of the component. Each scenario specifies a set of member functions, attributes, and associations and adds them into the design class diagram, as illustrated in Figure 1-38. Scenarios may also add classes to the design class diagram, and classes that are not involved in any scenario can be removed from the design class diagram. After all operations have been modeled as scenarios, and the design class diagram has been refined accordingly, the class diagram is ready for implementation.

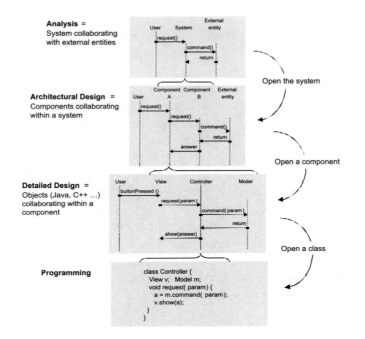

FIGURE 1-37. We use sequence diagrams systematically along the functional path of our process.

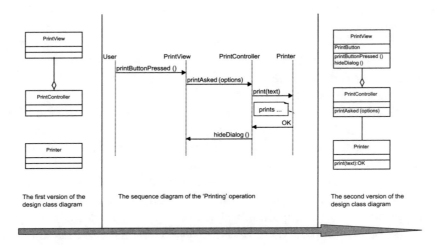

FIGURE 1-38. A sequence diagram improves the first version of the design class diagram.

Communication between objects will be implemented as function calls. Therefore, the messages of the sequence diagram should match with the final member functions. Whereas function calls always contain parentheses, return values are written without them.

One user's operation, modeled as an operation specification during analysis, may require design in more than one component. An example of such a case would be an application with a client component and a server component. The end user initiates an action in the client, which uses the services of the server to answer the original request. Although there is only one end user operation, it requires design in the two client and server components.

Let us now continue with the SMS example application. You draw a scenario including a sequence diagram of every component and operation. In practice, many operations are so trivial that there is no need to draw any diagrams. During detailed design, you draw only those sequence diagrams where there is some meaningful cooperation between the objects of the component in question. As in all phases, trivial diagrams are not only useless but even harmful. Large amounts of useless information hides the important diagrams from readers.

You decide to start behavior design with the "Sending a Short Message" operation. You draw the scenario illustrated in Figure 1-39, which illustrates the implementation of operation within the client component. According to the sequence diagram, the operation starts when the user presses the Send button in the application's main window. The first method that is called is the sendButtonPressed method, which is a member function of the MainView class. The method is a so-called *callback function* that is launched by the user's action.[11] The view object calls the Editor component to get the written message text. For this purpose, it uses the Text interface. After this, the Main-View object calls the sendRequest member function of the MainController. A view object can only *ask* a controller object to do something, because according to the MVC++ approach it is the controller that decides which actions should be taken. After this, the controller commands the view object to show an informative message in the user interface. Then, the controller loops through all selected recipients and uses the Phone object to do the actual sending. Thus, the communication between the application and the real physical phone has been implemented within the Phone class. The operation ends when the looping is over and the controller commands the view to inform the user.

Operation: Sending a short message.
Preconditions: Message is written, the recipients are selected.
Sequence Diagram:

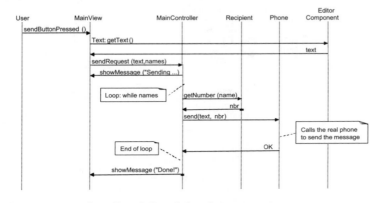

Exceptions: Sending fails: then show an error message.
Postconditions: The message is sent to the network.

FIGURE 1-39. A scenario illustrating the sending of a short message.

The scenario depicted in Figure 1-39 tunes the design class diagram of the client component. Whereas Figure 1-36 depicts the first version of the design class diagram, Figure 1-40 illustrates a new version of the diagram. The sequence diagram in Figure 1-39 causes the modifications. Various classes get new methods. Connections from MainController to Recipient and to Phone objects are established, because according to the sequence diagram they communicate with each other. An arrow from an object to another implies that there must also be a connection between the corresponding classes in the design class diagram.

After you have illustrated the first operation as a scenario and modified the design class diagram accordingly, you concentrate on the next operation. You select the operation "Entering recipients' information" and design it as shown in Figure 1-41. This operation invokes actions in the server component, too, and the actual Recipient class will be a part of the server component. Therefore, the client has only a proxy Recipient object, which imitates recipient for the client, and communicates with the real Recipient object living inside the server component. You decide to implement a remote proxy object within the client component as suggested by a GOF pattern named Proxy [Gamma et al.95].

A remote proxy is a logical representative for an object in a different address space. Based on the sequence diagram in Figure 1-41, you can now draw the second version of the design class diagram, as illustrated in Figure 1-42.

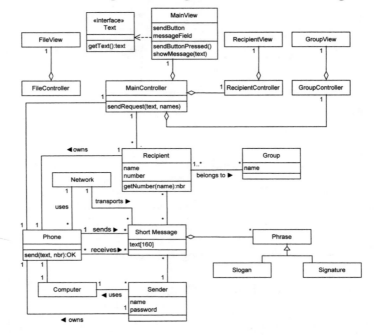

FIGURE 1-40. Design class diagram after first behavior modifications.

Operation: Entering recipients' information.
Preconditions: Server is up and running, The recipients dialog box is visible and user has entered a name and a phone number.
Sequence Diagram:

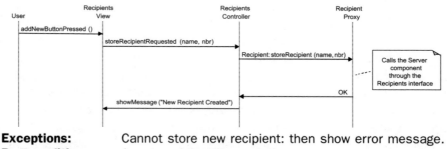

Exceptions: Cannot store new recipient: then show error message.
Postconditions: A new recipient is created.

FIGURE 1-41. Entering recipients' information.

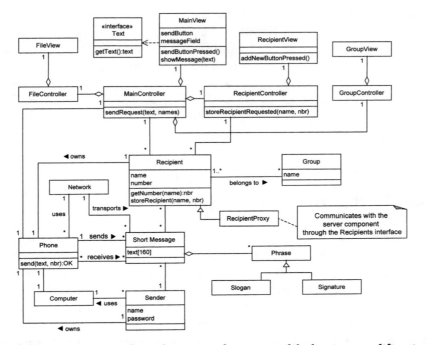

FIGURE 1-42. Design class diagram after second behavior modifications.

After all operations are visible as scenarios, the design class diagram is ready for implementation. The final member functions and data members are specified, associations between objects are tuned, and some new classes are discovered. Sometimes some objects of the first version of the design class diagram are not used at all. Those objects are removed from the final design class diagram. For example, the "Computer" class will probably be finally removed from the design class diagram, because it will not be used in any sequence diagram. Also, some associations that are relevant in the real world may not be needed in design. If two objects do not communicate with each other in any sequence diagram, the association between them is removed from the design class diagram.

The code of a GUI-centered, event-driven application is often difficult to read, because all functionality spreads into tiny member functions. These functions respond to events, and control moves frequently from one object to another. In traditional sequential applications, the flow of control typically is coded into the main program. Event-driven applications cannot include such a fixed control, because you cannot predict the sequence of events coming into the application. Also, each object takes care of only a part of the functionality, and the cooperation of objects cannot be read from the code of a single class.

Sequence diagrams can clarify the flow of control within an application. They illustrate the flow of control that cannot be seen anywhere else. Because the control is divided among the objects of an application or component, reading only the code of one particular object at a time gives a very limited view of functionality. Sequence diagrams, on the other hand, illustrate the cooperation of the objects. In the object-oriented application, this is the most important view of functionality.

Design Patterns: An Example

Design patterns, one of the recent software engineering problem-solving disciplines, provide tested solutions to common problems in software architectures. Problems—such as how to separate the construction of a complex object from its representation or how to define a one-to-many dependency between objects so that when one object changes state, all its dependents are notified automatically—emerge over and over again. It would be fortunate if software designers could apply good and tested solutions to these common problems. Although a process model, such as ours, gives the framework for software development by providing a process through the phases and a means to visualize development work, design patterns provide tools to produce high-quality decisions within the process in use.

Practical and tested solutions should be advocated and supported within organizations. Based on our experiences, one of the most beneficial reusable solutions is the MVC++ approach we discussed earlier. Another very useful concept is the one of *abstract partners* used also with the MVC++ approach. Let us therefore take a look at the abstract partnership in the form of a design pattern. The template of the presentation originates from the Gang-of-Four book [Gamma et al.95].

Abstract Partner

Intent

Provide a way to implement type-safe callbacks between two or more objects without connecting objects too closely or preventing their use with other objects.

Problem and Motivation

Object-oriented programs are made up of objects with various kinds of relations between them. In many cases, one object uses another. In a typed language, such as C++ and Java, the user object must know the type of the object it is using. This is not a problem if the utilized objects are implemented before their users, and users can be implemented to use the object of certain types. Problems occur if this is not the case.

For example, you may want to implement an object within an object library so that this library object *calls its user back*. When such an object is used, some methods of the user object itself are called back by the library object, as illustrated in Figure 1-43. In the middle of the serviceRequest() method, the library object calls the questionRelatedToTheRequest() method of the user object. If the library object is supposed to be reusable, this should be possible regardless of the type of the user object.

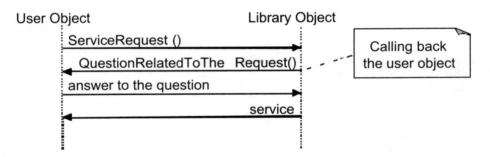

FIGURE 1-43. A library object communicating with its user object.

Let us take a more concrete example. Suppose that you want to implement a class imitating an engine. In designing the engine, you presume that it will be used with another class imitating a car. Thus, the car will aggregate and use the engine, as illustrated in Figure 1-44. Figure 1-45 shows the classes in C++. Because you want to simulate a real engine, you need at least two methods for the engine: run and stop. The car will call these methods. You also want to have an attribute oilPressure for the engine to correspond to the oil pressure of a real engine.

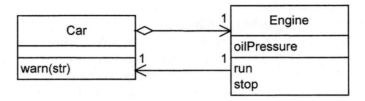

FIGURE 1-44. The car aggregates the engine.

```cpp
class Engine {
public:
   Engine(Car *c) {
      myCar = c;
      oilPressure = 100;
   }
   void run() {
      while (1) {
         // Engine is running ...
         if (oilPressure < 10) myCar->warn("Oil Pressure is Down!");
      }
   }
   void stop();
protected:
   float oilPressure;
   Car *myCar;
};

class Car {
public:
   Car() {
      boxer = new Engine(this);
      boxer->run();
   }
   void warn(char *str) {
      cout << str << endl;
   }
protected:
   Engine *boxer;
};
```

FIGURE 1-45. The car and engine classes in C++.

When the car calls the Run method of the engine, the engine starts running. This is easy to implement, because the engine is a part of the car, and the car can call all public methods of the engine. After the engine has been running for a while the oil pressure may drop below the acceptable level. In this case, the engine object must call the Warn method of the car object. Thus, while the car object calls the methods of the engine object, the engine object must also be able to call the Warn method of the car object, as illustrated in Figure 1-45. For this purpose, the engine object receives a reference to the car object, for example, as a parameter of the constructor. When the engine object calls the car object through this reference, the car object should show some error indicator such as an error message on the screen.

To allow reuse of the engine class, you decide to store it within a library. Suppose that, later, your colleagues want to use your engine object. Except this time they want to model a boat and use the engine with their boat. The colleagues plan to implement their boat as illustrated in Figure 1-46, but unfortunately this proves to be impossible. Their boat can easily call all the methods of the engine found in the library, but the engine cannot call the Warn method of his new boat. At the time you implemented the engine, you could not imagine that someone would want to use your engine with anything but a car. Therefore, you made the engine call an object of the type *car* when the oil pressure drops. This is a problem now that it is a boat using your engine.

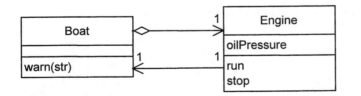

FIGURE 1-46. An attempt to use the engine with a boat.

Solution

To tackle this problem, you must implement objects that call back their users so that they do not make restrictive assumptions about the types of users. In the example, the engine object is an object that could be implemented within an object library. The engine object should have used its abstract partner to give a warning. Instead of calling the car object directly, it should have called it through the abstract engine partner, as illustrated in Figures 1-47, 1-48, and 1-49. The abstract partner is an abstract C++ class or a Java interface, which declares the methods that an object requires of other objects using it.

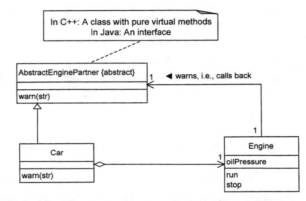

FIGURE 1-47. The engine uses the abstract engine partner.

```
class AbstractEnginePartner {
public:
   virtual void warn(char *str)=0;
};

class Engine {
public:
   Engine(AbstractEnginePartner *absP) {
      partner = absP;
   }
   void run() {
      while (1) {
         // Engine is running ...
         if (oilPressure < 10) partner->warn("Oil Pressure is Down!");
      }
   }
   void stop();
protected:
   float oilPressure;
   AbstractEnginePartner *partner;
};
```

FIGURE 1-48. The engine object using the abstract engine partner.

```
class Car : public AbstractEnginePartner {
public:
    Car(){
        boxer = new Engine(this);
        boxer->run();
    }
    void warn(char *str) {
        cout << str << endl;
    }
protected:
    Engine *boxer;
};
```

FIGURE 1-49. Using the engine with the car by inheriting the abstract partner.

Figures 1-50 and 1-51 illustrate the use of the engine with the boat. The car and the boat objects behave differently when the engine calls them, as shown in Figures 1-49 and 1-51. Whereas the car object only prints a warning message, the boat object also stops the engine. Thus, the user object decides how to respond to the calls of the library object. For example, you could have a boat that is not interested in warnings at all. This would be implemented in the boat class by coding an empty warn(str) method. The boat object would still fulfill the requirements set by the engine that it uses; from the engine's point of view, it would still take care of warnings.

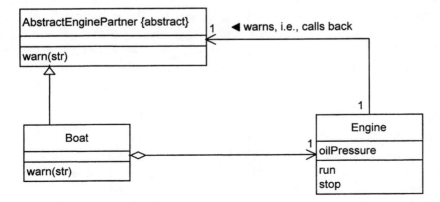

FIGURE 1-50. The engine uses the boat through the abstract engine partner.

```
class Boat : public AbstractEnginePartner {
public:
    Boat(){
        BMWDiesel = new Engine(this);
        BMWDiesel->run();
    }
    void warn(char *str) {
        cout << str << endl;
        BMWDiesel->stop();
    }
protected:
    Engine *BMWDiesel;
};
```

FIGURE 1-51. Using the engine with the boat.

The engine, together with its abstract partner, now forms a reusable component ready to be stored in an object library. Instead of naming the abstract class AbstractEnginePartner, you could call it Vehicle. On first sight, that may look even better, because a car and a boat are both vehicles. Still, it is better not to call the abstract partner classes by any "real name," because somebody might use the engine with a water pump, say, which most certainly is not a vehicle. By using the name *abstract partner*, you do not restrict the use of the engine object. Also, the name follows the rules of object orientation, because any class that uses the engine object *is* a partner of the engine, as inheritance is often specified.

Applicability

Use the Abstract Partner pattern when:

- You have two objects that call each others' methods.
- You must implement an object, for example, within an object library capable of calling methods of some unknown future objects.
- You do not want to tie objects too tightly together in a callback situation.

Structure

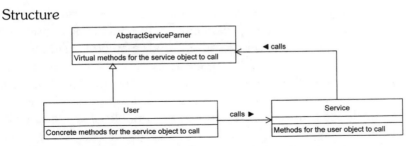

FIGURE. 1-52. Callback and abstract partnership.

Participants

User (car). Uses the service object directly. Implements the methods of the abstract partner to be used by the service object. Sends its 'this' pointer to the service object.

Service (engine). Can be implemented previously, for example in an object library. Calls the methods of an unknown user object through the abstract partner without knowing the exact type of the user object. Holds a pointer to the user object as a type of abstract partner.

AbstractServicePartner (AbtsractEnginePartner). An abstract class (C++) or an interface (Java). Forms a reusable component together with the service class.

Known Uses

Used in Nokia NMS series of products.

Using Abstract Partners and MVC++

According to the presented MVC++ approach, the controller objects *instantiate* the view and model objects. Although view and model objects should be as reusable as possible, the controller objects alone can hardly ever be reusable. Therefore, application components must be able to use model and view objects with new and different controllers in future implementations. Even more importantly, developers must be able to implement reusable MVC++ triads, for example, PrintView-PrintController-Printer combinations, and use them in any future software.

The controller classes are typically implemented for a particular application component and can therefore explicitly call known view and model objects. View and model objects, on the other hand, may be implemented earlier within libraries without a hint of future controllers or their types. Thus, the controller can directly call the methods of the view and model because their types are known. The view and model objects, on the other hand, should not call the controller directly. Instead, they should be capable of working with the controllers of different types.

Abstract partners solve this callback problem. Let us first study their use with a view object. The view object uses the abstract view partner interface implemented by the controller object. Each time the view object needs to call the controller object, it does the calling through the abstract partner interface, as illustrated in Figures 1-53, 1-54, and 1-55.[12]

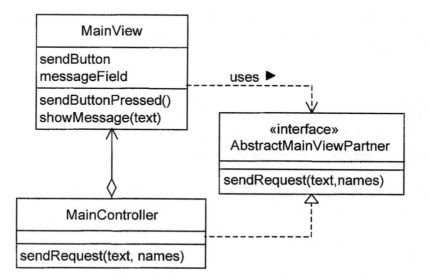

FIGURE 1-53. An abstract view partner interface between the view and the controller in Java implementation.

```
import java.awt.*;
import java.applet.Applet;
import ...

interface AbsMainViewPartner {
   public void sendRequest(String text, String names[]);
}

public class MainView   extends Frame
            implements ActionListener {
   private AbsMainViewPartner vp;
   ...
   public MainView(AbsMainViewPartner abs) {
      //Connect to instantiated main controller
      vp = abs;
      ...
      sendButton.addActionListener(this);
   }

   public void actionPerformed(ActionEvent e) {
      ...
      vp.SendRequest(text, names);      //calls the controller through
                                        //abstract partner interface

   }

   ...
}
```

FIGURE 1-54. View and its abstract partner.

```
import MainView;
public class MainController implements AbsMainViewPartner
{
    private MainView mainView;
    public MainController() {
        mainView = new MainView(this);
        mainView.init();
    }

    public void sendRequest(String text, String names[]) {
        ...
    }

    public static void main(String args[]) {
        MainController controller = new MainController();
    }
}
```

FIGURE 1-55. Controller.

We use abstract partners in many places. One of the best places is to use abstract controller partners to implement reusable model-view-controller collections. For example, you may want to allow the reuse of the PrinterView—PrinterController—Printer triad illustrated in Figure 1-56 in future applications. Because you cannot be sure whom the PrintController will communicate with in future applications, you must provide an abstract controller partner interface. Now, whoever wants to use the PrinterView—PrinterController—Printer triad must program a class that implements the abstract partner interface. Thus, you can now use the reusable printing triad with the MainController, as illustrated in Figure 1-56, but you can also use it with controllers of any given type.

We also implement model classes capable of calling whatever controller classes they are attached to. For time-consuming printing operations, for example, you may want the model object named Printer to call a controller object and inform the progress of the printing, as illustrated in Figure 1-57. For this purpose, you use abstract model partners.

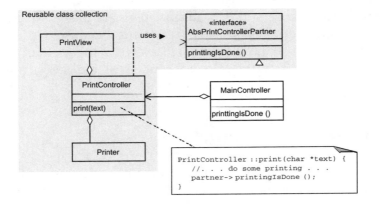

FIGURE 1-56. An abstract controller partner.

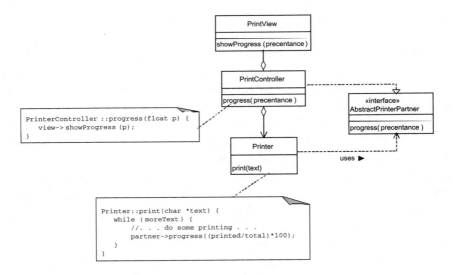

FIGURE 1-57. An abstract model partner.

MVC++ approach advocates the use of abstract partners as an interface between the model, controller, and view layers. The abstract partners keep the parts of the application independent. We can change and reuse model and view classes and even entire model-view-controller triads. This keeps the application robust for the unavoidable changes later in the project, as well as in the future projects to come.

Using abstract partners between the layers of MVC++ is a standard procedure. Everybody expects to find abstract partners there. We do not, therefore, draw them into design class diagrams because we avoid adding unnecessary information into diagrams. However, if the abstract partnership is used elsewhere apart from the MVC++ context, all the classes are drawn into the diagrams.

Documenting Design

In our software projects, we produce two types of documents during design: Architectural Design documents and Detailed Design documents.[13] A project producing or enhancing a single application produces only one architectural design document. In addition, such a project produces one detailed design document for each component of the application in question. In small applications of only a few components, the architectural and detailed design documents can be merged.

We maintain the design documents after the software project. It is especially important to maintain the architectural design documents.[14] They provide a visual and concrete view of the structures and behavior that the components implement. Such a high-level architectural view is almost impossible to extract afterwards from the code. For detailed design, the document maintenance is not that important, especially if tools that extract low-level design information directly from code are available.

Each project typically creates one architectural document and several detailed design documents, one for each application component. The purpose and content of the documents are illustrated as follows.

1. Architectural Design Document
   - Specifies the technical architecture of the application in terms of components.
   - Components (run-time and/or development view).
   - Scenarios including sequence diagrams illustrating collaboration of components.
   - Data management solutions, such as selecting the persistence mechanism.
2. Detailed Design Document
   - Specifies the technical architecture of a component in terms of programmable classes.

- Interfaces.
- Design class diagram.
- Scenarios including sequence diagrams illustrating collaboration of objects.
- Component test plan.

Programming

The programming phase refines the phase products of the design phase into a programming language. You could also say that programming is the last phase of design. Many low-level design decisions are made only during programming. Whereas class structures are modeled as class diagrams, and object collaboration as sequence diagrams, programming concentrates on the implementation of individual classes and their member functions.

The class declarations, that is, the public interfaces, originate from the design class diagrams, and the code of individual member functions reflect the sequence diagrams. It is important that you have already modeled the most important classes, their interfaces, and the cooperation between their instances during detailed design. Based on such design, you can now concentrate on one class only and one member function at a time during the programming phase.

We do not typically use any notations to illustrate the internal functionality of a single object. In some rare cases, low-level state or activity diagrams can assist the implementation of the most complicated and state-intensive classes. In most cases, there is no need to assist the implementation of a single class with any additional graphical notations. A programming language itself is the most powerful tool for this purpose.

There are tools that can generate code based on different graphical models. Typically these tools, such as GUI builders, database tools, and application wizards, can produce code for the limited portions of the system only. We have found such tools very useful. On the other hand, we do not use any *CASE* tools that would generate code from class diagrams and sequence diagrams for an entire system. Therefore, we do not draw design models with all details for this purpose.

Our class and sequence diagrams are not detailed enough for code generation because they include only the most important classes, methods, and attributes. Therefore, the most detailed design is actually performed during programming. This is why we, for example, write and review the first versions of class declarations together with the design class diagrams. The details of design can only be seen from code itself. Such practices help us keeping our documents up-to-date. Not every single modification in low level design requires changes in the documents.

Let us go study the SMS example application one again. Figure 1-58 illustrates a partial implementation of the Short Message Application MainController class depicted in Figure 1-42. The sequence diagram in Figure 1-39 has given you the basic structure of the sendRequest member function. You have made all the code-level design decisions while writing the code. The constructor instantiates the MainView class and all the needed subcontroller classes. In addition, it instantiates a set of model classes.

Integration and Testing

Integration and testing are among the most important parts of software development. We use three-stage testing. In the first stage, programmers of single components test their components. This is called *unit* or *component testing*. These unit tests are actually considered an essential part of the programming phase. A test plan including the test cases is reviewed and approved as a part of detailed design. Thus, a component is ready only after it has been successfully unit-tested. By using tools such as *test coverage analyzers* and *test-beds,* software designers run their code to find bugs. Each class must be tested, and the completeness of tests typically is monitored by the quality assurance function in milestone reviews.

The second testing phase performs *integration tests*. The unit-tested components are integrated into applications, and applications are integrated into systems. After that, the integration-testing phase may start. The software designers perform the test by running the integrated components together with the entire system. While module tests are typically performed in designers' own workspaces, integration testing happens in controlled laboratory environment. Carefully managing versions of the operating systems, windowing environments, compilers, developed components, and other such elements is important.

Component and integration tests check the outcome of the programming and design phases. The purpose of these testing phases is to find flaws in

```
import MainView;
import RecipientController;
...

public class MainController implements AbsMainViewPartner,
                                        AbsRecipientControllerPartner
{
   private MainView mainView;
   private RecipientController recipientController;
   ...
   private Recipient recipient;
   private Phone phone;

   public MainController() {
      mainView = new MainView(this);
      mainView.init();
      recipientController=new RecipientController(mainView);
      ...
      recipient = new Recipient();
      phone = new Phone();
   }

   public void sendRequest(String text, String names[]) {
      int i = 0;
      String nbr;
      boolean ok;
      mainView.ShowMessage("Sending...");
      do {
         nbr = recipient.getNumber(names[i]);
         ok = phone.send(text,nbr);
      } while (ok);
      mainView.showMessage("Done!");
   }
...

   public static void main(String args[]) {
      MainController controller = new MainController();
   }
}
```

FIGURE 1-58. The Java implementation of the MainController class.

design and programming. The phases determine whether there are any bugs in the system. It is practical to verify the whole software functionality during integration tests immediately after the system is stable enough. This verification requires that you go through all the requirement statements, use cases, and operations and test the integrated system against these specifications.

The third phase is the *system test phase*. It determines whether the system does what it is meant to do. In other words, the system test phase tests the system against the outcome of the analysis phase—mainly against the use cases. During this phase, separate system testers, not the designers, run and test the entire system. Their view is the view of the end user, and they try to find errors in the functionality of the entire system. Typically, they also find problems in usability, especially in the cases related to the different workflows of end users.

In addition to these basic testing phases, we may need to test the application once again at the customer's site. However, this additional testing depends on the type of the system being developed. Whereas the customers can install and test simple systems by, the developers or their representatives must install and test more complicated systems in the customer's environment. This testing is called *acceptance testing*.

Projects and Project Types

There are many different ways to arrange software development projects. Some projects can be organized well as waterfalls, where a long analysis phase is followed by a massive design, programming, and testing phase. Other projects are better organized in an iterative manner, or as spirals. Such projects perform the phases of our process model little by little without trying to complete all at once. Based on our experiences, there are benefits and problems in each approach.

We utilize two major types of phase structures for software projects. Let us call them *waterfall* and *incremental* approaches. In both approaches, software development must be controlled. Controlling means establishing and using proper project planning and management functions. Also, the phases of software development produce visible phase products to be used not just in progress tracking but also in future projects to come. The phase products are reviewed and approved properly. Thus, we use reviewed documents and incremental software builds during software development projects. Rapid development that would not produce anything visible except the final code does not meet our standards.

Waterfalls

The waterfall approach has a bad reputation—and mostly for good reasons. Its rigid structure does not take into account the nature of software very well. Waterfalls do not allow software designers to back up and refine decisions made in earlier phases. They assume that everything can be done perfectly at outset and in many cases, this is not true.

On the other hand, there are some clear benefits to the waterfall approach. The approach is easy to understand for different people related to projects. Methods and process models are easy to document according to a waterfall model. It is an easy model to manage, and most project managers prefer to design and monitor projects according to its rigid structure. A clear waterfall allows an efficient use of baselines and milestones. Thus, there are also many good sides to this approach. It is the nature of software development that makes efficient use of the model often difficult. However, we have used the waterfall model successfully in many software projects.

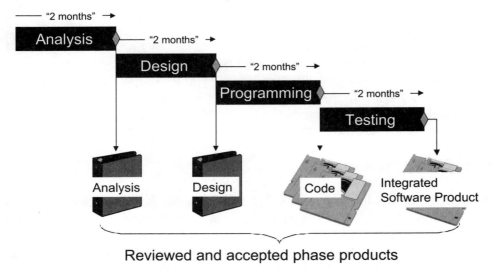

FIGURE 1-59. A classical waterfall project model.

In the waterfall model, software development phases follow each other, as illustrated in Figure 1-59. Each phase, typically lasting some months, produces reviewed and accepted phase products. The phase products serve as both the physical evidences of achieved milestones and the baselines for future phases. The design phase builds on top of the analysis phase; the programming phase builds on top of the design phase, and so on. None of the phases question or enhance the outcome of the previous phase. Waterfall assumes that everything is prefect at the outset. In some cases, this may be true.

Based on our experiences, the waterfall, with some modifications, can succeed in many projects. We have developed large telecommunications software systems according to the waterfall model. These projects, consisting of tens and hundreds of software developers, have succeeded mainly because they enhanced and developed further some established products. In addition, the projects used proven technology and utilized experienced software developers. In such cases, software designers knew what they were doing already at the outset. Thus, based on our experience, a waterfall project can succeed if:

- You develop new features on top of your established software product, that is, just the next release of the product.
- You know the domain well.
- You master the development tools and methods.
- You have a clear and stabile set of requirements.

Even if these conditions are true, however, we suggest certain modifications to the original waterfall model. We have made two modifications to the process to improve the model without sacrificing its simplicity too much: The modifications are the *feasibility study phase* and the *early launch of a next phase*. Let us first take a look at the feasibility study phase.

Feasibility Study

The *feasibility study* phase precedes the actual software development project.[15] It aims at the decision to start the project. A group of the most experienced and talented software designers perform the feasibility study, together with product planners and managers. During the feasibility study process, we collect the first versions of the requirements, construct the use cases, specify and analyze a set of solution suggestions, and estimate the workload and schedules of the future project.

In practice, feasibility study peeks at the future phases of software development and actually performs all project phases in a limited form. Thus, feasibility study includes the first iterations cycle of a software development process, as illustrated in Figure 1-60. When software designers collect requirements and write use cases, they actually perform the first iteration of analysis. Then, the software designers design different solution possibilities. They propose, for example, various architectural solutions, possibilities to purchase or subcontract parts of the software, and hardware to be used. Software designers try to design the best possible technical solution. The solution should meet the collected requirements and enable the implementation of the system according to the use cases. While doing this, software designers typically test various aspects of their solutions by designing subsets of the entire system or even by programming small prototypes. All this work, including analysis, design, and programming, is utilized during the actual project to come.

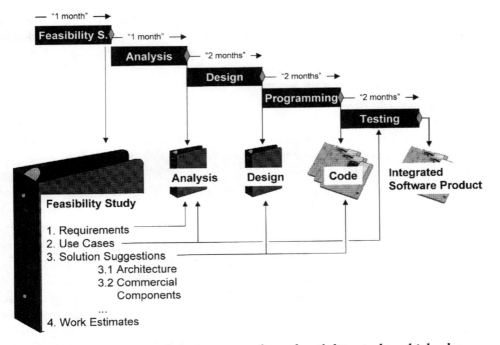

FIGURE 1-60. Experienced designers perform feasibility study, which also provides specifications and code for the actual development project.

Early Launch of Next Phase

Industrial software development requires discipline. It is unacceptable if the code itself is the only physical evidence of its activities. Therefore, software projects produce various phase products, typically in the forms of documents including diagrams and other specifications. These documents are reviewed and accepted according to the quality standards of a company.

If a project is organized in a waterfall form, its phases follow each other sequentially. This leads to a common misunderstanding: software designers and project managers seem to think that it is bad to think about design issues during analysis, for example. However, in real projects you should *think about* and *take into account* the consequences your decision have to the phases that follow; but you should not *mix* the models and artifacts produced during each phase. It is only beneficial to understand how decisions made during analysis affect design, for example. Therefore, a certain amount of design oriented thinking during analysis is suggested.

Also, the best way to test the design artifacts is to program some selected hot spots of the design during the design phase. For example, you may decide to use a certain library component to implement communication between your software and an external device, say with a mobile phone. You should test the connection by coding as soon as possible. Try implementing a simple connection between your software and the device during design or even during feasibility study. Programming during design is a way to ensure that your design is adequate in the context of the used tools and environments.

In practice, waterfall projects must have clear milestones and phases, as illustrated in Figure 1-59. A *phase product*, typically a physical document, concretizes each milestone. The phase products are reviewed and accepted according to the project and quality plans. Each phase product forms a base-line, which cannot be changed without being reviewed and accepted again. However, during each phase, software designers should already anticipate the next phases. During analysis, they should already write design issues to the design document. Design activities are done already during analysis, but they are documented in design documents to be finalized during the design phase. During design, software designers test their design decisions by programming selected parts of the software, testing drivers and other modules, or by implementing small prototypes. Based on our experiences, this is how the most talented software designer work, in any case. Such approach, illustrated in Figure 1-61, enables software designers to be flexible—even in waterfall projects. In addition, clear milestones and the waterfall structure keep the project simple and much easier to understand and manage.

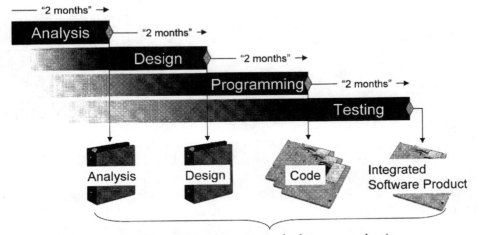

FIGURE 1-61. Each phase starts already during the previous phase.

Increments and Iterations

The waterfall project model does not fit in all projects. Thus, you should not use the waterfall project if:

- You are developing a totally new product.
- You are developing a one-time customer specific solution.
- You are entering to a new domain.
- You are not sure about the requirements.
- You have new major technical elements in use, such as operating systems or programming languages.

If some of these conditions are true, an incremental and iterative way of organizing software projects has a better chance to succeed. However, such an approach requires more work and skills from project managers. Incremental and iterative projects have a built-in mechanism for late changes. Project plans are expected to change during project, and project management, customers, and other such parties must take this into account. After all, if changes were not going to happen, we would recommend waterfalls!

Incremental and Iterative Projects

Incremental and iterative projects do not perform just one analysis, design, programming, and testing phase, but several of each. Software does not evolve at once, but little by little. The key slogan of the incremental software development is "Deliver something early." The goal is to get a selected portion of the software ready as soon as possible and integrate the components of the application as early as you can. Additional functionality is implemented later, as increments during the following iteration cycles.

One of the key sources for our practices is the spiral model of Boehm [Boehm 88]. He suggests that, during software development, the most difficult parts should be tackled first. He proposes that each project should first identify a subproblem which has the highest risk associated with it and then find a solution for that problem. We apply his suggestions with use cases.

Iterative and incremental software development projects are best arranged around use cases. You should first identify and write all the use cases of the entire software. Among the use cases, select one or two of the most important for the first increment. These use cases should typically be selected based on the most severe risks of the project. For example, if you are entering to the new domain, and you are about to start the implementation of a product to the new markets, the functional requirements are probably vague. You are not sure what the end users and customers expect from the product that you plan to develop. In such a case, you should select one or two use cases that you believe to be the most important from the end users' points of view. On the other hand, if you plan to carry your application from UNIX to Windows NT, for example, you should test the most critical technical issues during the first iteration. In such a case, you select the use cases including the key technical challenges with which to start.

Whichever use cases you select, your project should first implement software including only those use cases. These use cases are implemented and integrated to form an executable version of the product. After that, the project iterates all phases once again, and the next iterations learn from the first cycle. The phase products of analysis, design, and programming is revised and refined. Then, the following cycles take care of the next use cases, as illustrated in Figure 1-62.

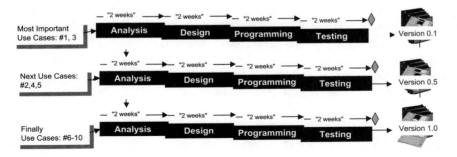

FIGURE 1-62. A use case oriented software development project.

Incremental and iterative projects also need to be controlled using visible phase products. However, a formal review of the analysis document after each analysis iteration, for example, is probably be too laborious for the most of the projects. It is often better to accept a single increment as a complete phase product in one phase review. These phase reviews study the executable software together with the documentation. These review sessions are also in the interest of the customers and end users, because they can now test and run software and give feedback to the development team during the project. This would not be possible if only documents were reviewed.

We have used such an incremental and iterative approach, especially when developing the first commercial version of a new product type. You should not mix the approach with pure prototyping. Such projects develop simple throw-away prototypes or mockups to study a technology or a product concept. Such software trials are typically for internal use only. Our incremental approach discussed here is for different kinds of projects. In the presented approach, even the very first version produced by the first iteration loop remains and stays alive within the final product. This kind of incremental development requires a solid architectural vision and practices to permit continuous expansion.

There is a risk of having a need to reimplement all the software in each and every iteration. This is the case if the first iteration loop produces poor architectures. To avoid this, architecture should be most modular consisting of components with strong cohesion and weak coupling. A modular architecture is the best means to prepare software for unexpected needs.

Inside the components themselves, design patterns and frameworks, such as our MVC++, approach promote modifiability. MVC++ enables us to add increments to the components without changing the architecture after each iteration. Each new use case typically introduces some new model, view, and controller classes and adds some methods and attributes to the old classes. Such common architectural style makes it fairly easy to implement the needed modifications. Also, because the whole organization uses the same approach, everybody knows the basic architecture of each application, and additional increments can be designed and implemented even by different designers.

Iterating Design and Programming

In addition to the presented use case oriented iterations, we have efficiently used a more fine-grained iteration. This iteration happens during design only, and its purpose is to reduce risks during design. Especially if you are not familiar with the programming language and environment, architecture, operating system, or any used development tool, you should not perform design without early programming trials.

Programming is one of the best tests for design. Programming can point out design flaws, and should therefore be used often during design. Actually, design and programming should interfere in a rapid iterative manner. The sequence diagrams can support such work.

Our process model uses sequence diagrams in the design of behavior. This happens along the functional path. First, you select the most important operation from the component's point of view. Then, you illustrate the behavior of the component with one sequence diagram. Immediately after this, you open your programming environment and program the classes and methods presented in the very first sequence diagram. Instead of drawing all sequence diagrams and modifying the design class diagram accordingly in one go, you test sequence diagrams with early and frequent coding during design. Finally, when you get more experienced with the architecture, the methods, and the tools you can design successfully without continuous programming trials.

Let us take a look at the Short Message System application. Let us suppose that you have just drawn the first design sequence diagram illustrated in Figure 1-39. You have then modified the design class diagram into the form illustrated in Figure 1-40. Now, immediately after this, you open your Java builder and program the first, limited version of the component. The component should include only the classes and methods presented in the first sequence diagram. Thus, the first programmed version implements the design class diagram illustrated in Figure 1-63. You implement only the actual sending of messages. You do not include the editing of messages, the selecting of recipients, the managing of groups, and so on, into the very first version. You deal with them during the next iterations.

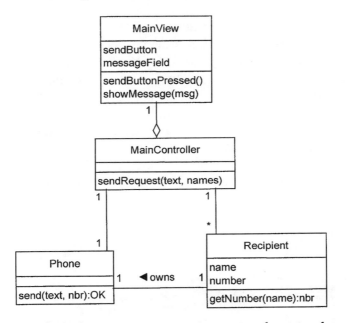

FIGURE 1-63. The first design-programming iteration loop implements only a very limited application component.

Solving Waterfall Problems with Increments

There are problems in the waterfall project model. Above all, rigid waterfall assumes that everything goes as planned. Also, it assumes that software developers successfully construct high-quality specifications at the outset. Projects may have milestones, such as "The analysis document is reviewed and accepted." Unfortunately, no good means exist to analyze the quality of such documents.

In some cases, the documents may be of good quality and provide a sound base for the phases to come. In other cases, such documents only *look* adequate, and the subsequent phases reveal their unfinished and even erroneous nature. Thus, delays in waterfall projects show too late—only during programming and testing.

Real life is tough. Almost all software projects run late or they are not capable of implementing all that was planned. Unexpected delays emerge during projects due to implementation problems, changes in personnel, and changing requirements. In waterfall projects, such delays are fatal.

Figure 1-64 illustrates a typical waterfall project running late. According to the project plan, each phase lasts two months, and the project starting January 1st should deliver a complete functioning software system on August 31st. In the real project, analysis and design seem to proceed as planned. This is natural, because their milestones are based on documents and specifications. Project pressures force designers to finish these phase product in time, even if it was not really complete. The quality of such phase products is hard to evaluate, but the project personnel are eager to agree that the milestone has been achieved in time.

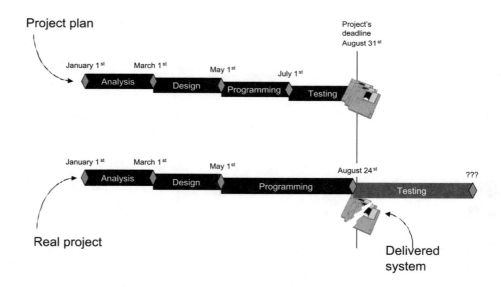

FIGURE 1-64. Waterfall: plans and reality.

After analysis and design, the project starts the programming phase. In the example illustrated in Figure 1-64, the analysis and design phases have been sloppy. Therefore, the programming phase encounters severe problems and lasts almost twice as long as planned. Like almost all projects, the project has a definite deadline and fixed resources. This means that the programming phase cannot be extended, nor can the project hire more programmers. However, the project needs to deliver the system on the due day. Other projects and customers are depending on it.

August 31st is a nightmare for the project manager. He can say almost nothing about the final system. He can assume that it is *almost* complete or that, say, 88 percent of code is implemented. But the quality of the implementation is unknown, nobody knows which parts have been implemented, and everybody expects that there are many faults in the system because the testing has not even started yet. Customers will not accept such a system. Because the problem arise late during programming and the project aimed at one complete system, nothing can save the project.

The incremental and iterative project model can successfully solve the presented problems. Such projects use functioning and tested increments as the main milestones of the projects. Instead of having a milestone "Specification ready," the project has a milestone "Use Case #3 implemented and tested." Such milestones have executable increments as concrete evidence. It is easy to verify that the phase, that is, the iteration loop, has performed as planned. A running system does not lie as much as documents do. And if it tries, testing reveals its nature.

The iterative approach enables projects to meet changing requirements and modify remaining iterations in case of unexpected problems. Every iteration starts with the analysis of current situation, it learns from the previous iterations, and it modifies the remaining project phases. Thus, iterative projects have a built-in mechanism for changes that always emerge during projects.

Projects face similar problems, regardless of their types. They tend to run late. Incremental and iterative projects can take this into account, as illustrated in Figure 1-65. The project plan includes three iterations, each building an increment of the final system. The iterations have been designed based on use cases. The first iteration implements the two most important use cases, the second iteration the next use cases, and the last iteration implements the use cases that are the least important or whose requirements are not yet stabilized.

Once again, the due date and the personnel are fixed, and programming and testing exceed their schedules. At the end of the project, the system is not ready. Several parts are missing. There is a big difference compared to the waterfall projects, though: The project manager can say exactly what is available and what is missing. He can say that the use cases numbers 1–4 are complete, integrated, and tested. The increment built on July 25th is worth delivering to customers, and in most cases it satisfies the customer. It includes the most important use cases in a fully tested and functioning form. Instead of delivering an 88-percent ready system of unknown quality, the project can now deliver a fully tested system implementing a well-known portion of planned functionality. The missing use cases can typically be postponed to future projects, or they can be delivered after the deadline as a separate update release.

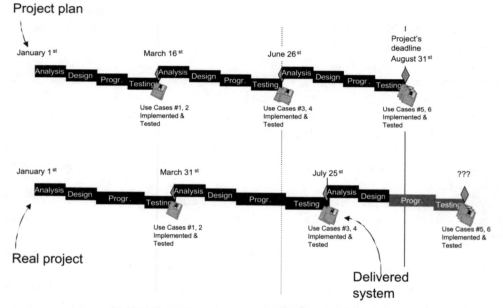

FIGURE 1-65. Increments—plans and reality.

For us, incremental and iterative project types are means to manage risks. We admit that projects tend to run late, we do not understand the system at the outset, and unexpected problems emerge. However, we must be able to run our project machines under these conditions. In all cases, the projects must deliver useful systems in time. We guarantee usefulness by prioritizing the use cases and assuring that the most important use cases will be implemented in any case. We guarantee time-to-market by building many increments into the project. Because each increment is fully tested, it can be delivered if needed. Thus, after the first iteration we can deliver a functioning and tested system at any point of time.

Utilizing Project Teams

Individual programmers can implement amazing amounts of functionality if they work alone. It is well-known fact that when the project team grows, the productivity of an individual on the project decreases dramatically. It is therefore important to offer a *sandbox* for an individual software developer. A developer can work in such sandbox almost as if he worked alone. The sandbox should have only a minimum number of well-specified dependencies with the sandboxes of others.

Such sandboxes enable concurrent development of software systems. Each software developer can develop his portion of the system concurrently with others. The development view of architectural design, explained in the section "Component Specification with Run-Time and Development Views," allocates the sandboxes. The view illustrates the architecture of the system in terms of components that are developed independently. In addition, the view specifies the interfaces, that is, the dependencies between the components.

We trust in the good will and ethics of individual software designers. We believe that the vast majority of developers do their best to meet project requirements. Project managers must be able to trust in their project teams. They monitor the project and its progress but they do not monitor designers' willingness to work adequately. If this is not the case, the necessary control structures of projects jeopardize the efficiency of project teams. Bureaucracy emerges. In an ideal case, software developers can implement their components the way they prefer, as long as the components implement the interfaces and meet their functional and other requirements. The architecture of the system and the project structure must support such a way of working, that is, independence and concurrent work of software professionals.

Figure 1-66 illustrates a project that aims at concurrent development of software components. The project team consists of four professionals building software as two increments. During analysis and architectural design, parallelism is rather difficult although not impossible to achieve. For example, the construction of use cases can be allocated to different software designers. Each designer constructs the first version of his use case. Then, these independently written use cases are discussed and enhanced together, and common parts are harmonized.

Architectural design can also be performed partially concurrently. Individual designers can sketch preliminary architectures independently. One chief architect collects the sketches and forms a unified proposal of the entire

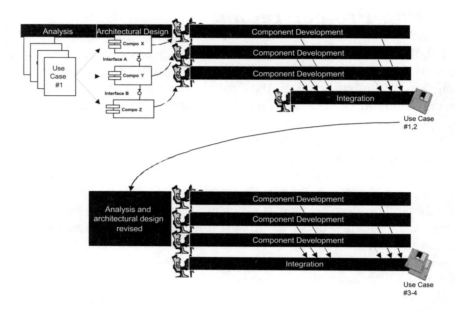

FIGURE 1-66. Concurrent engineering in component sandboxes.

component architecture. The final architecture is then polished together. The functionality of use cases is allocated to individual components, as already explained in this book. This allocation activity also specifies the interfaces between the components.

The components of the system are developed concurrently, as illustrated in Figure 1-66. All components of the development view are allocated to individual software designers. Software developers design, implement, and unit-test their own components to meet the requirements. The trusted developers work independently, according to the agreed-upon guidelines of the company.

In addition to the developers, an independent integrator is working on the project. The integrator's main responsibility is to make components work together. Such a role is necessary because each developer is mainly interested in his or her own component only. Integration of such components requires extra work, and it does not happen automatically. This simply demonstrates the law of entropy.

The integrator pulls components to the integration as soon as there is something to be integrated. He does not wait for any official versions of components.

Instead, as soon as possible, he starts begging developers for any code that possibly could be integrated and run together. He continuously tries to integrate even unfinished components to provide feedback to component developers and the project manager, to build the integration environment, and to get ready for the final integration. This enables integration to proceed concurrently with the development, thus shortening time to market. In addition, it helps software developers implement collaborative components without sacrificing the individual sandbox mentality necessary for concurrent software development.

Discussion

Unnecessary phases, notations, and project activities are harmful. With real software projects, there is no time to play around with useless diagrams or theories. Therefore, all project activities must prove their usefulness in real projects, and you must discard all tasks and artifacts that seem beneficial only in theory. Typically, professional software developers take care of discarding the unnecessary. They refuse to draw diagrams and write documents that they do not find beneficial. Such practicality has affected our approach significantly.

Based on our experiences, some phases and artifacts have proven to be more beneficial than others. The following communicates these experiences.

Essential Elements

Use cases have proven to be one of the most widely accepted tools within our projects, and also elsewhere. Very different people, including project managers, customers, technical writers, testers, and software developers, have found them quite beneficial. Use cases are easy to produce and understand and can be integrated easily into any software development project.

Some people complain that use cases lack formalism and are poorly specified as a concept. This is probably true. However, for us, use cases are merely tools we use to discuss and analyze requirements, and their alleged shortcomings do not matter. On the contrary, we do not want to add any formalism to use cases but rather want to keep them as simple as possible. We do not even use any graphical notations that would prevent nontechnical people to understand our use cases.

Use cases are something that a software designer would create even without any method in use. Based on our experiences, software systems are typically first expressed through the functionality they provide, that is to say as use cases, and only after then as concepts or objects. This is true especially among customers and end users. Objects are not that intuitive, after all. It is the functionality that counts—not objects alone.

Object analysis that produces the analysis class diagrams is very useful when developing the first version of the application or when entering into a new domain with a new product concept. Analysis class diagrams help in building a common vocabulary of key concepts and their relations. However, analysis class diagrams do not appear to be absolutely necessary. This is the case especially when we work with a well-known domain or develop some new functionality on top of an existing system. If analysis class diagrams are not produced, object design needs more discipline because the design class diagram should always reflect the concepts of the domain. Thus, object analysis is necessary in any case although projects might not document the analysis class diagram as an independent phase product.

Behavior analysis produces operation listings and operation specifications. The majority of the operations are extracted from use cases. When we have a small application under development, we may skip the construction of the operation specifications and analysis sequence diagrams. This is especially true if the system do not have complicated communication with the external world. However, we do create a simple list of operations extracted from the use cases; such a list is easy to create and maintain.

Based on our experiences, software designers often draw dialog sketches or even some kind of story boards if they need to design complicated user interfaces. These sketches easily turn into dialog diagrams. Our dialog diagram has proven to be on the right level of abstraction. Operation lists from the behavior analysis and the dialog diagram are clearly beneficial artifacts.

Technically, it is easy to implement a GUI prototype without any inner functionality, that is, just the view classes of an application. You simply draw the dialogs. But to get any useful feedback from such a prototype is time consuming and laborious. In almost all cases, a separate GUI prototype is just a waste of time, and projects can not afford such a phase. However, rapid white-board sketches in use case or GUI specification meetings do seem beneficial. The details of the user interface are volatile, and projects should not even try to freeze them too early.

Instead of dummy GUI prototypes, it is better to arrange the software project on an incremental basis. Such projects do not create a separate user interface prototype. Instead, they implement all parts of the application concurrently. During the first iteration, the projects implement an increment capable of performing just a few use cases. Then they collect feedback from the customers based on the first use cases. Such a limited application is far more useful in getting end users' feedback than would be a GUI prototype having no inner functionality but the entire user interface part was complete. Instead of the user interface alone, projects get feedback on how the application fits for its use, that is, can the users perform the use cases successfully. GUI alone is just a part of this.

Architectural design is of vital importance for the projects of multiple software designers and large systems. The phase products of architectural design, such as interfaces, components, and their collaboration, enable concurrent engineering and the communication of individual designers. These artifacts help the designers work toward common goals. The detailed design, on the other hand, concentrates on "programming-in-the-small" and does not require such common discipline. Although all projects should concentrate carefully on architectural design, some projects may even skip the steering of detailed design. This is the case especially if the project team consists of experienced designers, who can well perform detailed design independently, in the ways they want.

During design, projects should be economical and should perform only what is needed to implement software products of proper quality. Projects should not waste time with unnecessary theories or notations. Based on our experience, the use of sequence, class, component, and implementation diagrams as presented is a good compromise. Projects clearly need two levels of design: components and classes. They also need tools to visualize the communication of these elements: sequence diagrams. We have not seen benefits from using any other notations during design.

Software designers find sequence diagrams most intuitive, and the diagrams are how designers model the functionality of software systems in almost any case. *State* diagrams, on the contrary, do not appear to be very beneficial, excluding their use in GUI specification as dialog diagrams. We have encountered many method books and scientists who love state diagrams. However, the vast majority of software designers whom we have met seem to dislike them. They rather model the systems as collaborative entities reacting for various stimuli than as entities with complicated state behavior. Thus, state machines seem far too over-advertised. Also, the collaboration diagrams of UML are useless in our cases and they overlap too much with the sequence diagrams. We do not claim, though, that state or collaboration diagrams are somehow wrong or theoretically weak. Within tight project schedules we must concentrate only on essentials, thus, we use a limited set of tools.

Need for a Controlled Process

Large software systems cannot be developed without a systematic process and common architectural vision. Although small systems can be developed through the heroic achievements of highly talented individuals, large organizations with large system development projects cannot rely on such heroism. When used correctly, processes and architectural models improve software development by setting standards, unifying development teams, and providing adequate freedom for individual software designers. They also serve as a definition base for project metrics, project management decisions, quality control checkpoints, and scheduling.

A process is the target of software process improvement activities. Only visible, controlled, and managed processes can be improved. Arbitrary actions without certain phases and phase products cannot be assessed or evaluated. Thus, such work cannot be systematically improved.

A process model must be usable, that is, easy and effective to use. A method is more likely to be used when it is simple, clearly effective, and small. We have noticed that most object-oriented software development methods are too big and complex to be used in real software projects. It should be clear for every software developer why each figure or text is produced and how they support software development. A usable method helps the designer concentrate on the most important concepts in each phase and helps her work at a proper level of abstraction. A usable method allows the designer to clearly present the problems and solutions to the problems. A usable method is also easy to learn and does not produce unnecessary phase products. Keeping this in mind, we also continue to streamling our approach.

Notes

1. GSM (Global System for Mobile communications). A digital cellular system approved by almost all European and Asian countries.
2. Use cases were first introduced by Ivar Jacobson [Jacobson et al. 92]. We claim that the current problem with use cases is that they are too loosely defined. Therefore, we have been forced to define our way of using use cases. For us, they are a means of communication between software developers and users.
3. Some sources, such as [Fowler and Scott 97] on page 43 suggest that almost any fragment of functionality can be modeled as use cases. We have seen that this jeopardizes the communicative nature of use cases, and we have reserved the word use case for the functional entities big enough to provide measurable value to the user.
4. More about features; see Chapter 3 of this book.
5. The Summary of this book gives a more detailed table of contents of the documents.
6. See also Chapter 3 of this book.
7. See Chapter 3 of this book for further information about logical view.
8. Database issues are explained in Chapter 2 of this book.
9. See Chapter 4 of this book to see a simpler architectural solution.
10. Chapter 2 of this book explains how to deal with persistence in detailed design.
11. How the actual calling of the method is implemented depends on a windowing system and programming language in use. With Borland Delphi and MS Visual Basic, for example, you just double-click the button and the skeleton of the callback method opens. In Java, you would use the listeners. In X Window you use the AddCallback functions of the toolkit to connect a button and the callback. In any event, you must finally connect at he pressing of a button with a member function of the view class in question.
12. In C++, the abstract partners are classes containing only pure virtual methods and the controller class inherits the abstract partner. In Java, abstract partners are interfaces and the controller implements the abstract partner.
13. The Summary of this book gives more detailed table of contents of the documents.
14. For more information about how to arrange architectural blueprints related to a large software product, see Chapter 3 of this book.
15. See "Feasibility Study" sections of Chapter 1 and 3 of this book to learn more about our feasibility study process.

CHAPTER 2

Object-Oriented Data Management

It is hardly possible to imagine real-life information systems that would not need to store the information they manipulate onto some persistent storage media. Practically all applications need to either share common data with each other or store information on disk to make the data accessible—even when the application that created the data no longer exists. Just think about the variety of management information systems that support the value chains of every company: sales and marketing support systems, planning systems, manufacturing support systems, process automation, and so on. Good data management is the key to creating useful applications. The novel application areas such as multimedia and video-on-demand are setting requirements that are even more demanding for storing and manipulating complex data.

It is justified to say that succeeding with data management is by far one of the most critical aspects in modern software development, be it based on the object paradigm or not. However, it has been somewhat surprising to notice that object-oriented data management solutions have been poorly covered in the plethora of textbooks, articles, and magazines written to describe object-oriented software engineering.

During the last few years, we have looked into a number of unsuccessful object-oriented software projects. Some of the reasons for failure appear to relate to data management solutions. Failed development efforts seem to fall into three categories:

- **Lip Service Projects:** These are projects where the phrase *object-orientation* has been used to give the project a credible and fashionable flavor. In these cases, practical deeds and object-oriented software development ideology do not necessarily meet at all.
- **The End Justifies the Means Projects:** In these projects, the intent is clearly trying to make use of the object-oriented paradigm, but the actual outcome and keeping of schedules are judged far more important than following a certain software development model. Typically, analysis and maybe even design phases have been carried out by rigorously following some object methodology. Moreover, typically an object programming language, such as C++ or Java, is being used in the actual implementation phase. However, a remarkable majority of this kind of project seems to fall short in interfacing with the database, resulting in complex and bizarre class implementations. There is a risk that further development and maintenance of these applications can be troublesome and laborious.
- **Purist Projects:** These projects are typically staffed by idealists who really want to apply object-orientation from the very beginning to the very end. When it comes to data management solutions, quite often this kind of approach leads to taking high technology risks, due to the temptation to deploy unproved, immature middleware or data management products.

We believe that the right approach is somewhere in between the latter two approaches described above. You have to have a goal-oriented attitude. At the end of the day, no one will care about the elegance of your solution if it does not work, is unreliable, or comes too late. On the other hand, by looking into the most successful projects, it seems that better productivity in software engineering and the real benefits from object orientation can be gained by closely following the object paradigm all the way from the very first analysis sketches to the actual programming phase—from A to Z. When you have drawn a box to depict a Customer class into your class diagram you should be able to work with this same Customer class from the very beginning to the very end.

Interfacing with databases is an area where you may be tempted to give up object orientation, because the mainstream implementation options are based on a functional approach rather than object orientation. This is especially true when you are working with relational databases. You will find it hard to match certain object concepts with SQL, tables and columns, ODBC, triggers, stored procedures, and all the numerous features that are characteristic of relational database products. Sometimes, the *impedance mismatch* is used to depict the problem of having to change one's way of thinking temporarily from object orientation to functional and back, just to be able to store information on disk. The fact that relational databases have not offered reasonable interfacing capabilities for object-oriented developers has been one of the driving forces for the development of object databases.

Naturally, dozens of ways are available to manage object persistence in your application. It appears that the most typical situation in the industry is for C++ programs to interface with the database directly. Database access is embedded in the logic of the applications. But, when it comes to productivity of software development and clarity of software design, you should consider implementing database interfaces via *persistent objects*, that is, making the actual objects capable of storing themselves onto disk.

The concept of persistent objects is examined in the following sections. Implementing classes, objects, associations, and other typical expressions such as *aggregation* and *inheritance,* on top of different data management solutions, are presented in detail.

Persistent Objects

Let us first look at the basic concepts in object-oriented data management and practical means to manipulate database-resident objects.

Persistent and Transitory Objects

Let us start this section with a definition of *persistent objects*: *An object can be regarded as persistent if its lifetime is longer than the lifetime of the process that created the object.*

Not all the classes in a class diagram are persistent. Some classes may be transitory by nature. Their lifetime is either shorter or equal to the lifetime of the process that created them. Typically, programming languages such as

C++, combined with some added-value class library such as the Standard Template Library, provide excellent means to cope with transitory objects. However, when it comes to persistent objects, the mere programming language is not enough. In practice, this means that to make objects persistent, it must be possible to store an object's information into some persistent storage, such as files provided by the operating system or some database management system. In the most naïve sense, persistence means only the possibility to store an object's information onto disk and get it back when required. In practice, the requirements for data management are much more demanding.

- **Queries and navigation:** You should be able to access the stored data from your application. Database management systems typically provide a higher-level query language such as SQL that enables you to define arbitrary complex queries which return the stored data that matches with the conditions given in the query. When it comes to object-oriented software development, there is also another natural data access mechanism that should be available: navigation from one object to another by following the relationships of objects. You should have means to access objects and their data by following the links that the objects have with each other.
- **Simultaneous access:** You must enable simultaneous access to persistent objects' data by many different applications. It is possible that these other applications will be written in a different programming language by unknown developers, who may have not even heard of object-oriented thinking.
- **Security:** In many cases, you must be able to provide a solution in which it is possible to restrict access to information for some objects or restrict privileges to carry out some operations, such as deleting or updating an object.
- **Backing up and recovery:** When it comes to a data management solution for a real-life application, it is usually vital to try to protect the system against physical as well as logical failures. Moreover, if the worst has happened—due to a hardware failure, a malfunctioning application, or human error—it should be as easy and as fast as possible to bring the system up again.
- **Performance:** Good performance is usually one of the most important issues regarding the usability and actual deployment of an information

system. Traditionally, the object-oriented paradigm has been blamed for causing systems to run slowly due to using several software layers. Somehow the object-oriented approach may invite you to make architectural design-time data management-related decisions that may cause performance problems.

- **Flexibility to unpredictable access requirements and class diagram evolution.** Information systems usually evolve through several succeeding generations. Requirements keep changing over time. It should be easy to project the changes in the underlying class diagram to an actual data management implementation. In fact, we consider this to be possibly the most neglected of all the requirements for a data management solution. It can be extremely tedious to upgrade a system and its database if the persistence solution has been solved without paying attention to database schema evolution issues.

We will next look at the more difficult parts of object-oriented design when you are implementing an application that stores its data into a database. A number of pitfalls await the object-oriented beginner. During the design time, you have to address questions such as the following:

- How to model and manipulate sets of objects? Is there a counterpart for a database query in the object-oriented world?
- How to access and manipulate the persistent objects in an application?
- How to define the database interface?
- How to design the database schema to support object persistence?
- How to manage the concept of a database transaction in an object-oriented application?
- What kind of a database system should I use? Should I consider object databases or stick to the relational ones?

We will next present simple practices you can use to overcome these typical problems. Let's start with one of the trickiest ones: how to manage sets of objects in an application.

Collections

When you try to marry object orientation with data management, you will find manipulation of groups of objects to be poorly supported. The more you have previously worked with relational databases, the more you will find it somewhat disappointing that there are no good means to model subsets of object instances in your class diagrams.

Set operations, such as updating millions of data rows with one single SQL command, are very powerful operations in relational databases. When you are used to thinking about application development from the relational point of view, that is, through sets and queries, you will miss similar possibilities when you start with object-orientation.

How do you model these in your class diagrams? If you have drawn a Document class in your diagram, what should you do if you know that in addition to accessing Document objects one-by-one, you would also like to model some subset of all the instantiated Documents and define operations for these sets of objects?

In our approach, a special class called Collection has been introduced to tackle the problem of manipulating sets of objects. A very similar concept is being deployed in practically all the most popular object-oriented database products.[1]

A collection is like an in-memory array or a set of objects of the same class. It always uses similar methods for manipulating the set—methods for populating the collection with the results of a database query, for inserting a single object into the collection, for removing an object from the collection and for updating an object in the collection, for asking for the number of objects in the collection, and for accessing the objects in the collection one-by-one. It is also possible to add application-specific methods, such as mass updates, for the collection class.

There are several commercial class libraries that offer useful data structures for use as collections, such as USL, Tools.h++, and Standard Template Library (STL).

We use collections in a controlled way. After having identified a need to model a subset of objects in the design phase, we introduce a new class into the design class diagram named: <class_name>Collection.

We use a simple example—the *Virtual Library*—throughout Chapter 2 to demonstrate the ideas of object persistence with concrete examples and code fragments. The Virtual Library could be an information system targeted to controlling all the documents and books within a company, for example. There is no central physical library in this case. Instead, the information system maintains information on the locations of the documents, authors of the documents, current reservations, and so on. The basic idea is that you could order any printed or online document and it could be located anywhere within the organization. You could also make simple queries based on authors, abstracts, keywords, and other bibliographic information.

Let us first look at collections by using this Virtual Library example. For instance, if we have discovered that we will need to manipulate and define operators for a collection of Document objects, we define a new class called DocumentCollection. Figure 2-1 presents a set of methods that this DocumentCollection class has.

DocumentCollection()	Creates an empty collection.
~DocumentCollection()	Removes the collection.
Add(Document &instance)	Adds an object into collection.
Remove(Document &instance)	Removes an object.
Clear()	Empties the collection.
Contains(Document &instance)	Tests existence of an object.
NumberOfObjects()	Returns the number of objects.
operator [ ](int index)	Iterator for sequential access.
PopulateFromQuery(char &query)	Fills the collection with the results of a database query.

FIGURE 2-1. Methods for a collection class.

It is possible to add more methods to the DocumentCollection class that provide more powerful object manipulation for a specific application, such as MarkBorrowed (date EndDate).

By introducing a consistent and coherent way to manipulate object subsets, we gain the benefit of clarity and efficiency in design. We are always able to solve similar problems in a similar way. An additional benefit of deploying in-memory collections is the tempting possibility to gain good performance for operations if we are deploying collections in a suitable way in constructing the application logic.

Navigating with Persistent Objects

One of the most interesting mechanisms the object-oriented approach provides is navigation between objects via association links. Whenever you have access to an object, you should be able to access the other objects that your object refers to via associations. Object-oriented programming languages such as C++ or Java make this easy. You just need to follow a pointer to get a hold on an object across an association link. You can also do this with persistent objects—this is called navigating with persistent objects. We will next look at the issue of how to give the persistent objects navigation properties.

Object navigation is quite different from working with sets and queries for those with a relational background. Figure 2-2 illustrates associations between two classes.

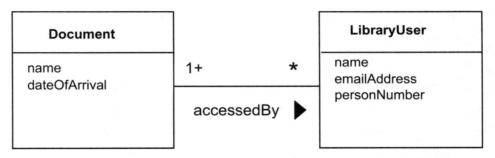

FIGURE 2-2. **You can navigate between the persistent objects of the classes Document and LibraryUser by using the accessedBy association link.**

When designing persistent objects, we always give a name to those associations that are to be used for navigation. The names for associations can be deployed later in giving names for methods that enable association management in the application.

Our guidelines suggest that a standard set of methods should be defined for *every* persistent class that has associations. One method is introduced for attaching an object to an association, one for removing an association between the objects, and one for accessing all the objects that are being referred to through the association link.

Figure 2-3 gives an example of methods needed to manage an association (see also the example of Figure 2-2).

```
AddToaccessedBy(LibraryUser *instance);
RemoveFromaccessedBy(LibraryUser *instance);
GetaccessedBy(LibraryUserCollection *cltn)
```

FIGURE 2-3. An example of methods for management of associations.

By using these navigation methods, you can construct your application logic so that new objects of different classes can be attached to each other just like the class diagram suggests. Whenever you have access to an object in your program, you can also get a hold on the other objects across the association link easily.

Making Objects Persistent

Traditional database design seems to be more art than science. Dozens of good books and hundreds of innovative articles have been written about the relationship of traditional analysis means (say, ER charts) and relational database schema design. However, little has been said about these issues on the object-oriented side. It would appear that the object-oriented community has not considered database-related issues too exciting. A standard answer to object data management problems preferred by a number of object practitioners would be a suggestion to start deploying object database technology.

Our guidelines provide simple yet object-like support for interfacing with databases:

- Identify persistent classes from your analysis class diagram.
- Add collection classes to your design class diagram if needed.
- Separate application-dependent parts and data management-related parts of the implementation by introducing a *database partner class* for every persistent class to take care of data storage manipulation and navigation via association links.
- Add classes to manage database connections, transactions, and other database services.

Several factors favor solving data management in this way. First, this approach is very object-like. Second, this approach is flexible to changes in the underlying middleware. It is possible to change the database product or even the database technique from relational to object database or even from files to a relational database afterwards, with little effort. In the following sections, we present some design patterns to implement persistent objects. Naturally, the effort needed varies a lot depending on the database technique and middleware used. However, the ideas presented are quite general by nature and applicable in a number of real-life cases.

Identifying the Persistent Objects

A class diagram evolves through several phases during the software development process. In the analysis phase, a first version of the class diagram is created. It presents the fundamental concepts of the application modeled as classes and their associations with each other. In the design phase, the initial class diagram is transformed into a design class diagram. User interface issues and other implementation-driven factors (such as inheriting some reusable component classes) are taken into account. Likewise, object persistence should be taken into consideration in the design phase.

It is preferable to start thinking about object persistence from the pure analysis class diagram. Finding the persistent classes from the analysis phase diagram is usually straightforward. All the relevant concepts and their relations have been identified already. The class diagram of the analysis phase has not yet been loaded down with irrelevant implementation-driven classes. Typically, persistent objects have concrete counterparts in the real world, such as *invoice*, *document*, or *room*. They model the very fundamental concepts of the application domain. If you use MVC++, as we proposed earlier, then you can easily identify the persistent classes from the model part of the design class diagram.

Note that if you have once defined that some class is persistent in one class diagram, it does not necessarily imply that classes with the same name would be also persistent in other diagrams. You have to think about the role of the class in the model, and the lifetime of the objects of that class.

After we identify the persistent classes, we document the findings into the design class diagram. For example, we document by giving these classes a suitable prefix (P_<class_name>), using UML stereotype string ´persistent', or coloring these classes with some background color, or using whatever means the OOA/OOD tool used provides.

Database Partners

We will next look into a design pattern—the *database partner*—that can be used to provide object persistence in a flexible way. We have noticed that an adapter layer between the database access operations and the actual domain-specific functionality of a persistent class is useful.[2] We should have an easy way to encapsulate the changes needed if the database solution should need to be changed one day. A situation may arise in which you need to upgrade to a new, major version of the existing database product, to replace the existing database with a totally new database product, or even change from, say, a relational database to an object-oriented database.

To achieve feasible levels of encapsulation of database management-related issues and application-dependent issues, a separate class called the database partner is defined per *every* persistent class. The database partner has all the methods needed for database manipulation and navigation via association links. The actual persistent class inherits the database partner class and thus gets the ability to manipulate data stored in a database. All the methods discovered by looking into scenarios are defined for the actual persistent class. Thus, clear distinctions in the roles of these classes are evident. The database partner takes care of data manipulation-related issues, and the persistent class implements application derived methods by deploying the inherited database methods.

Let us look at an example. Suppose that you have identified the Document class to be persistent, and you have correspondingly changed the name of the class to P_Document to depict its persistence. You should once more modify the design class diagram by replacing P_Document with an inheritance chain of a database partner—named, for example, DP_Document—that is inherited by P_Document and change the associations to point to the database partners of other persistent classes. This is illustrated in Figure 2-4.

To have a consistent way of defining methods for the database partners, it is favorable to define the methods for the database partner by following a precise policy. First, you need to have methods for database manipulation: a constructor for creating a database partner instance, a method for deleting a database partner object, Get<attribute> methods for accessing attributes, Set<attribute> methods for updating attributes, and finally query methods for fetching the database partner objects from the database according to a given database query.

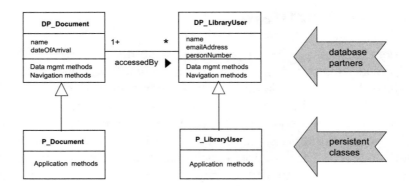

FIGURE 2-4. Adding database partners and persistent classes to a class diagram.

You also need to add the navigation methods for manipulation of associations: AddTo<association>, RemoveFrom<association>, and Get<association>. You should define these methods for every association in which this class participates. This way you can navigate by using the persistent objects.

Let us consider complete design-time specification of the persistent class P_Document and its database partner DP_Document. See Figure 2-5 for an example.

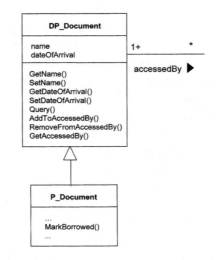

FIGURE 2-5. A complete specification of a persistent class and a related database partner.

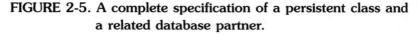

The application methods for a persistent class are implemented by using the data manipulation and association navigation methods provided by the database partner. The code fragment in Figure 2-6 clarifies writing an application method by using the services of the database partner.

```
// Mark the document borrowed. Check first that the
// document is already available for borrowers
// (= dateOfArrival has a value).

void P_Document::MarkBorrowed(DP_LibraryUser *user,
int &status)
{
    if (GetDateOfArrival())
    {
        AddToaccessedBy(user);
        status = OK;
    }
    else
        {
            status = NOT_YET_AVAILABLE;
        };
}
```

FIGURE 2-6. An example of implementing an application method by deploying the services of a database partner.

Other Database Services

We also should have means to make a connection to the database server and disconnect from it, as well as some means to manage database transactions. An object-oriented way to handle these is to define separate classes for database connections and transactions. This kind of policy is in use in many object database products, too.

We define a class Database that has methods Connect and Disconnect. These are used to establish a connection with a given database and to close the connection, respectively.

When it comes to manipulation of database transactions, we define a class Transaction that has methods Commit and Rollback. It is sensible to define the logic of these two methods so that ending a transaction implicitly starts a new one. Some databases do this for you automatically. Many modern database products provide sophisticated features such as optimistic concurrency management, checkpoints, and so on. It is easy to add support for these new features by adding new methods to the Transaction class.

Let us review a bit. What do we have so far? We have a way to isolate the database product-dependent parts of implementation from the application domain dependent parts. We have a consistent way of defining methods for database manipulation. We know how to manage object collections and how to navigate between objects as defined in the class diagram.

Introduction of database partner classes has given us some degree of freedom in implementation. For example, if we would like to change the underlying database product later for some reason, all the changes focus on database partners—we do not have to touch the persistent object classes at all.

A natural way to divide implementation work in an object-oriented R & D organization is to give a set of classes to be implemented to one designer and another set of classes to another. Well-defined interfaces between classes enable this option. Database partners make this division of work so that the database gurus of the organization can focus on data management issues, such as implementation of database partner classes, and the application domain experts can focus on the puzzles of the application area. You can implement classes to model a complex system while knowing practically nothing about database issues. This division of work and responsibilities could also be used as a boundary in subcontracting. It is easy to test the database partners independently from the application logic-dependent parts.

Later in this book, we will also look into the possibilities of automatically generating the database partner classes (see the section "Object Layer Generators" later in this chapter).

Selecting the Persistence Mechanism

There are several feasible data storage options. The most interesting options we will look at in more detail are: the file system of the operating system, relational databases, hybrid object-relational databases, and pure object databases. In addition to these, a multitude of other data storage alternatives is available, such as hierarchical and network databases and numerous different indexing mechanisms.

Each of these data storage mechanisms has its pros and cons. Quite often, the database selection is considered a technical issue only. Such consideration certainly is not adequate. Several other non-technical aspects should be considered as well.

Implementing Object Persistence with Files

The earliest trials with persistent objects presented in literature were based on using the file system of the operating system. If you want to make objects persistent, you simply implement Save and Open methods for *every* persistent class. You store the object onto disk by calling the Save method and correspondingly load it back into memory structures by calling Open method. As simplistic as this approach may sound, it is quite applicable in many cases.

If you are more ambitious and want to implement all the object abstractions—such as inheritance, aggregates, and associations—with files, you will need to work hard at it. To present complex abstractions with files, you will need to discover clever file syntaxes and coding and decoding algorithms. It is not so straightforward to store information implemented as pointer references in your program into files.

In practice, it is not even sensible to try to design a full-blown, file-based, generic framework for managing persistent objects. It is much too laborious to implement all the necessary logic to cope with object inter-relations with simple files. Even if you *can* make it all work, the framework probably will not perform adequately, it will cost too much, it will not enable multiuser updates, or it will become useless after the very first changes in the class diagram.

Some commercial class libraries or application development environments such as Microsoft Foundation Classes include persistence services that are based on using files as a storage solution for persistent objects. In a number of simple cases, these persistence services may satisfy your needs adequately. Nevertheless, a file system-based persistence mechanism is not a long-term solution for a multiuser information system.

Using Relational Databases to Provide Object Persistence

We will next look into providing object persistence with relational databases. There is no denying the fact that relational databases are *the* Database Solution today. The vast majority of R & D projects are based on relational solutions. According to analysts, the market share of relational databases is today somewhere over 70 percent. During the next few years, the market dominance of relational databases is predicted to approach 90 percent. [Gartner]. Due to indisputable popularity of relational databases, also object-oriented software developers face the fact that applications should be able to store their information in relational databases. We will next examine the special characteristics of interfacing relational databases in more detail.

Relational databases have been available for more than 20 years. The market is dominated by a group of very strong players. It is quite difficult for newcomers to gain a foothold in this arena. On the other hand, this clear market situation has helped to create the current firm position for relational databases. It is actually quite easy to select a relational database product. Only a few credible options are available, and the products themselves have become very much alike when it comes to their technical features, pricing, and support services. One product may lead in some respect for a while, but the other vendors release equivalent features in their next releases. Some may disagree, but today we think it does not really matter very much which relational database product you select. *Oracle*, *Informix*, *Sybase*, *Microsoft SQL Server*, *IBM DB/2*, and *CA-Ingres* are the strongest players in terms of market share.

Basic Relational Concepts

Information is stored into two-dimensional *tables* in a relational database. A table consists of *rows* and *columns*. All the elements in a column have the same *type* and *domain*—that is, logically, they have the same meaning.

The remarkable difference between relational databases and, say, flat files is that you access the information stored in a relational database only by its logical structure instead of by physical storage structure. In other words, you are not interested in from which byte offset some data begin and end on the disk. Instead, you formulate a logical query and let the database management system take care of fetching the data for you. In fact, you do not even *know* how your data are located physically in a relational database.

Structured Query Language (SQL) is an interface for communicating with the database. Official bodies such as ISO and ANSI have standardized SQL—or, more precisely, parts of it. The SQL standard itself has been revised several times. Now, practically all database products support the SQL-2 level of the standard.

Relational databases are able to serialize database transactions. Several users may simultaneously access the same data, and the data management system takes care of transaction consistency. Practically all the commercially available products implement transaction management in a *pessimistic* way— using locks to avoid simultaneous updates until the application that has caused data to be locked either commits or rollbacks the transaction. Some relational database products, such as *Solid Server*, support *optimistic* concurrency control, in which no locks are used; instead, consistency of data is inspected in the commit phase only. Optimistic transaction management can give somewhat better performance in certain cases where simultaneous updates to the same piece of information are rare.

Relational databases have been the forerunners of the two-tier client-server architecture. A powerful database server executes SQL queries sent by client processes. The server and the client can locate physically in different computers across a LAN or even a WAN. Typically, client computers are remarkably lighter than the server in terms of processing power and price. Perhaps the most common hardware configuration in many application areas during the last few years has been a setup of a UNIX database server connected via TCP/IP LAN with a number of PC clients running some version of Microsoft Windows. Java and the rapidly growing interest in platform-independent development may change the general computing model in the future. But these anticipated changes do not necessarily reflect to data management in a remarkable way.

Practically all the big relational products are targeted for continuous usage (24/7), meaning that it should be possible to run the database without ever shutting down the server. In practice, never shutting down is not possible whatever product you use, due to the time required for upgrading the database. However, some credit should be given to RDBMS vendors for enhanced on-line backups and archive-logging features.

Indexes are typically *b-trees* or *hash tables* that can be built for tables toto speed up queries. Query *optimizers* in relational databases try to deduct optimal access paths for queries by deploying statistical information about data distribution and available indexes. Query optimization is one of the few areas where relational database vendors try to differentiate and find short-term competitive advantages over competitors.

Interfacing with a Relational Database

Figure 2-7 depicts the most common ways for an object-oriented application to interface with a database server.

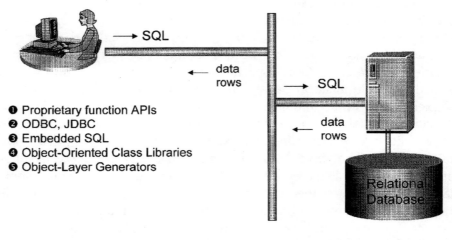

① Proprietary function APIs
② ODBC, JDBC
③ Embedded SQL
④ Object-Oriented Class Libraries
⑤ Object-Layer Generators

⑥ Stored procedures

FIGURE 2-7. The most common ways for an object-oriented application to interface with an RDBMS.

Proprietary APIs

The relational database management systems typically have a function *application programming interface* (API) for the application to communicate with the database. Virtually all the commercially available RDBMS products have at least a proprietary C programming interface. In some products, this interface is really meant for application development—it has been properly documented and its usage described in manuals. On the other hand, most vendors have not documented the proprietary interface at all. They want other means to be used in interfacing the database. It should be noted that none of the RDBMS vendors provide a native C++, Smalltalk, or Java interface to their products. Perhaps the most discouraging part is that all these proprietary function APIs of different RDBMS products are totally incompatible with each other.

ODBC and JDBC

Microsoft has been advocating the *Open Database Connectivity* (ODBC) interface. ODBC is a simple C function API that has been implemented on top of virtually every data management product. ODBC has become popular. Nearly all the current Windows productivity tools and 4GLs are built to use ODBC in database communication. As Java has gained continuously more and more popularity among the software development community, an ODBC-like interface called JDBC has been developed for Java programmers.

Embedded SQL

One of the most common ways to interface with a database is with *embedded SQL*. You include database manipulation statements beginning with some prefix like EXEC SQL or $ into your source code. Before compiling your source with the programming language compiler, you must preprocess your source code with a translator that converts embedded SQL statements into function calls of the RDBMS API. Embedded SQL is quite popular. The syntax is simple, and portability to other database products is feasible. There are embedded SQL precompilers for several programming languages. Recently, some database vendors have launched precompilers for C++ as well.

Stored Procedures

During the past few years, RDBMS vendors have implemented the possibility of running part of the application in the database server. You can write more complex SQL procedures with embedded logic, give them a name, and store them in the database server. These *stored procedures* sound intuitively nice. It is easy to buy into all the claimed benefits of stored procedures: improved performance, architectural clarity, reuse aspects, and so on. Nevertheless, somewhat surprisingly, it looks like stored procedures have not become as widely used as one might expect. People are complaining about non-existing standards for stored procedure languages and practical problems in defining adequate database server resources (caches, memory, and so on).

General Third-Party Database Class Libraries

Commercial class libraries are available to interface with the database from an object programming language. This has become a niche market, because C++ quickly gained a strong foothold as a programming language but the relational vendors did not implement C++ interfaces to their products in time to meet the demand. This delay paved the way for small companies to enter the market.

Perhaps the best-known database class libraries for relational databases are *DBTools.h++, CommonBase, SQL*C++,* and *SQLObjects.* You can also find nice public domain class libraries on the Internet.[3]

These class libraries have very similar motivations. They aim to hide the native database interface with their own interface—often a bit simpler and more general one. Applications are written on top of these classes. Thus, you can achieve a degree of portability by using these class libraries.

The class diagram that these class libraries offer is very close to the concepts of the relational model. They contain classes such as Table, Column, Query, Cursor, and so on. You have to solve all the problems of mapping your own class diagram with the database schema. A code fragment in Figure 2-8 gives an example of the use of a database class library.

Object Layer Generators

During the past few years, a new product category has evolved: the *object layer generators.* These are tools that generate a tailored C++ object interface to a database based on the class diagram fed into them.

You introduce the class diagram to the generator by giving a description of the diagram and giving hints to the generator on how to map objects and

```
// Find the room where the library user resides.
Room * LibraryUser::GetresidesIn()
{
    . . .
    // introduce classes and corresponding tables
    DBTable libuser (db, "LIBRARY_USER");
    DBTable room (db, "ROOM");

    // define aliases for attributes
    DBColumn &room_id = *room["OID"];
    DBColumn &room_nbr = *room["NUMBER"];
    DBColumn &user_id = *lib_user["OID"];
    DBColumn &resides_in = *lib_user["RESIDES_IN"];

    // define the attributes to fetch from LIBRARY_USER
    DBSelectList selList1 (resides_in);
    // introduce a cursor to fetch data
    DBCursor cursor1(db, DBSelect(selList1, user_id == oid));
    // get data
    cursor1.Fetch();

. . . now we know the right oid for the room

    // define the attributes to fetch from ROOM
    DBSelectList selList2 (room_id,room_nbr);
    // introduce a cursor to fetch data
    DBCursor cursor2(db, DBSelect(selList2, room_id == resides_in.value));
    // get data
    cursor2.Fetch();

    . . .
    return new Room(room_id.value, room_nbr.value);
}
```

FIGURE 2-8. An example of the use of a database class library.

attributes and associations with tables and fields. Typically, these tools enable use of products from several database vendors.

One of the pioneers in this area has been *Persistence* from Persistence, Inc. It is able to generate C++ code that can be used to interface with the biggest relational players and even with some object database products. With Persistence, the decision to use a particular product can be deferred until linking time. In principle, you do not have to modify your source code to make your persistent classes run on different database products.

There are also other relevant options in this category, like *Oracle Designer/2000 C++ Object Layer Generator, SubtleWare, Secant Persistent Object Manager, Crosslogic Universe,* and a number of others.[4]

Figure 2-9 illustrates usage of the database API generated by a database interface generator. Note that all the methods used in this example have been generated automatically, based on the class diagram description.

```
// Find the authors of the document.

void Document::FindAuthors(char *authors)
{
    // get the relevant document entry
    DocumentEntry *de;
    de = this ->GetDescribes();

    // get the bibliographic entry
    BibliographicEntry *be;
    be = de->GetHasBibliographicEntry();

    // copy the authors attribute
    strcpy(authors, be->GetAuthors());
}
```

FIGURE 2-9. An example of using the code generated by an object layer generator.

Mapping Class Diagrams onto Database Tables

So, how should you use all the fancy features of modern relational databases in object-oriented development? A number of tricky questions need to be addressed: How to convert class diagrams onto database tables? How to use indexes for optimal performance? How to manage transactions? And finally, what kind of interface to use for the actual object-oriented application development?

Dr. James Rumbaugh, the father of the OMT method, with his colleagues has presented several practical ways to map class diagrams onto relational database tables. In the following sections, we will look at these basic mappings and present some comments about practical considerations.[5]

Objects and Classes

The basic idea is simple: A class maps into a table, the objects belonging to that class map to rows, and attributes of the object are columns of the table (see Figure 2-10).

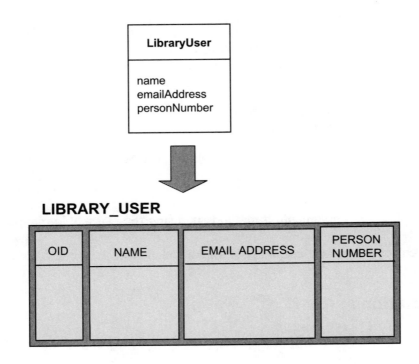

FIGURE 2-10. Mapping a class to a relational table.

Every object should have a unique identity. The easiest way to offer this identity is to add a special column Object Identifier (OID) into the table definitions and to use sequence generators available in all the major RDBMS products to provide unique surrogate keys. In other words, whenever we are inserting a new object (row) into the database, we embed calling of the sequence generator into the SQL insert statement. Let us summarize: We create a database table for the persistent class. The columns of the class are the attributes of the class and an extra column for OID. From the data management point of view, making an object persistent simply means inserting a row into that table.

Figure 2-11 shows an example that demonstrates the key ideas in the implementation of some basic methods with Embedded SQL /C++.

```
— CREATING A PERSISTENT OBJECT IN CONSTRUCTOR
void Library_User::LibraryUser(name, email, person_nbr)
{
        ...
        — get a unique OID from the seq. generator
        ...
        EXEC SQL INSERT INTO library_user
                VALUES (:oid,:name,:email,:person_nbr);
}

— DELETING A PERSISTENT OBJECT
void LibraryUser::remove()
{
        EXEC SQL DELETE FROM library_user WHERE oid = :oid;
}
```

FIGURE 2-11. Implementing methods by using the class-table mapping.

Stored procedures are useful in the implementation of these methods, as well.

Associations

You can implement associations between objects when using a relational database in several ways. The different design patterns differ in terms of flexibility, extensibility and performance.

It is not possible to save pointers in a relational database. To overcome this deficiency, we use *foreign keys* to present dependencies between data rows of tables. Foreign keys are columns in a row that are used to link the row with some other data in another table. The principles of *mappings* are based heavily on the foreign key concept.

There are two fundamental approaches: You can use foreign keys or you can make an *association table*—extra table for the association. An easy naming convention in database design is to use the name of the association in giving a name to the foreign key (option 1) or to the association table (option 2). Figures 2-12 and 2-13 demonstrate the differences of these two options.

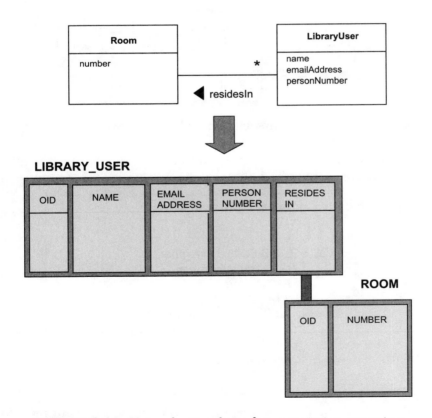

FIGURE 2-12. Using foreign keys for association mapping.

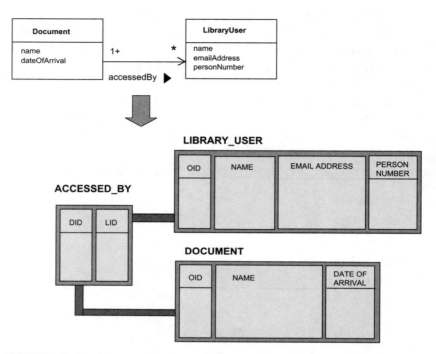

FIGURE 2-13. Using an association table for association mapping.

Figure 2-14 clarifies the idea by giving an example of implementing an association management method by using the foreign key mapping option.

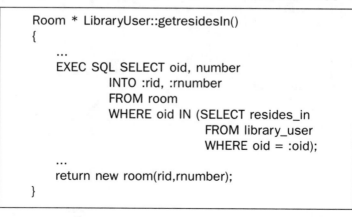

```
Room * LibraryUser::getresidesIn()
{
    ...
    EXEC SQL SELECT oid, number
            INTO :rid, :rnumber
            FROM room
            WHERE oid IN (SELECT resides_in
                            FROM library_user
                            WHERE oid = :oid);
    ...
    return new room(rid,rnumber);
}
```

FIGURE 2-14. An example of writing an association management method by using the foreign key mapping.

Many-to-many associations always must be implemented by using a separate association table. One-to-one or one-to-many associations can be alternatively implemented by using embedded foreign keys in the tables.

In general, using association tables is more flexible than foreign keys. On the other hand, accessing objects via associations results in extra joining of tables. *Joins* are always tricky in relational databases in terms of performance. However, query optimizers and indexing techniques have been continuously improving in RDBMS products. Thorough planning of indexing makes using association tables efficient enough.

Aggregates

There is no native way to express containment hierarchies of objects with pure relational databases. You cannot define tables to be comprised of other tables[6] or rows to be comprised of rows in other tables.

In practice, though, this situation is not so difficult. It is possible to replace an aggregation with an expression where named associations are used to depict inclusion of other classes. If we want to express that an aggregate class contains a subclass, we use an association and give it the name has<contained class>. Correspondingly, we can use isPartOf associations to indicate that the class belongs logically to another class.

After this kind of conversion, we can follow the design patterns presented for association mappings in the "Associations" section. Figure 2-15 illustrates this kind of a transformation.

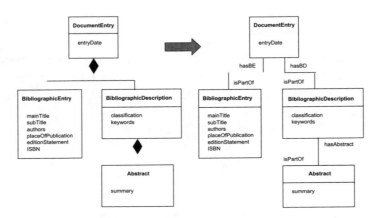

FIGURE 2-15. Converting an aggregate to named associations.

To support the idea of atomicity included into the concept of aggregated objects in object-oriented modeling, we should have a means to manage the cluster of tables involved in the aggregation as a single, atomic entity. Relational database products provide a nice way of doing this: *integrity constraints*. For example, we can define integrity rules to delete relevant rows automatically also from the referred tables whenever a row from the master table is being deleted. This deletion prevents the tables from becoming filled with garbage rows.

Inheritance

Inheritance is one of the most powerful—and most used—object modeling concepts. Object programming languages such as C++ and Java make use of inheritance easily. Declaring a C++ class to be derived from another class is straightforward. Unfortunately, the same does not hold for persistent objects when using a relational database. There is no built-in way of implementing an inheritance hierarchy with tabular structures and SQL.

However, you can use a few alternative design patterns to support inheritance:

- Table-per-class approach.
- Leaf-class approach.
- One table approach.

Table-Per-Class Approach

Make the base class and all the derived classes self-standing database tables. The table that stores the base class objects has all the base class attributes as columns. The tables that map into derived classes have only the extra attributes as columns and a special IS_A column that is used to combine the extra attributes with the base class table attributes when assembling an object. In other words, whenever you want to access a derived object, you have to make a join with the base class table. See Figure 2-16 for an example of the table-per-class approach.

An example of accessing leaf objects (on-line document objects) of the inheritance chain by using this inheritance mapping structure is given in Figure 2-17.

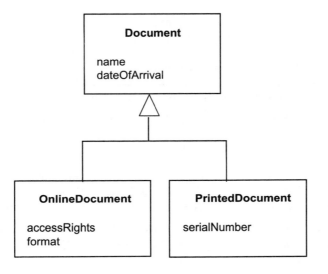

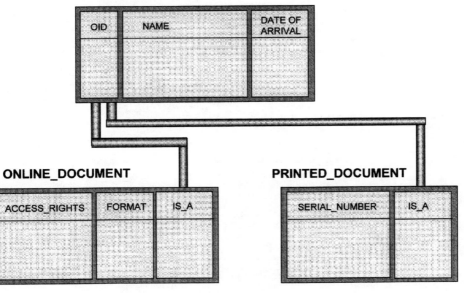

FIGURE 2-16. Table-per-class approach.

```
select      d.oid, d.name, d.date_of_arrival,
            o.access_rights, o.format
from        document d, online_document o
where       o.is_a = d.oid;
```

FIGURE 2-17. A SQL query for accessing the leaf objects of the inheritance chain by using the table-per-class mapping.

Leaf-Class Approach

Replicate base class attributes to derived classes and implement only leaf classes of the inheritance hierarchy as database tables. You do not need any joins when accessing derived objects. On the other hand, if you want to instantiate base class objects, you must make a union of all the tables present in the inheritance hierarchy mapping. See Figure 2-18 for an example of this mapping option.

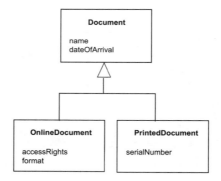

FIGURE 2-18. Leaf-class approach.

Figure 2-19 gives an example of accessing all base class objects (document) by using this inheritance mapping structure.

```
select      oid, name, date_of_arrival,
from        online_document
union
select      oid, name, date_of_arrival,
from        printed_document
```

FIGURE 2-19. A SQL query for accessing the base class objects of the inheritance chain by using the leaf-class mapping.

1-Table Approach

Make only one table for the entire inheritance hierarchy. All the attributes are collected into that table. If some attribute is not relevant to a certain object, a NULL value is used to indicate invalidity of that attribute. Besides, you will also need an extra column CLASS that contains the name of class. See Figure 2-20 for an example of this mapping.

This approach is very efficient. You will never need joins, unions, or any other time-consuming operations. Relational purists might not love this kind of an implementation option. It breaks the normalization principles. If you have many attributes in your classes or very deep inheritance hierarchies, this approach is not practical, because your tables will become very wide.

An example of accessing leaf objects (on-line document objects) of the inheritance chain by using this inheritance mapping structure is given in Figure 2-21.

Note that you have to know in your program that the attribute serial-Number is not relevant for the class OnlineDocument. Alternatively, you could introduce a couple of "metadata" tables that contain information about attributes of classes and how they map to fields of tables. The penalty of this approach is that you have to access the metadata tables every time you want to access persistent objects. However, this repository approach is used in many commercial object-oriented productivity tools that are able to map objects to a relational database.

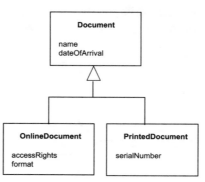

DOCUMENT

OID	CLASS	NAME	DATE OF ARRIVAL	ACCESS_RIGHTS	FORMAT	SERIAL_NUMBER

FIGURE 2-20. One-table approach.

select	oid, name, date_of_arrival, access_rights, format
from	document
where	class = 'ON_LINE';

FIGURE 2-21. A SQL query for accessing the leaf objects of the inheritance chain by using the table-per-class mapping.

Common Pitfalls and Problems

As we have seen, more or less straightforward ways are available to manage persistence of objects in a relational database. However, tricky pitfalls also are lurking for an object-oriented developer.

First, it is very easy to underestimate the amount of work needed. The code needed to make objects persistent is simple. By following the well-known design patterns—like the ones we have just described—it is quite easy. The database schema becomes surprisingly well normalized. If the class diagram has been well designed, the rules presented yield a schema in the third normal form where no data needs to be replicated to several tables. The SQL statements needed are simple, and the logic required in your code is not too complex. It is not too difficult or time-consuming to have the *first* version of your implementation up and running.

The problems relate to the *next* versions of your implementation. You will find that you may have to make some modifications due to unsatisfactory performance, or you may need to modify your class diagram—add new attributes, change associations or add new ones, and so on. This kind of modification may be very time-consuming and result in several changes to the database schema, endless type conversions in your classes, and so on. We strongly urge you to make decent regression tests for persistent classes. Type conversions have proven to be very error-prone, although they are seemingly straightforward to do.

Implementing Persistent Objects with Object-Relational Databases

Object-relational databases (ORDBMS) are database systems that are able to implement object-oriented abstractions on top of the relational model. Initially, there were two reasons why ORDBMS product development started approximately ten years ago: new data management requirements and object-oriented programming.

First, industry segments such as *CAD*, *CAM*, *CASE*, and *multimedia* set new requirements for data management. Relational databases did not provide features, such as *long transactions*, *optimistic transactions*, *data versions*, or *history data support*. Naturally, some of these features can be implemented on relational databases, but the effort can prove laborious and time-consuming.

The second main motivation for ORDBMS development was set by the object-oriented programming community. Relational databases do not provide direct support for many of the dominant concepts in object-oriented programming such as *inheritance*, *aggregation* and *abstract data types*.

The essential features of an ORDBMS were described in *Third Genera- tion Database System Manifesto* for the first time in 1990. This manifesto was written by a group of relational database experts who wanted to put up a defense against the emerging object database community [Committee 90]. The manifesto explained how current relational database products could be enhanced to provide support for the growing application requirements.

There is no commonly accepted definition for an object-relational database. A basic requirement is that the DBMS incorporates the concept of an object in some form. In practice, a database system product can be considered to be an object-relational database if it implements some of the object-oriented modeling abstractions in its data model for example, abstract data types and inheritance.

During the past few years, several ORDBMSs products have entered the market. These products have very diverse backgrounds in terms of their origin. Some products have been developed from scratch, some are old rela- tional databases that have evolved into ORDBMSs. Some relational database products have been integrated with object data management technology acquired by the RDBMS vendor.

The strongest players on the ORDBMS arena are currently *UniSQL*, *Oracle8*, *Informix*, *CA-Ingres* and *DB2*. *Oracle8*, *CA-Ingres*, and *IBM DB2* have evolved from a pure relational database while *UniSQL* is built from scratch. *Informix* is integrated with an object-relational database product *Illustra* originally built from scratch.

The data management features and the object-oriented features the ORDBMS products provide vary considerably from one product to another. Not all products offer support for inheritance in their data model, even though it is a fundamental concept of object orientation.

In principle, all of the ORDBMS vendors advocate the *SQL3* query lan- guage as the means to communicate with the database. However, the actual implementations of the query language differ to some extent. This difference is partly because of the products' incoherent data models. But the real problem is that SQL3 is not yet completed. It is a standardization work in progress at the time of this writing.

Status of the SQL Standard

Current relational database products implement some level of the SQL2 standard also known as SQL-92. The conformance can be *entry level, intermediate level*, or *full*. Today, SQL2 has become partly obsolete even in the non-object-oriented world because many relational database products implement a set of new features that are not supported by SQL2. Examples of these unsupported features are *triggers* and *stored procedures*. Additionally, relational database vendors have been adding new object-oriented features into their products for several years now. Therefore, the value of SQL2 as a standard has declined. In effect, portability of database applications utilizing these new features has become worse.

ANSI, ISO, and certain other standard bodies are working on a draft of the SQL3 standard. Currently, this draft includes roughly two thousand pages.[7] A great deal of work on the standard still remains to be done, and it will most likely be at least 1999 when it is finished.

The SQL3 specification work has proven to be ambitious. One sign of this is that a few of the features originally planned for SQL3 have been already dropped to the next-generation SQL standard specification (SQL4). However, SQL3 can be considered to be a standard for object-relational databases when it is completed.

SQL3 Features

In this section, we go into the details of the most significant parts of the upcoming standard from the point of view of object modelings. As a whole, SQL3 will be a very large standard; it defines many remarkable new features, such as extensions to *table* and *type* concepts, *procedural* capabilities, and support for certain *object-oriented abstractions*. The features presented and the syntax used follow the standard draft as it was in the spring 1998 [ANSI 98].

Extensions to the Table Concept

Each table has an implicitly defined data type, called a *row type*. You can also create *named row types* separately from table definitions. A row type consists of a field name and data type pairs that the columns of the table having this row type will have. A row in a table is an instance of its row type and each row in a table has the same row type. Inheritance can be applied also to named row types.

The row type feature is defined in SQL3 in order to implement *table references*, to provide the possibility to pass rows as arguments to *routines*, to return rows as return values from functions, and to store rows in variables.

SQL3 gives you the possibility of defining *object identifiers* (OIDs) for rows. You also can use OIDs to reference to a row in other tables. You can define any table with a named row type to contain an object identifier by supplying the table definition with the WITH REF VALUE expression. The type of this *reference value* indicates the name of the row type with which it is associated. The object identifier is placed in a system-maintained column of the table. This column can be used in SQL clauses like any other column. A few relational database products have already implemented concepts very near the reference value concept of SQL3.

Any table can be a declared as a *subtable* of one or many *supertables*. Inheritance can be defined with the UNDER clause in a table definition. When a subtable is defined, it inherits all the columns of its supertables. Additionally, it can have columns of its own. A table with subtables but without a supertable is called a *maximal supertable*. A maximal supertable and all its *direct* and *indirect* subtables form a *subtable family*.

A row in each subtable corresponds to one row in each direct supertable. A row in a supertable corresponds to zero or one row in its subtables. The semantics for the insert, delete, and update operations keep the rows in subtable families consistent.

You can associate routines with tables to implement object-like operations for rows. You can also employ *polymorphism* by redefining more specific routines for subtables. Routines are associated with tables by adding a reference value as an argument to the routines of a table.

Extensions to the Type Concept

So far, relational databases have been capable of handling *primitive built-in* data types only, such as strings, numbers, and dates. In addition to these built-it data types, SQL3 defines *abstract data types* (ADTs). You can use the ADTs in a similar way as the built-in types. For example, you can define a column in a table to have an ADT as the data type.

An ADT defines a set of attributes to represent a single entity. Attributes of an ADT can be both built-in data types and abstract data types. ADTs can have *operations* associated with the ADT definitions. When defining an ADT, certain operations (for example, ordering operation) are compulsory (see Figure 2-22).

The operations are implemented with routines. A routine can either be a *function* or a *procedure*. A function has a return value, whereas a procedure does not. In practice, a routine can be either a SQL routine stored in a database or an *external* routine written with a programming language.

Any ADT can have one or more *supertypes* and one or more *subtypes*. The inheritance is defined with the UNDER clause in the subtype definition. The ADT inheritance has the common features of the object-oriented inheritance concept. An instance of a subtype is considered an instance of all its supertypes, and an instance of a subtype can be used where an instance of any of its supertypes is needed.

```
CREATE ABSTRACT DATA TYPE library_user_adt (
name              VARCHAR NOT NULL,
email             VARCHAR NOT NULL,
person_number     NUMERIC NOT NULL,
ORDER FULL BY RELATIVE compare_library_users )
```

FIGURE 2-22. A simple abstract data type definition.

There are similarities between the table and the ADT concepts of SQL3, but, there are certain significant differences as well. When you want to store ADT instances persistently, the ADT has to be a column in a table. In a database, there is no central place where all the instances of ADTs are stored. The instances are always stored in tables which have columns of this ADT. Furthermore, there are two kind of inheritance in SQL3, namely the ADT inheritance and the table inheritance. The ADT subtype concept is totally distinct from the subtable concept.

SQL3 introduces several other, new data types not defined in SQL2: *Boolean*, *REF type*, *binary large object* (BLOB), and *character large object* (CLOB). The Boolean data type can have only values TRUE or FALSE. The REF data type can reference another table in a database. When you want to define a reference to another table, you define a column to the referring table with a data type REF(<named row type>). The REF column actually contains the reference value (OID) of the referenced row type instance.

The BLOB data type offers the possibility of storing large binary data objects, such as *images*, *video,* or *audio* in the database. The CLOB data type can be used to store large amounts of text into a single column. SQL3 defines also the concept of *domain* which can have a set of permissible values from a certain data type.

SQL3 provides three types of *collection* data types: *SET, MULTISET,* and *LIST*. A MULTISET is a non-ordered collection that can have duplicate values; a SET is a non-ordered collection that cannot have duplicate values; and a LIST is an ordered collection. A collection can contain values from a built-in type, an abstract data type, a row type, or another collection type.

New Statement Types

A number of new statement types have been added to SQL3 toto make it a *computationally complete* language. Many of these statement types are related to adding procedural logic capabilities to the SQL language. These statements include, for example:

- IF ... THEN ... ELSE ... ELSEIF and CASE statements for implementing *conditional* execution paths to SQL routines.
- LOOP, WHILE, REPEAT and FOR statements to implement *repeated execution* to SQL routines.
- RETURN statement for returning values from SQL functions.
- *Exception handling* mechanisms to implement error handling to SQL routines.

Interfacing with an Object-Relational Database

The application programming interfaces offered by the object-relational database products can be divided into two categories: SQL3 *query language interfaces* and *navigation interfaces*. Usually the navigation interface is built on top of the SQL3 query language interface.

You can issue SQL3 statements to an ORDBMS via an embedded SQL3 interface, function interface, or an ODBC-like interface—depending on the product, of course (see Figure 2-23). SQL3 does not define a complete navigation interface; nor does it define mappings between SQL3 ADTs and classes in object-oriented programming languages.

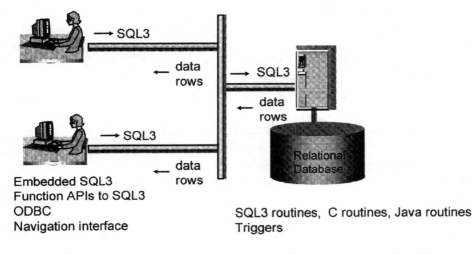

FIGURE 2-23. Interfacing with object-relational databases.

In general, navigation interfaces fit better with the object-orientation paradigm, because they make it possible to navigate in the class diagram of an application via *association links*. Thus, it is desirable that the products would offer some type of navigation interface in addition to the query language interface. Usually the navigation interfaces are generated from the application class diagram or from the database schema. However, not all ORDBMS products have a navigation interface at all and the navigation interfaces currently implemented vary considerably.

At the moment, no such navigation interface generators are available that would work with multiple ORDBMS products. This lack does not mean that there is no need for this kind of tool. It means that the current products have very different query language interfaces. Whenever there is a navigation interface available, you should use it in your applications, although it is advisable that you implement the database partners on top of the navigation interface of the ORDBMS—even if the interface provides you with C++ or Java classes. This implementation enables better *encapsulation*, and therefore you are able to change the database system more easily, if required. Another reason is that the navigation interfaces offered by the ORDBMS products might not provide you with all the abstractions needed for implementing complete class diagrams. You probably still need to use the SQL3 query language to some extent in the database partner layer.

If there is no navigation interface available, you have to implement your database partner layer completely using the SQL3 query language. In any case, the layer will be much simpler than with relational databases, because object-relational databases implement certain object-oriented abstractions in the data model of the database system.

Implementing Class Diagrams

SQL3 and object-relational database products are good news for object-oriented developers. Several ways of mapping the object abstractions to the ORDBMS data model are available. Naturally, all the mappings presented earlier for relational databases are available also with ORDBMSs. The mappings described in this section follow the SQL3 features and syntax as it was in the spring of 1998.

The objective in this section is to present the different alternatives SQL3 offers compared to the pure relational data model. The code fragments presented emphasize the DML operations and ignore database connection, transaction, and error-handling issues.

Furthermore, many of the ORDBMS implementations that are currently available offer more elegant data model than is specified in the SQL3 standard draft.

Classes and Objects

In SQL3, you can use named row types or ADTs to encapsulate a set of attributes together to implement classes. You can implement the object identity easily by using the reference values in tables. For ADTs there is not an own identity concept, such as the system generated OIDs are for tables.

Furthermore, you can implement operations as routines and associate the routines with tables or ADTs, as described earlier. You can implement the routines with the procedural SQL or a programming language, such as C, C++, or Java. The most effective implementation alternative depends on the desired functionality of the routine.

There are three steps you have to take when you implement classes with named row types in an ORDBMS. First, define a named row type to represent the attributes of your class; include also the OID attribute to the named row type definition. Second, create a table for the row type and define that the values for OID are generated by the database system (see Figures 2-24 through 2-26). Finally, you can create the operations of your class as routines.

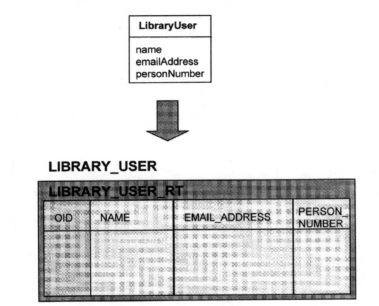

FIGURE 2-24. Mapping a class into a table in an ORDBMS.

If you are using ADTs to implement classes, you have to first create an ADT to represent the attributes of your class. Secondly, you have to create a table that has the columns ADT and OID. And lastly it is time to implement the operations.

In Figure 2-25 we create a row type and a table for the LibraryUser class. In the row type definition, the _rt extension stands for row type. In Figure 2-26, we define a database partner method (a constructor) for creating a new persistent object from the LibraryUser class.

Implementing classes is actually easy and straightforward in SQL3, as in SQL2. However, SQL3 supports the class concept better than SQL2 because you have the named row types and ADTs available.

```
CREATE ROW TYPE library_user_rt (
oid                REF(library_user_rt)
name               VARCHAR(50) NOT NULL,
email_address      VARCHAR(50) NOT NULL,
person_number      NUMERIC NOT NULL )

CREATE TABLE library_user
OF library_user_rt WITH REF VALUE (
VALUES FOR oid ARE SYSTEM GENERATED )
```

FIGURE 2-25. Defining a row type and a table for this row type.

```
LibraryUser::LibraryUser(name, email, personNbr)
{
...
EXEC SQL INSERT INTO
library_user(name,email_address,person_number)
VALUES (:name,:email,:personNbr);
...
EXEC SQL SELECT oid
INTO :oid
FROM library_user
WHERE person_number=:personNbr;
...
}
```

FIGURE 2-26. A constructor of the database partner class.

Associations

In SQL3, you can implement *one-to-one* and *many-to-one* associations with a new data type REF. With this data type, you can reference only to a row type—not to an ADT, for example. The REF data type enables simple navigation via association links between the tables (see Figures 2-27 through 2-29). This slightly raises the abstraction level of the associations, compared to pure relational databases where you have to always deal with the foreign key in these association types. However, in SQL3 you also have to implement the *many-to-many* associations with a separate association table as with relational databases.

However, the REF data type enables only *unidirectional* navigation. The SQL3 data model does not provide navigation to both directions of the association. Naturally, you can define references to both ends of the associations, but the DBMS does not keep the references automatically up to date when the other end of the association is updated. Of course, you can preserve the *referential integrity* with stored SQL procedures and triggers, but that is quite laborious.

The REF data type always refers to a named row type, and a row type can be used in several tables. Therefore, you have to define explicitly the table from which to look for the row type. This is declared with a SCOPE clause in the table definition.

In Figures 2-27 and 2-28, we create row types and tables for the LibraryUser and Room classes and implement the association with the REF data type. In Figure 2-29, we define a database partner method for navigating via the association defined in Figure 2-28. Note that there is no need for an explicit join operation in the SQL query.

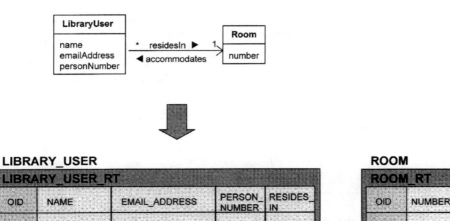

FIGURE 2-27. Mapping an association into tables in an ORDBMS.

```
CREATE ROW TYPE library_user_rt (
oid                  REF(library_user_rt)
name                 VARCHAR(50) NOT NULL,
email_address        VARCHAR(50) NOT NULL,
person_number        NUMERIC NOT NULL,
resides_in           REF(room_rt) )

CREATE TABLE library_user
OF library_user_rt WITH REF VALUE (
SCOPE FOR resides_in IS room,
VALUES FOR oid ARE SYSTEM GENERATED );

CREATE ROW TYPE room_rt (
oid                  REF(room_rt)
number               VARCHAR(10) NOT NULL )

CREATE TABLE room
OF room_rt WITH REF VALUE (
VALUES FOR oid ARE SYSTEM GENERATED );
```

FIGURE 2-28. Defining row types and tables for the association.

```
Room * LibraryUser::getResidesIn()
{
...
EXEC SQL SELECT resides_in>oid, resides_in>number
INTO :roid, :rnumber
FROM library_user
WHERE oid = :oid);
...
return new Room(roid, rnumber);
}
```

FIGURE 2-29. A database partner method for the association.

From the perspective of object modeling, SQL3 does not offer very much that is new for the association manipulation. The reference feature is inherently unidirectional, and you still need an association table to model the many-to-many associations. There is almost as much functionality necessary in the database partner layer as with traditional relational databases.

Aggregates

You can implement the aggregation by embedding ADTs or named row types within each other. You can do this embedding by assigning an ADT or a row type as a column data type. You can define a one-to-one aggregation, as well as a one-to-many aggregation, in this way (see Figures 2-30 through 2-32). SQL3 provides three types of collection data types that you can use in one-to-many aggregations: SET<type>, MULTISET<type>, and LIST<type>.

When you are modeling the aggregation in such a way, you do not have to worry about keeping the referential integrity consistent when deleting object instances, because the whole aggregate object is stored in one row of one table.

In Figures 2-30 and 2-31, we create a named row type for the DocumentEntry aggregation and ADTs for the three aggregated classes. We use a collection type attribute to implement the attributes authors and keywords. In Figure 2-32, we define a database partner method for fetching aggregated objects.

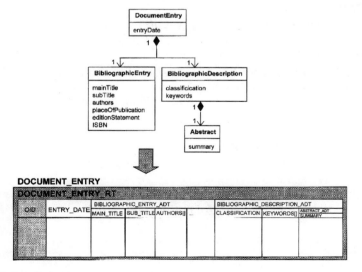

FIGURE 2-30. Mapping an aggregation hierarchy into tables in an ORDBMS.

```
CREATE ABSTRACT DATA TYPE abstract_adt (
document_summary              VARCHAR(2000),
EQUALS ONLY BY STATE )

CREATE ABSTRACT DATA TYPE bibliographic_desc_adt (
classification                NUMERIC,
keywords                      SET(VARCHAR(20)),
abstract                      abstract_adt,
ORDER FULL BY RELATIVE        compare_bibliographic_desc)

CREATE ABSTRACT DATA TYPE bibliographic_entry_adt (
main_title                    VARCHAR(50),
sub_title                     VARCHAR(50),
authors                       SET(VARCHAR(50)),
place_of_publication          VARCHAR(50),
edition_statement             VARCHAR(2000),
isbn                          VARCHAR(15)
ORDER FULL BY RELATIVE        compare_bibliographic_entry)

CREATE ROW TYPE document_entry_rt (
oid                           REF(document_entry_rt)
entry_date                    DATE NOT NULL,
bibliographic_entry           bibliographic_entry_adt,
bibliographic_desc            bibliographic_desc_adt )

CREATE TABLE document_entry
OF document_entry_rt WITH REF VALUE (
VALUES FOR oid ARE SYSTEM GENERATED )
```

FIGURE 2-31. Defining row types and tables for the aggregation hierarchy.

```
Abstract * BibliographicDescription::getAbstract()
{
...
EXEC SQL SELECT
bibliographic_desc>>abstract>>document_summary
INTO :summary
FROM document_entry
WHERE oid = :oid //oid of document_entry
...
return new Abstract(summary);
}
```

FIGURE 2-32. A database partner method for the aggregation.

Note that, when you implement aggregation as described, there is only one OID for the whole aggregation hierarchy. If you need OIDs for aggregated classes as well, you have to implement them yourself.

It is easier to implement the aggregation with SQL3 than with SQL2-level relational databases. In SQL3, you have the concepts of collection, named row type, and ADT that you can utilize when implementing the aggregations.

Inheritance

You can implement inheritance by using the ADT inheritance or the table inheritance, which both support *multiple inheritance*. The concepts of subtype and supertype, and subtable and supertable, correspond to the familiar object-oriented concepts *parent class* and *children class*.

When you are implementing table inheritance with SQL3, you first have to create a named row type for the parent class and for the children classes. The sub row types inherit the super row type representing the parent class. Then, you have to define a table for each created row type. The inheritance is defined for the tables as well (see Figures 2-33 through 2-35). If you are using ADTs to implement classes, you can define the inheritance in the same way than with row types.

In Figures 2-33 and 2-34, we create named row types and tables for each class in the Document inheritance hierarchy, utilizing the table inheritance. In Figure 2-35, we define a database partner method for fetching an instance according to a super class attribute.

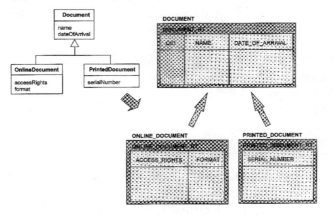

FIGURE 2-33. Mapping inheritance into tables in an ORDBMS.

```
CREATE ROW TYPE document_rt (
oid                    REF(document_rt),
name                   VARCHAR(50) NOT NULL,
date_of_arrival        DATE )

CREATE ROW TYPE online_document_rt UNDER
document_rt(
access_rights          VARCHAR(20) NOT NULL,
format                 VARCHAR(10) )

CREATE ROW TYPE printed_document_rt UNDER
document_rt(
serial_number          VARCHAR(20) NOT NULL )

CREATE TABLE document
OF document_rt WITH REF VALUE (
VALUES FOR oid ARE SYSTEM GENERATED )

CREATE TABLE online_document UNDER document
OF online_document_rt;

CREATE TABLE printed_document UNDER document
OF printed_document_rt;
```

FIGURE 2-34. Defining row types and tables for the inheritance hierarchy.

```
OnlineDocumentCltn * OnlineDocument::queryByName(char *)
{
...
EXEC SQL SELECT oid, access_rights, format
INTO :doid,rights,format
FROM online_document
WHERE name = :name
...
}
```

FIGURE 2-35. A database partner method fetching a super class attribute.

As you can see from the examples, the implementation of inheritance is easy with SQL3. The support for inheritance is a remarkable improvement from pure relational databases. You do not have to solve the complex problem of mapping the inheritance hierarchy to the relational database schema.

Issues to Take into Consideration

When you are considering using an object-relational database you should consider the issues mentioned in the following section. These issues differ somewhat from the world of pure relational databases and you should take them into account.

Standardization

Because the object-relational database products and the query languages they implement are vastly different, the portability of applications from one ORDBMS product to another is poor. The way these products seem to be evolving indicates that convergence among these products is taking place, but quite slowly. One reason for this is that the only standardization effort relating directly to these products is the SQL3 work, which is still unfinished.

One reason for slow progress of the SQL3 work is the number of players in the standardization committees. Furthermore, none of the players is superior compared to others, unlike SQL, which became the de-facto query language of RDBMSs. At that time, IBM was the superior player, and others followed it. Therefore, it is easy to predict that SQL3 standardization still will take some time. In addition, it is likely that this standard will not be very explicit and coherent because of the number of compromises the players have to make.

Furthermore, having followed the SQL3 standardization work, it would not be a wonder if some notable SQL3 dropouts would still appear to get the standardization work finished.

Interfaces

Some object-relational database products do not have a native, object-oriented programming language interface with a navigation facility. These products communicate with the user only via SQL-like query language. The database has its own type system, and host languages have their own type systems. Nevertheless, these type systems can be closer to one another compared to the situation with SQL2 and C++, for example. Still, the *impedance mismatch* problem is present with these products, even if the problem is not that severe anymore. The data format has to be converted from one type system to another when transferring data between the database and host languages; this conversion also leads to the fact that, in the short term, we cannot expect our applications using an ORDBMSs to be very portable.

Performance

Even though the data model of relational databases is simple and straight-forward, the performance of the these products is not always satisfactory. *Indexing* techniques are still developing rapidly, and new types of *query optimizers* are being introduced.

If you think about how complex the data model of an ORDBMS is compared to its predecessors, it is easy to predict that these ORDBMS products can suffer from substantial performance problems. It will probably take several years before query optimization and indexing techniques satisfy completely the level of complexity introduced by the data model of an object-relational database.

Because the ORDBMSs have evolved from RDBMSs, they rely mainly on similar client-server architecture. All the processing is done at the server side. The client merely communicates with the database engine via query language clauses. This defines much of the performance profile of the ORDBMS products. However, a *client-side cache*, used by certain products, can boost the application performance in certain situations considerably if the cache is properly integrated with the navigation interface.

Conclusions

Extending the relational model is a feasible way of satisfying the new requirements set by the new application areas and object-orientation. Nevertheless, when a relational model is extended to an object-relational model, the *complexity* of the data model increases considerably. Thus, understanding all aspects of the data model to take full advantage of it requires some effort.

However, for organizations with a strong relational and object-oriented background, object-relational databases offer a tempting transition path to a more object-oriented data management environment. The fact that ORDBMS products are not completely compatible should not prevent you from taking advantage of this new and promising technology. You cannot deny the fact that ORDBMSs are a huge step up from pure relational databases. Especially when it comes to object-oriented software development, object-relational databases are a step in the right direction.

Object Databases for Storing Persistent Objects

At the beginning of the '90s, a totally new database system type entered the data management arena: *object databases* (ODBMSs). A few object enthusiasts even predicted at that time that these products would overtake the relational database market completely within a few years. This is not quite how it turned out, but in certain application areas, such as structural documentation databases, object databases have gained a strong foothold.

The motivation for pure object database system development was mainly the same as for ORDBMS development, that is, the new data management requirements set by new application areas and requirements set by the object-oriented programming community. However, the approach taken by object databases is totally different. First, the ODBMS vendors chose to integrate the database manipulation with the application programming language. Object databases strive to minimize the difference between the database manipulation language and the application programming language, like C++ or Java. Secondly, the architecture of object databases is very different compared from that of their predecessors. The client takes part in the database system processing, unlike in relational databases.

One major argument on behalf of object database products is the productivity gained from the integration of the database manipulation language and the application programming language. This integration solves the *impedance mismatch* problem that is strongly present with other database system types.

There are several definitions for object databases that emphasize different aspects of these products. Following is a definition given by the *Object Data*

Management Group (ODMG), the standard body for ODBMSs. This definition emphasizes the differentiation aspect of object database products compared to ORDBMS. [ODMG 97]

> *"We define ODBMS to be a database management*
> *system that integrates database capabilities with*
> *object-oriented programming capabilities."*

ODMG

The features of an ODBMS were described for the first time extensively in the *Object-Oriented Database Manifesto* in 1989, written by a group of qualified object orientation specialists. Part of the features mentioned in the manifesto are related to *object model* and part to *architecture* of an object database. [Atkinson et. al 89]

The object model features defined in the manifesto are support for *complex objects*, *encapsulation*, *object identity*, *types* or *classes*, *inheritance*, *overriding* combined with *late binding*, *extensibility*, and *computational completeness*. The features related to database architecture are *persistence*, *ad hoc querying*, *secondary storage management*, *concurrency*, and *recovery*.

The requirements set by the manifesto are, mainly, fulfilled by the current object database products. Interestingly, these requirements do not explicitly specify the database manipulation integration with the application programming language, which seems to be an essential feature of the current ODBMS products.

Additionally, many object database products implement other new features that are desirable in many application areas. These features include, for example, *object versions*, *nested transactions*, and *optimistic transactions*.

As a whole, the object database market is quite small. According to analysts, the market share of RDBMSs is more than one hundred times bigger. On the other hand, the market of ODBMSs has approximately doubled *every* year for the past few years; however, the markets for database systems in general have grown considerably overall.

There are more than a dozen object database products in the market, and the competition is tough. It is highly likely that a struggle to survive is taking place among the these products at this very moment. It is crucial for the vendors to concentrate on the application areas that the object databases best suit because they cannot be utilized as broadly as relational databases can. The strongest ODBMS players currently are *ObjectStore, Versant, Objectivity/DB, O2, GemStone,* and *Poet.*

Object Database Standardization

The first ODBMS products in the beginning of the '90s differed quite a bit from each other. They did not have a common object model or a query language, which was the major obstacle for the success of the object databases. At that time, it was extremely risky to start a development project on top of an object database. To solve this obvious credibility problem, the biggest ODBMS vendors decided to make an exceptional move. They set up a working group called Object Database Management Group (ODMG) in 1991. The voting members of the group in the beginning were Object Design Inc., Objectivity Inc., O2 Technology, Ontos Inc., and Versant Object Technology. Currently the group is called Object Data Management Group.

The mission of ODMG was to develop a "SQL-like" standard for the object database products. They tried to take the best out of the existing products and avoid inventing a whole new standard from scratch. The first version of the standard, ODMG-93, was released in 1993. Currently, the latest version of the standard is 2.0, which was released in May 1997.[8] The voting members of ODMG have promised to support the ODMG 2.0 standard by the end of 1998.

To be exact, ODBMG 2.0 is not a formal standard—yet. However, it will be submitted to both *ANSI* and *OMG.* So far, OMG has accepted parts of the former releases of the ODMG standard.

ODMG 2.0

In this section, we first look at the scope of the ODMG 2.0 standard. Then we take a closer look at the object model defined by this standard. The section describes only the features of the ODMG 2.0 object model that are of interest from the point of view of our process. However, the object model is much richer, and the other aspects of the model can be studied further from the ODMG 2.0 standard specification.

Scope of the ODMG 2.0 Standard

The ODMG 2.0 standard is quite large. It defines the following:

- The *object model* for the object database products. The object model is based on the *core object model* of the *Object Management Group* (OMG). We describe the object model later in more detail.
- *Object Definition Language* (ODL), which corresponds semantically to the *data definition part* of SQL. ODL is based on the *interface definition language* (IDL), of the OMG. ODL is a programming language independent language. Additionally there are programming language specific versions of ODL for each supported programming language in ODMG 2.0 (for example, *ODL/C++*).
- *Object Interchange Format* (OIF), which can be used to populate databases or exchange objects between databases, for example. This is a good example of the pragmatic approach ODMG has practiced. Relational databases have been around more than 20 years, but even today there is really no common way of transferring data from one database to another.
- *Object Query Language* (OQL) that is a declarative query language like SQL. OQL can be used for fetching and inserting objects. A notable difference from SQL is that OQL does not enable updating objects—like SQL does. Objects are always updated with methods that can be invoked from OQL clauses. SQL is used as the basis of the OQL query language, but this is not clearly visible in the syntax of OQL.
- The *C++-binding,* which defines how the database manipulation is integrated with the C++ programming language. This is called the *C++ object manipulation language* (C++/OML). The goal of the C++ binding was to give the user a feeling of using only one programming language when implementing applications that utilize a database.
- The *Java and Smalltalk bindings* define the bindings between these programming languages and ODMG object model (ODL and OML).

There was a lot of criticism against the first version of this standard from the relational database community when it was published. Part of this criticism was well justified, especially when it comes to defining the almost completely new query language, OQL. In practice, the majority of object database products implement a SQL3-like query language and not OQL.

Object Model

The object database products do not have a common strong mathematical background like the *relational algebra* of the relational databases. Therefore, the object models of the ODBMS products used to differ considerably, especially among the first products. Luckily, to a large extent the products now seem to follow the object model specified in the ODMG standard.

The object model defined in the ODMG standard is programming language-independent. Thus, for example, the basic concepts of ODMG object model are vastly different from the object model of C++. Furthermore, there is not a corresponding concept in the C++ object model for *every* ODMG object model concept.

The basic modeling primitives of the object model are an *object* and a *literal*. Every object has an unique identifier, whereas a literal does not. The identity of an object separates the object from all other objects within the database. The literals are identified by their values, as opposed to objects. The object model defines simple literals, such as a character string or a number, and structured literals, such as a date.

The values of attributes and *associations* (*relationship* in ODMG terminology) of an object determine the *state* of the object at a given point in time. These are the *properties* of an object. A value of an attribute can be an object or a literal or *collection* of objects or literals. The *behavior* of an object is determined by a set of operations that can be executed on or by the object.

Objects and literals can be categorized into *types,* which are also objects. All elements belonging to a type have a common behavior and a common range of states. An association is a property that is defined between two types. An association can be one-to-one, one-to-many, or many-to-many.

A type has a *specification* and one or more *implementations*. There can be one implementation for each used machine architecture, for example. The object model supports the inheritance schema of C++. However, the whole inheritance schema of the object model of ODMG is considerably richer because the object model is programming language-independent.

The ODMG object model defines five different kinds of collections: *set, bag, list, array,* and *directory*. Arrays and lists are ordered collections, whereas sets and bags are not. Bags and lists can contain duplicate objects—sets and arrays cannot. Directories are unordered sets of key-value pairs with no duplicate keys.

A common misunderstanding is that an ODBMS would store whole objects. This is not true, because the majority of the ODBMS products store only the states of objects, namely the attribute and the association values. You have to implement the behavior of the objects, that is, the *methods*, with an application programming language, and store them along with your application binary code. This is actually against the object orientation paradigm because the methods are not encapsulated in the database with the objects. Very few ODBMSs offer anything corresponding to the stored procedure concept of RDBMSs and ORDBMSs.

If you want the database to maintain a collection of all persistent objects belonging to a type, you have to define the database to maintain an *extent* for the type. This is not done by default in ODBMSs, unlike in relational databases, where you can always fetch all rows from a table.

If an extent is defined for a class, it is possible to define additional *keys* for this class as well. An object can be uniquely identified by the value of its key, in addition to OID. A key can consist of one or more properties of a class. However, the C++ binding does not support keys.

The data model enables individual objects to be *named* in the database. These objects act as database *roots* where the navigation in the database can begin. There is one global *name space* in the database, and every object can have multiple names.

The object model just described is a high-level description of the object model of the ODMG 2.0 standard. This object model defines the basis of the ODBMS products. Compared to the relational model, this object model allows the user to define very complex data structures in the database. Furthermore, many current products have even more extensive object models. They can contain, for example, the possibility of storing object versions in the database.

Architecture

The architecture of object databases differs totally from that of their predecessors. The ODBMS products support the *client-server* model but they implement it differently than do relational databases (see Figure 2-36). Actually, there are two kinds of client-server models the object database products use: *page server* and *object server* models. These two models differ in many aspects, such as in how much processing is performed in the client and what is the *locking granularity* [Cattell 94].

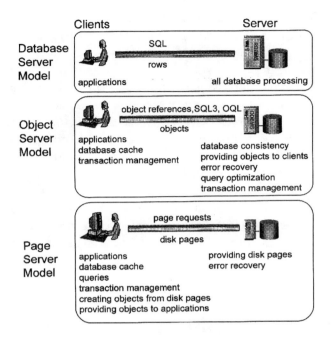

FIGURE 2-36. Different database system architectures.

The object server model balances the database system processing load between the client and the server. Unlike in relational databases, the processing power of the client is deployed as well. The server takes care of, for example, *database consistency*, *query optimization*, *transaction management*, *error recovery*, and sending objects to the clients. The client takes care of providing objects to the applications and takes also part in transaction management. The locking granularity is usually one object.

In the page server model, more of the processing is performed in the client. The main responsibility of the server is to fetch the *disk pages* the clients need from the disk. The disk page is also the locking granularity. Error recovery from many error situations is performed on the server side. All other processing is done on the client in the same environment where the applications execute.

These client server models that are used by the object databases provide the possibility to implement a *cache* on the client to improve performance of object applications. In practice, there is one cache per client—not one cache per application. This enables the applications to reference an object extremely quickly if the object is already in the cache of the client. In practice, the cache can best be utilized when the user navigates the class diagram of an application.

To a large extent, the client-side cache determines the difference of object database and relational database performance profiles. It explains most of the perceived performance differences in relational and object databases. In applications where the object server or page server architecture fits well, a remarkable improvement in performance can be achieved, compared to relational databases, for example. Of course, there can be a great variation in the two architectures of object databases in terms of performance in many situations.

Naturally, in these client-server models that the object databases use the user has to pay a price. To be able to implement efficient systems utilizing object databases, the client workstations must have more processing power than in systems implemented with a relational database or with an object-relational database.

Interfacing with Object Databases

Interfacing with an object database is remarkably different compared to the other common database system types. The navigation interfaces of object databases forces you really to think your data object wise and not relation wise.

Navigation vs. Query Language Usage

Navigation is the main method of object interaction with object databases. The object database products usually support navigation very efficiently. The explanation for the efficiency is the client-side cache we discussed earlier. The usage of the navigation interface is also considerably more productive than the traditional query language usage, because the user can manipulate persistent objects with programming language clauses.

However, all application requirements cannot be satisfied with the navigation interface. You might have a need to perform *ad hoc queries* or *reporting*, for example. The navigation interface is not usually the answer to these needs. The object database products should always provide a query language interface in addition to the navigation interface.

A few of the first object database products did not offer a query language interface at all. However, quite soon it was evident that this is a compulsory feature, and these days, all the ODBMS products have a query language facility. In practice, most of the products offer a SQL3-like query language. Only few products have adopted OQL as the query language.

In modern database systems, the query language clauses can usually be issued to the database system via an interactive interface or from applications. With most of the relational database products, the user can perform any *Data Definition Language* (DDL) or *Data Manipulation Language* (DML) operations interactively via an interactive interface, for example. Regarding object databases, the situation is very different. Not all products offer an interactive interface; nor does ODMG 2.0 define one. With the ODBMS products that do offer the interactive interface, the user can typically perform only a small subset of the DDL and DML operations.

Programming Language Interfaces

Most of the ODBMS products offer a primary interface to the C++ programming language. A few products offer an interface to Smalltalk and Java as well. Some products offer a function interface even to languages such as C and Ada. Naturally, as Java is fast gaining more and more popularity among developers, it can be expected to become a serious candidate for the primary interface in the future.

The database manipulation can be integrated with C++ in two ways. First, a C++ class library can provide the needed methods for the database manipulation. Secondly, the database manipulation can be done with an extended C++. In the latter case, the C++ code has to be precompiled before compiling it with the C++ compiler (see Figure 2-37).

Many products support the ODBC interface that is a familiar interface from the relational database environment. It is noteworthy in the context of object databases because it gives the user a possibility of using general purpose tools which were originally built for relational databases. Because the ODBMS products are quite new, not many reporting and 4GL tools have been available for them so far. However, ODBC does not provide the possibility of utilizing the efficient navigation features of object databases, as it is designed for query language usage.

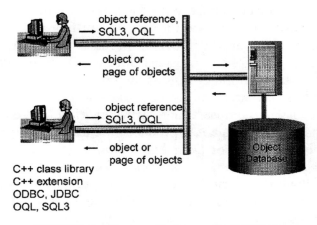

object reference,
→ SQL3, OQL

← object or
page of objects

object reference
→ SQL3, OQL

← object or
page of objects

C++ class library
C++ extension
ODBC, JDBC
OQL, SQL3

FIGURE 2-37. Interfacing with ODBMSs.

When you are using an object database, the role of the database partner diminishes, because the database system product offers the same kind of services and methods as the database partner. On the other hand, the database partner layer enhances the portability of the application from one object database product to another, and even from an ODBMS to another database system type. Additionally, the database partner layer can enhance the maintainability of the system because it gives you an abstract layer for the persistent object manipulation.

If you choose to use a database partner layer in your system, the methods are very simple and fast to implement. Using the database partner layer offers you an easy way to change the data management product. You might need to change it if the ODBMS does not turn out to be a success in terms of performance, for example. In the beginning, using the database partner layer requires more engineering resources, but in the long run you might end up saving money.

Implementing Class Diagrams

In general, you can implement your class diagrams with an object database in an easy and straightforward manner. The ODBMS products support the essential object modeling concepts inherently in their data model.

In the following section, we use the syntax of the ODMG 2.0 to implement the object abstractions. [ODMG 97] The presented code fragments emphasize the DML operations and ignore database connection, transaction, and error handling issues.

The database schema of an object database is basically the design class diagram of your application, or more specifically, the persistent objects from this class diagram. You can describe the class diagram to an ODBMS with ODL/C++. The ODL/C++ description is run through ODL/C++ preprocessor, which generates the C++ classes that provide the methods for the manipulation of the persistent objects.

Classes and Objects

If you want the objects of your C++ class to be able to be stored persistently, you should have the class inherit the public d_Object class from the class library the ODBMS product offers. This makes the objects of this class persistent-capable. The d_-prefix is used in all global names the ODMG 2.0 C++ binding defines.

The attributes of a class are defined just like you define any attributes in C++ class definitions (see Figures 2-38 and 2-39). The operations are defined also to the class definition as usual with C++. However, the implementation of the operations is a set of normal C++ methods, and they are not stored in the database. Thus, we ignore the operations in this section. The ODBMS will automatically create and maintain the OID for each persistent object stored in the database.

In Figure 2-38, we define the LibraryUser class as a persistent capable class with ODL/C++. In Figure 2-39, we create a new LibraryUser object to myDB database.

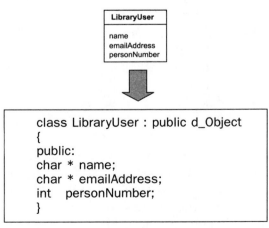

```
class LibraryUser : public d_Object
{
public:
char * name;
char * emailAddress;
int   personNumber;
}
```

FIGURE 2-38. Defining a class in ODBMS.

In C++, you can create persistent objects with an overloaded version of the new() operator. For each persistent-capable class, there is a template class d_Ref<your_class>, which you can use to reference the persistent objects (see Figure 2-39).

```
...
d_Ref<LibraryUser> newUser;
newUser = new(myDB,"LibraryUser") LibraryUser(name, email, personNbr);
...
```

FIGURE 2-39. Creating a persistent object to an ODBMS database.

Associations

One-to-one, one-to-many, and many-to-many binary associations (*relationship* in ODMG terminology) are supported inherently in the data model of ODBMSs. Referential integrity is automatically maintained by the database system when the associations are updated. With object databases, you do not need any intermediate constructs such as an association table to model many-to-many associations.

When you are defining an association, you have to describe it to both classes taking part in the association (see Figure 2-40). This enables *two-way* navigation and the ODBMS to maintain the referential integrity when either end of the association is updated. The C++ class library provides the template classes d_Rel_Ref<class>, d_Rel_Set<class>,and d_Rel_List<class> that are needed in association definitions.

In Figure 2-40, we define the LibraryUser and Room classes with the association as persistent-capable classes. In Figure 2-41 you see an example of how to navigate to the room where the user RootUser resides. RootUser is an explicitly named persistent object in the database myDB.

Associations can be easily manipulated with C++, since there is no impedance mismatch problem and the navigation can be bi-directional (see Figure 2-41). Of course, you can query values of associations with OQL or SQL3 depending which query language is available.

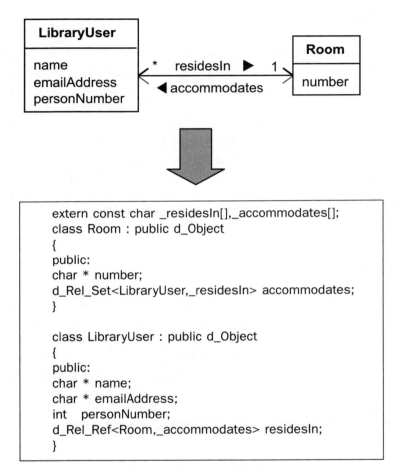

FIGURE 2-40. Defining an association to an ODBMS.

```
   ...
   d_Ref<Room> myRoom;
   d_Ref<LibraryUser> myUser;
   myUser= myDB->lookup_obect("RootUser");
   myRoom = myUser->residesIn;
   ...
```

FIGURE 2-41. Navigation via associations.

Aggregates

You can describe aggregation by using *object references* (d_Ref<class>) and collections in ODL/C++ class definitions (*see Figure 42*). Aggregations are *one-way* and thus you cannot navigate from the *aggregated* object to the *aggregating* object. The aggregation type can be one-to-one or one-to-many. The type of the many side can be any of the collection types described earlier. According to the ODMG 2.0 standard the referenced objects are treated as literals in aggregating classes and thus they do not have their own OID. These "objects" are always an integral part of the aggregating object.

In Figure 2-42 we define the DocumentEntry aggregation as persistent capable. In the Figure 2-43 you can see how to reference an attribute of an aggregated object.

Inheritance

You can define *inheritance* exactly as you can in C++ (see Figure 2-44). This simple way to represent inheritance in a database is one of the most remarkable benefits of object databases as compared to relational databases.

In Figure 2-44, we define the Document inheritance hierarchy as persistent capable. In Figure 2-45, you see an example of how to use the classes.

Issues to Take into Consideration

When you are considering using an object database you should consider the issues mentioned in the following section. These issues differ remarkably from the world of pure relational databases.

Standardization

The ODMG standard sets the goal for portability much further than what has been reached with the SQL standard of the relational databases. If all the object database vendors would fulfill the ODMG 2.0 standard completely, you could port your application to another ODBMS environment in terms of programming language bindings, database schema structure definition, and query language clauses.

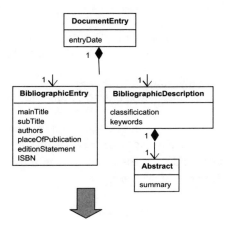

```
class BibliographicEntry : public d_Object
{
public:
char * mainTitle;
char * subTitle;
d_Set<char*> authors;
char * placeOfPublication;
char * editionStatement;
char * isbn;
}

class Abstract : public d_Object
{
public:
char * summary;
}

class BibliographicDesc : public d_Object
{
public:
char * classification;
d_Set<char *> keywords;
d_Ref<Abstract> abstract;
}

class DocumentEntry : public d_Object
{
public:
char * entryDate;
d_Ref<BibliographicEntry> bibliographicEntry;
d_Ref<BibliographicDesc> bibliographicDesc;
}
```

FIGURE 2-42. Defining a persistent aggregation hierarchy.

```
...
d_Ref<DocumentEntry> myDocumentEntry;
myDocumentEntry = myDB->lookup_object
 ("ODMG standard");
cout<<myDocumentEntry->
bibliographicDesc.abstract.summary;
...
```

FIGURE 2-43. Navigation via associations. Print the abstract of the **DocumentEntry** instance that is named to the database **myDB** as "ODMG standard".

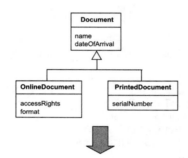

```
class Document : public d_Object
{
public:
char * name;
char * dateOfArrival;
}

class OnlineDocument : public Document
{
public:
char * accessRights;
char * format;
}

class PrintedDocument : public Document
{
public:
char * serialNumber;
}
```

FIGURE 2-44. Defining the inheritance hierarchy to an ODBMS.

```
...
d_OQL_Query myQuery("select o from onlineDocuments o where o.name=$1");
d_Ref<OnlineDocument> myOnlineDocument;
char * name="John"
myQuery<<name;
d_oql_execute(myQuery, myOnlineDocument);
...
```

FIGURE 2-45. Fetching an OnlineDocument instance according to a super class attribute name with OQL. There is an extent in the database named *onlineDocuments*.

Currently, most of the ODBMS products support earlier releases of the ODMG standard to some extent. Nevertheless, the portability of applications using the ODBMS products is not very good. If your application has to be ported to another environment, you must be prepared to do some serious work. An intermediate layer—such as the database partners—makes these kind of porting efforts easier and faster.

A few noticeable shortcomings in the ODMG 2.0 standard exist. It does not define the *database schema evolution* at all, for example. If you think how complex the schema evolution operations are that can result from the ODBMS data model, you can imagine that it is not easy to implement all these schema evolution possibilities.

You can find the corresponding schema evolution operations in ODBMSs as in RDBMSs. These operations are fairly simple. The schema evolution operations that can be derived from object-orientation are clearly more complex. Most of the ODBMS products support the easier schema evolution operations, but usually the more complex schema evolution tasks require manual work to some extent. An example of a complex schema evolution task is creating a common super class for multiple existing classes.

Another ODBMS 2.0 shortcoming is the lack of an *authorization* system in the ODBMS products. A few products implement the authorization in the operating system or in an implementation-defined segment level. However, you cannot find the same kind of versatile authorization possibilities that the RDBMS products have. The ODMG 2.0 standard also does not define: optimistic transactions, long transactions, or object versions. There are many implementations of these features available in different products, but they vary considerably from each other.

Mission-Critical Aspects

In their early days, the ODBMS products were used mainly in design systems and not so much in mission-critical environments which set tight requirements for *uptime*, *security*, and *performance*. Earlier, the object database products used to provide weaker means to implement continuous operation and data security, for example.

Currently, the ODBMS products implement the uptime, security, and performance features rather well, but still you should pay some attention to this issue. During the past few years, object databases have also been used in many mission-critical systems.

Performance

Currently, all the ODBMS products offer some kind of query language facility. A few products execute the queries in the server, and some products execute them in the client. If the queries are executed in the client, the necessary objects are first transferred to the client over LAN. Of course, this might take a great deal of time if the query involves a large number of objects.

When using queries, you should think carefully about the consequences of your queries in terms of database processing. To a large extent, the architecture of the ODBMS products determines the query performance. Remember that the architectures of different object databases differ considerably.

Additionally, you cannot expect to see the same level of query optimization as you do in relational databases. Query optimization is still in its infancy in many ODBMS products. It will take some time until you will be able to gain query language performance comparable to that of relational databases.

Navigation is the main method of object interaction with ODBMSs. If most of your database access involve query language clauses, instead of navigation via association links, it is possible that you will run into performance problems. The problems are due to the fact that ODBMSs are fast, particularly if the client-side cache can be utilized. Navigation utilizes the cache, and queries do or do not, depending on the database system architecture. Navigation does not use the query optimization either, because it utilizes the predefined association links.

Because of the architecture of the ODBMSs you cannot expect the products to perform well in a situation where there are many simultaneous users accessing and manipulating the very same objects. This would imply a lot of network traffic between the server and the clients, because the cache in all clients have to be kept up to date.

If you want to write well-optimized code to optimize the ODBMS performance to the maximum, you have to remember that different products use dissimilar means to tune the database performance. For example, you have to implement clustering in ODBMS products in several different ways. In some products, the clustering is defined in the database schema level, whereas other products require the programmer to give the database system clustering hints when a new persistent object that could be clustered is created. *Physical data independence* is not as good in many ODBMS products as it is in relational databases.

As a whole, ODBMSs perform very differently from their predecessors. Some database operations are remarkably faster, and some are slower, depending on the application and the specific operation that is being executed. Additionally, the performance difference among different ODBMS products is great because of their architecture differences. These cold facts can make a developer feel a bit uncomfortable when experimenting with object databases. It seems that you simply cannot anticipate the performance of your application as well as you could with relational databases.

Choosing the Right Object Database Product

Choosing an object database product is more difficult than choosing an RDBMS product, because the features the ODBMS products provide vary considerably among the products. Additionally, you can find many sophisticated features from ODBMSs that you cannot find from RDBMSs. These features include long transactions and support for object versions, for example. Depending on your application area you might find a few of these new features to be very crucial and therefore, this might dictate your ODBMS choice.

Because the ODBMS products are based on different architectures, the performance differences among the products are great. You should carry out your own performance tests before deciding on the product you will use in your system. A couple of *benchmarks* are available, such as *001* and *007*. However, these benchmarks do not directly indicate whether a product suits your needs or not.

Because the ODBMS products are quite new, they support only the most common hardware and operating systems platforms. If your system uses an uncommon platform, you should pay attention to how it is supported by different products.

Far too many ODBMS products are in the market compared to their potential business volume. It is highly likely that many of the current object database products will vanish or merge in the near future. Only the strongest can survive. Most of the object database vendors operate on venture capital, and it is quite difficult to estimate the long-term credibility of any particular vendor.

Choosing the right object database product for your system is more difficult than choosing an RDBMS product, because the products differ so much. When you are choosing an ODBMS product, you should take the following steps, in this order:

1. Identify the ODBMS features that are most important to your system.
2. Find the ODBMS products that support your operating system and hardware platforms. These are your candidate object database products.
3. Perform a paper evaluation and find out which products provide the features that are important to you. Also take the credibility of the object database vendor into account. Shortlist one or two products to continue the evaluation with.
4. Define and implement your own benchmark that represents the time-critical parts of your system.
5. Choose the product that performs best. If the performance is not satisfactory, take a look into other database system technologies.
6. Talk to the vendor's other customers.

Conclusions

Object databases are an attractive option for a serious, object-oriented developer. Implementing class diagrams is easy and straightforward with ODBMSs. ODBMS products offer more extensive support for object abstractions than do ORDBMSs, for example, in mapping the associations to the data model of the database system.

When you are using an object database, you really do not have to think how to map the class diagram used in your application to the data model supported by the database system. All the major object abstractions are supported inherently in the data model of the ODBMSs. The impedance mismatch problem is solved.

Choosing an ODBMS on your system implies strong, long-term *commitment* to object-oriented programming languages, such as C++, Java, or Smalltalk. With these languages, ODBMSs are very efficient if you are mainly utilizing navigational access to the database.

Even if the standardization situation is not perfect with ODBMSs, it is possible to take advantage of this novel technology. Especially, if the features of some ODBMS product fit well to your requirements, you should seriously consider the product. However, keep the issues that we discussed earlier in your mind when making the database decision.

Making the Right Database Decision

Implementation technology for object persistence is one of the most important decisions in an object-oriented software project. A data management solution is always a long-lasting decision. There are many factors that should be considered in your decision-making: money, attitudes, expectations, target hardware, and software environment—and the nature of the applications.

It seems that selection of database technology is often more a matter of religion than the result of analytical pondering. To sum up all the factors affecting decision-making, we have identified the following criteria that can be used to rate the situation:

Costs

- **How much does the developer's license cost?** It is a common observation that database licenses are expensive. And they are. Besides that, licensing terms are quite complex and prone to continuous changes.
- **What about run-time licenses and maintenance fees?** In the last few years, run-time pricing of major object databases and relational databases have converged quite a bit. Today, there are no large differences.
- **How expensive is it to acquire technical support, training, and consultancy from the database vendor?** This is an area where the market share of the database product is important. The more products there are

in the field, the more third party consulting firms that are ready to help in these issue—often at a remarkably lower price than the database vendor's own consultancy services.

Hardware and Operating System

- **Availability:** Surprisingly few data management options are available for some still common environments—say VAX VMS, AS/400, OS/2, and others. When it comes to Windows (NT) and UNIX, the problem rather is in selecting the right horse.
- **Technology Trends:** Established products move slower, a non-disputable fact. Young products and concepts still in the market entry phase need to move fast and adapt quickly to emerging technologies. On the other hand, because these young players do not have the burden of a massive installed base on the field, they may also abandon some hardware or operating system support with short notice in case the demand is decreasing.

R & D Organization

- **Existing knowledge and skills:** This factor seems to be among the most important ones in R & D organizations. Naturally, basic knowledge about the product should play a relevant role in the decision-making phase. But think about a situation in which the developers happen to know a certain relational database product well but have not used it before with object-oriented development. If the decision in this case is based solely on the fact that they know the database product per se, it is not on very solid ground.
- **Attitudes:** Database decisions, as well as other technology decisions—such as operating system, hardware, programming language, and so on—tend to be of religious nature among developers. Too often, decisions seem to be made based on subjective, superficial, vague beliefs, and incomplete information.
- **Selected technology management policy:** Every company should define its target position in terms of adopting new technologies. It should be crystal clear whether the company wants to pioneer with new, unproved technologies or to try and follow the 2nd wave, where a clear market for the new technology has already emerged. Some conservative companies may have a policy to rely on absolutely mature technology

only. All approaches have their pros and cons. Mapped to databases today, pioneers would probably choose object or hybrid databases from small vendors, 2nd wave companies object databases from the very biggest players or hybrid databases, and conservatives would stick to the top four relational databases.

Customer Organization

- **Company policies:** The bigger the customer is, the more likely it has a well-defined IT policy. Exceptions to approved hardware, operating system, or data management solutions are probably not desired.
- **Existing knowledge and skills:** From the customer point of view, a new database product means trouble and costs. You have to acquire administration and trouble-shooting skills. Payback time of a new information system that is based on unfamiliar database product may become surprisingly high.

Characteristics of the Application

- **Legacy information system interfacing:** Very often a developer faces a situation where part of the relevant information is stored and maintained by an information system developed ages ago. At that time, perhaps no one had even heard of object orientation. It may be very awkward and time-consuming to make these legacy systems interoperate with the system being developed. In such cases, relational databases are probably the best bet. Relational database products typically have a set of gateways to non-relational and also to other relational database products. If the legacy system has been built on a relational database, but the database schema incompatibility is the only problem, *views* can often be used to build an object-oriented structure on top of the old one.
- **Distribution requirements.** Both relational and object databases can be said to follow the client server paradigm in the architectural sense. But the point is that most of the rocessing in many object databases is carried out on the client side. And the role of the server is quite often very modest. The situation is precisely vice versa with relational databases. Relational databases do most of the processing on the server side. This situation leads to configurations with a very powerful database server and lightweight clients. It is an issue to be taken into consideration when thinking about hardware configurations.

- **Number of simultaneous users:** Relational databases are clearly more suitable for online transaction processing. As the number of simultaneous users grows, perceived performance can be assumed to deteriorate in a linear fashion. This is not the case with object databases. According to our experiences, with object databases, performance may suddenly *collapse* if the number of users is increased. This can be explained by the architectural differences with these different types of databases. On the other hand, if there are only few users in the system, the complex transaction management algorithms of relational databases may well be overkill.
- **Uptime requirements:** There seem to be impressive references about databases—both relational and object-oriented—that have been totally embedded into some devices[9] that do not have a user interface at all. Thus, embedded databases should be managed without any user-interrupted administration. This kind of management is really a tough requirement. Some products are better in this sense than others. If you are to develop this kind of application, request the vendor to provide you with provable and demonstrable references.

Development Tools and Software Process

- **Institutionalized software process:** Starting to deploy object-oriented development may cause changes to old ways of working and to division of responsibilities among people in the organization. For example, automatic code generation of parts of application (such as the idea of automatically generating database partners from the class diagram) changes the way and focus of testing.
- **Tools:** Most of the popular database design tools do not fit well in object-oriented development. Therefore, you may need to rethink your current tools.

The Future of Object Data Management

During this decade object databases and object-relational databases have entered the market. However, the relational databases still dominate the market to a large extent. In the following sections, we give you our opinion where the world of object data management is heading in the next few years.

The Struggle Between ORDBMSs and Pure ODBMSs

The object database technology has been a promising technology for several years. The market has grown rapidly, but the object database products have not grabbed much market share from relational databases. Probably, part of the software industry has been waiting for proper ORDBMSs to arrive.

The ODBMS products will not overtake the relational database market although they can be used in some traditional relational database areas. The object database market is located mainly in the *niche* application areas and there is still plenty of market potential available in these specialized application areas, where object databases can excel. Object databases can excel compared to other database system types with their novel data model or new data management features. Additionally, object databases offer a very different performance profile from relational databases.

One strong argument on behalf of object databases is the seamless integration between the database manipulation and the application programming languages. On the other hand, this is also a major disadvantage of these products. Object databases can be utilized most effectively with C++, Java, or Smalltalk. Application development with other tools is not so efficient and productive, because no native interfaces to non object-oriented languages are available, and the impedance mismatch problem there is strongly present.

If you think about large systems, you realize that the databases are usually accessed in a variety of ways: possibly with several programming languages, 4GL tools, query language scripts, and so on. Object databases can satisfy, usually, only one of these ways in a productive and efficient manner—namely, access from an object-oriented programming language. Other ways of database access (4GL, ODBC, scripts, C, and so on) are not so easy and efficient. Therefore, you should think very carefully before selecting an object database for a large, long-living system (see Figure 2-46).

The application areas where relational databases currently dominate are likely to take advantage, gradually, from ORDBMS products that have entered the market. Pure relational databases will be used extensively in the software industry, but for object data management these pure relational products probably will be used more rarely than nowadays. Nevertheless, this transition to ORDBMS products will take place quite slowly.

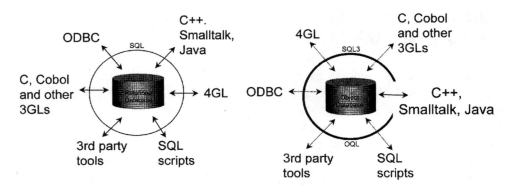

FIGURE 2-46. The difference in interfacing with relational databases and object databases.

SQL vs. OQL

The SQL3 and the OQL query languages partly overlap. There have been threats that ORDBMSs and object databases would develop their query languages in totally different directions.

A *merger group* was formed some time ago with intent to merge these two query languages. This group included participants from both of the standardization committees. The goal was to make OQL a read-only subset of the SQL query language. The reason for this goal is that SQL3 is a considerably larger language compared to OQL—it contains DDL, DML, and a computationally complete programming language. ODMG, in turn, has chosen to separate DDL into a separate language that is independent of host programming languages. The OML is integrated into application programming language. Thus, OQL as a query language lacks the DML operations INSERT, UPDATE, and DELETE. These operations are instead performed via method invocations.

There are also some other fundamental differences between the query languages. For example, OQL queries can return collections of objects, structures, or literals, whereas SQL3 query can return only tables.

This merging process was very promising from the users' point of view, because there would no longer exist two competing query languages in database systems that support objects. Unfortunately, the merger group has now broken up, and there are no signs about new cooperation. Still, it is quite likely that if the SQL3 scope is not reduced any more remarkably, the object databases will continue to support it as a primary query language even more than nowadays.

Notes

1. In fact, object database products and object-relational database products enable several different kinds of collections, like sets, bags and lists. However, the presented simple 'set' collection is as useful with relational databases for most purposes.
2. A very similar idea of having "broker" objects as mediators between database objects and domain objects has been presented in *A Pattern Language for Relational Databases and Smalltalk* by Kyle Brown and Bruce Whitenack. See www.ksccary.com.
3. Try the following keyword "database class library" with your favorite Web search engine to get more information about this subject.
4. Try the following keywords with your favorite web search engine to get more information about this subject: "object layer generator" or "database interface generator."
5. Very useful ideas and practical hints can be also found from Crossing Chasms pattern language developed by Kyle Brown and Bruce Whitenack. See www.ksccary.com for further information.
6. Actually, this kind of expression is being proposed to SQL-3 standard.
7. The first version of the SQL standard contained roughly 50 pages in 1989.
8. You can follow the evolution of the ODMG work from http://www.odmg.org.
9. Telecommunications application domain is full of these kinds of "zero-administration" devices, like switches or multiplexers, and so on.

CHAPTER 3

Large-Scale
Development

Creating great software is hard, but it's even harder when you try to do it in a scope of a large system. The good news is programming tools and methods have improved; the bad news is the average size of a software system is growing all the time. Increasing competition in the software business has pushed the software houses to deliver more and more feature-rich systems that provide users with innovative user interface solutions and better capacity than the systems in the past. This push is evident in software development and the average size of software projects increases year after year.

We consider a software system to be *large* if its size exceeds 200,000 lines of code. Such systems have two characteristic properties that bring special flavor to their development. First, they are far more complex than single applications; second, they tend to be evolutionary by nature.

The *complexity* is often considered an inherent factor in any software development, but for a small exercises such as "Hello world" it is not the case. Complexity is when you are debugging a poorly structured distributed system with some dozens of thousands of classes. Systems that are developed for years as a series of consecutive system releases are called *evolutionary systems*. The development of new functionality is mostly carried out by modifying the existing

185

design. An evolutionary system is not considered complete if there are new market needs to evolve it. The releases in the field are in maintenance phase but there are continuous development efforts on-going to create new releases on the basis of existing ones.

In the following we briefly discuss the characteristics of large and evolutionary systems. Then we propose some guide lines that can help you to meet the challenges of this kind of systems.

Evolutionary Systems

An *incremental approach* to software development is a practice of developing a software system gradually, piece by piece. The need for incremental development is obvious in large-scale development. Not many customers are willing to commit to a large project delivering a system that won't be released for several years.

The incremental approach to development is as valuable to a vendor as it is to the customer when time to market counts. It is of paramount importance to deliver at least the basic functionality if the window of opportunity for selling a system is open. Making a great software product a few years too late would not generate any positive cash flow, because the market may no longer exist.

Most best-known software life cycle models, be it the simple waterfall model or a more sophisticated variant of spiral model, are strongly biased toward one-time development of a system. A built-in assumption of many life cycle models is that you try to build a system for a foreseeable need. Of course, the requirements may be volatile and the process may be iterative and incremental accordingly, but the focus in the development work is fully in producing *the* release that meets contractual commitments. When the system is complete, you transfer it to *maintenance* phase.

The process of developing evolutionary systems partially resembles the process of fixing bugs. The development of new functionality usually requires that you modify the existing design, but we do not consider it maintenance. Is it maintenance if you extend the scope of a system with a life span of several years to new market segments by creating a set of completely new applications? We do not think so.

The need for continuous development of new features originates from the changes in customer's business environment or technology. As a rule, changes in business, such as major growth of business volume or a new mode of operation, introduce new requirements for the systems supporting the business. The technology changes may be minor, such as a new version of an operating system; or they may be major discontinuities, such as the Internet phenomenon. In the case of discontinuities, a set of products may be replaced by new ones, which means issues of new product development. The minor changes, that is, adding new functionality or enhancing the existing one, make it necessary to to upgrade the existing system with a new version of the system.

The macro process for evolutionary systems is like a *perpetuum mobile* that never stops[1] as depicted in Figure 3-1. Each cycle produces a new release of the system and lasts typically from a half a year to a couple of years depending on the system complexity and amount of delivered functionality. After the first release of the system, the next releases will be based on the available functionality provided by the once developed software. Development of new functionality will be assisted and restricted by the architecture and components created for previous releases.

Software life cycles developed for application development typically cover only the *feature development* phase of the process. Most of the documented best practices for software development apply well inside feature development, but they do not tend to address evolutionary system development.

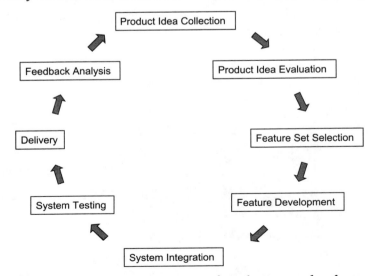

FIGURE 3-1. The macro process of evolutionary development for large-scale systems.

Cost of Evolution

Creating new functionality over an existing system by reusing the code of earlier releases and adding to it may sound like an easy way to make money, especially if the system has established a strong market position. We have experienced cases in which up to 80-90 percent of existing code from previous releases are reused in the development of a new release. Design and programming is easier with each release provided the architecture improves and higher-level reusable components are available.

Unfortunately, developing evolutionary systems is not that easy. For one thing, the architecture does not improve automatically over time. Often it does just the opposite, especially when several software developers touch the design in the course of the development without necessarily understanding the principles of architecture. Even if you managed to take good care of the architecture and truly save in design costs of new releases, this productivity gain is easily eaten by the extra effort required for testing, maintenance, and system upgrades. These costs grow with the growth of system complexity.

We claim that evolving large software systems in the same way you would develop smaller systems results in the effort and cost trends illustrated in Figure 3-2. This figure shows the relative effort necessary for requirements analysis, software design and programming, and testing to produce one new function point for a release. The cost of preparing procedures and programs for system upgrades is also included.

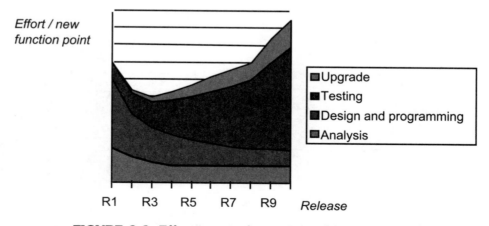

FIGURE 3-2. Effort required per a new function point.

We first look at the traditional phases of software development. The *design phase* includes architectural design and detailed design. Testing covers all testing phases such as unit testing, integration testing, and system testing, as well as the time needed for debugging the found bugs. Let's assume the amount of *new* delivered functionality in each release R1 ... R10 is about the same and the release cycle one year. Figure 3-2 presents thus the cost trends for a time period of about ten years.

The first release (R1) demands more requirements analysis and design than later releases, because the whole product concept needs to be clarified and the main directions of architecture set. The relative portion of analysis and design effort required to produce one new function point is quite high for the first few releases until the product's concept and architectural solutions stabilize. Then, the requirements analysis effort per one function point is about the same, but the software design effort starts to decrease gradually thanks to reuse of existing services, if the architecture allows.

As you can see from Figure 3-2, the testing effort required for the new functionality is continuously increasing, and most of the time and effort is spent on testing, which does not add any value to the product as such. The reason for this is the continuously increasing amount of *regression testing*, testing that the existing functionality still works. As the size of the software grows, more and more regression tests need to be run because the modifications due to fault corrections or system enhancements may have broken some parts of the system. As a result, you need to spend more time and effort per new unit of functionality in each release to test the system unless you take some actions to resolve this unwanted trend.

The need to enhance the existing systems with new features brings about the need to *upgrade* the delivered systems. A *system upgrade* includes such things as replacing a set of executables with new versions, adding or removing some executables, patching the configuration files and other system settings, and sometimes upgrading the database scheme and running required back-ups and conversions. A failing system upgrade could stop all business operations for a day or more, and therefore the upgrades, in particular, need to be planned and carried out carefully.

Whether the system upgrades are done manually, automatically, or a bit of both, you need to take into account the cost and time of planning, implementing, and testing the upgrade procedures and possible support tools. If the system architecture is not made extensible so that it is easy to upgrade, the unit cost of implementing upgrade procedures for new functionality increases as a function of system size and number of different configurations of installations.

The bottom line: after some point of time in system life cycle, the relative cost of developing new functionality increases due to rapidly increasing testing costs and costs of upgrading the system.

Cost of Maintenance

There is also a growing need to allocate more resources into maintenance work, which is more bad news on top of the increased testing and upgrading costs. If the software quality in terms of defect density[2] remains constant, you will observe a pattern of reported fault reports for a given time interval, such as that shown in Figure 3-3. The number of fault reports directly correlates with the effort needed for maintenance work.

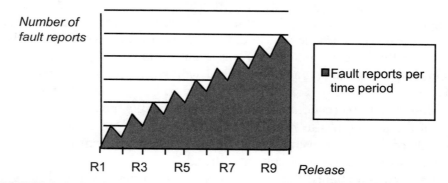

FIGURE 3-3. Fault reports per time interval in a multiyear, large project.

If you are successful in selling your system, your number of customers and users grows even faster than the size of code. After each release, there will be a peak in the number of fault reports when the deliveries have progressed to the state in which most of your customers are using the new system. Although you were able to fix the bugs efficiently, there will be more and more defects in each release because the size and usage of the system is growing—unless you succeed in improving the defect density dramatically.

If you have tens or hundreds of customers, many fault reports tell you about the same bug, but some work needs to be done to be sure the bug was really fixed. In many cases, most of the bug fixes need to be done by the software engineer who knows best the implementation.

The growing size of the system under development brings new ways to apply the system and more dependencies between various parts of the system. This, in turn, introduces new complexity and sources of errors constantly, making the testing and debugging more difficult and time consuming. The larger the software is, the more defects it will contain; and the more customers you have, the more the product is tested in the field, and so more defects are found.

There are mixed blessings in evolutionary system development. On one hand, existing software assets may be largely reused, which potentially provides a lot of chances to learn from past experience and create a flexible system architecture that ensures high productivity in the long run. On the other hand, developing new features on top of a legacy system can be tedious if the system architecture is not extensible enough. The effort required for testing, maintenance, and upgrades may tie up so many resources the new product development paralyzes. If the percentage of resources used for these tasks is higher in each consecutive release, you have less and less available resources for creating new value to the customers. The root cause for all these problems lies in the rapidly growing complexity of the large systems.

Growth of Complexity

The inherent complexity of large systems shows in many ways in the development and maintenance. For one thing, a larger system requires more man months to develop than a smaller one because there is simply more to be done. In addition, the performance of large projects in terms of delivered function points per person months is typically lower than in smaller projects because of organizational inefficiency and the inherently high complexity of systems to be developed.

Many large systems are complex business systems, such as telecom switches or air traffic control systems, that require such a wide range of domain knowledge that one small team of gurus cannot develop and support them. Therefore, the project organizations that develop large systems tend to be large and somehow hierarchically organized.[3] This makes the development process complex, resulting in inefficiency in decision-making and an increase in meeting hours.

We claim that a vast amount of overwhelming complexity of large system architectures is a consequence of poorly managed *dependencies* between the elements of the system.[4] If you do not know the dependencies among the pieces of the system, you can hardly understand the consequences of system modifications either. The growth of system dependencies resulting in complexity is rather quadratic than linear as the number of classes in the system grows, unless the system architecture is particularly well designed. To illustrate this, consider a system having 1,000,000 lines of C++. Such a system can have about 5,000 classes, probably even more. Understanding such a large piece of software obviously calls for properly structured architecture. Managing the object collaboration patterns of 5,000 classes is close to impossible for average software designers, but still the designers need to understand them to a great deal if they need to do major modifications to the system.

Understanding all the dependencies among thousands of classes challenges a designer's mental capacity if the system is poorly structured. Figure 3-4 illustrates the number of *possible* dependencies of software systems having 2, 4, 8, and 5,000 classes. As the number of classes increases, the number of possible dependencies grows quadratically according to formula $n*(n - 1)/2$, in which n stands for the number of classes. Given the example of 5,000 classes, there could be 5,000 x (5,000 -1)/2 = 12,497,500 possible dependencies between 5,000 classes!

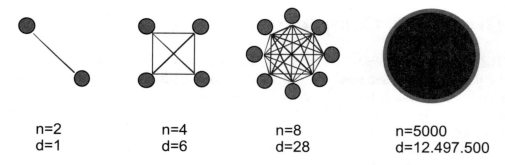

| n=2 | n=4 | n=8 | n=5000 |
| d=1 | d=6 | d=28 | d=12.497.500 |

FIGURE 3-4. Number of possible dependencies (d) for systems having 2, 4, 8, and 5,000 classes.

The number of real dependencies is smaller, because not all classes refer to each other. However, many dependencies are *transitive* by nature. Consider the illustration in Figure 3--5, in which class C1 depends on class C2, which, in turn, depends on class C3. It follows that a change in class C3 may change the behavior of C2, which again may break the behavior of C1. This indirect dependency between C1 and C3 is called a *transitive dependency*.

Due to transitive dependencies, the total number of real dependencies may be surprisingly high. At least it is more than likely that the growth of complexity follows a steeper curve than the growth of software in terms of lines of code. So, a system having 1,000,000 lines of code is far more than ten times more complex than a system having 100,000 lines of code. This makes it particularly challenging to develop large systems cost-efficiently and pinpoints the value of solid and clear architecture in large-scale development.

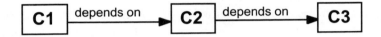

FIGURE 3-5. Transitive dependency: C1 depends on C2 directly and on C3 indirectly.

Size and Cycle Time

A natural, yet unfortunate consequence of developing complex systems is the long development cycle time. Project lead times for large systems may be even several years in worst cases. Inherent inefficiency of large organizations and the growing complexity of systems explain this only partially. The third fundamental reason for the long development cycles is stated by Frederick Brooks in his legendary essay "The Mythical Man-Month" [Brooks 95]:

> *"The number of months of a project depends upon its sequential constraints. The maximum number of men depends upon the number of independent subtasks. From these two quantities one can derive schedules using fewer men and more months. (The only risk is product obsolescence.) One cannot, however, get workable schedules using more men and fewer months. More software projects have gone awry for lack of calendar time than for all causes combined."*

The point is you could obtain only limited benefits by adding more resources to typical bottleneck areas belonging to the late phases of project, such as testing, customer documentation, or development of upgrade instructions and scripts, because they are not independent from each other or from software development tasks. Installation and upgrade procedures cannot be made without your knowing many final design decisions, such as the database schema, use and structure of system configuration files, names of all executables, and so on. Customer documents cannot be completed before the final versions of user interface applications have been frozen. Black box test cases cannot be prepared before the specifications are available, and the glass box test cases, used in low-level testing and integration, require the detailed design to be complete.

Unfortunately, minor changes in upstream information may cause extensive rework of downstream deliverables, and a lot of communication is necessary to do the required changes properly. There is always some optimal number of developers for a project, and adding more eventually makes the projects take *longer* because of burdens in communication and other overhead.

Long development cycle times constitute a major challenge for any system vendor providing large systems for open markets in which competition exists. The world is changing faster than ever, as are the business needs for software. Waiting more than a year for a new, critical software release is too long even today, never mind in the future.

Market pressures for shorter and shorter product development cycles are obvious: rapidly changing business environments call for quick solutions to keep the business going. If a customer needs some critical new functionality *now* and you can deliver it only in three years, your customer satisfaction surveys will not be favorable, to say the least.

There are two unfortunate phenomena that we aim at breaking by improving the practices for large-scale development:

1. The larger the system, the higher the relative cost of a new unit of functionality.
2. The larger the system, the longer the relative cycle time of delivering new functionality to the system.

The first claim says that the cost of delivering similar functionality to a larger system is higher than if delivering to a smaller one. The second, in turn, says that delivering similar amount of functionality to a larger system takes more time than if delivering to a smaller one. To make them concrete, consider a case in which you want to make just one new feature to an insurance information system that has been developed for five years resulting in

1,000,000 lines of code. The design, implementation, and testing of that feature might take a couple of months, but you may need to test the whole system for several weeks or months to ensure that the modification did not break the existing functionality. Then you could deliver the new release containing the new feature to a customer or two, but making a new system product that meets the expectations of a large customer base is another story. You may need to update hundreds of pages of customer documentation, prepare and test general upgrade procedures for the database, update product descriptions, and do many other things that are required to make the software to become a *product*.

Because it would not be cost-efficient to do all this for only one small feature, you normally develop a release that has other features as well. Rarely are the cycle times for developing the features similar, so some smaller features always need to wait for larger ones to be ready in many phases. This lengthens the cycle time as perceived by customers waiting for some particular feature.

There are no magic tricks which could make the inherent complexity of large systems vanish as such, and same goes for the need to evolve them. It is obvious that the often proposed silver bullet candidates, such as CASE tools or the most recent programming languages, cannot alone solve any of the fundamental problems of large systems. To work out some solutions to these core problems, you need to attack the essential issues of complexity and evolution. It is obvious that the architecture of the system contributes most to the success of large-scale development. Because the root cause for the problems of large systems is that they are *too* large, the obvious solution is that you partition the system into smaller pieces. If you are able to manage the evolution of the pieces as if they were small stand-alone applications and integrate them into a consistent whole, you can deal with the development of the pieces themselves by using the best available practices for smaller projects.

In the following, we present some practical guidelines for breaking a large system into suitable kind of subsystems.

Subsystems

It matters how you decompose a large system into subsystems. We claim that a clever decomposition can help you to gain dramatic reduction in time-to-market and increase in overall productivity. We will show how establishing suitable kinds of subsystems can contribute a lot on effectiveness of project work. We will use a case study from the domain we know best—management of telecommunication networks—to demonstrate our solutions for large-scale development. In the following we will introduce this case study that is used throughout the rest of the sections discussing large-scale development.

Case Study: GSM Network Manager

Many of the practices presented in this book were created to provide productive means for the development of network management systems at Nokia Telecommunications. These systems were developed using object-oriented methods and tools from the outset. In general, network management is an excellent area for exploiting object technology, because it is natural to model the networks so that the network nodes are considered as collaborating objects. The network nodes (that is, the network elements) send and receive messages from each other and from the management system. Therefore, it is not surprising that a relatively large portion of case studies and experience reports came from the domain of network management in the early years of object technology.

The examples represented here are based on our own solutions within the development of Nokia NMS product line but we have simplified them a great deal to make them easy to understand. We call this imaginary and simplified network management system as *GSM Network Manager* to make it easy to refer to, and to distinct it from Nokia's real products.

GSM Network Manager is a system that is targeted to the technical network management of GSM[5] networks. To make a long story short, GSM networks are digital telecommunications networks based on cellular radio access that provide users with free mobility. The mobile phones communicate with base stations that are connected to GSM network infrastructure needed in establishing calls.

Technical network management of any network—be it a large telecom or a small PC network—is mostly about managing faults, configuration, accounting, performance, and security of the network.

Consider a network management system a sort of user interface for the network operator to the network. It enables an operator to perform use cases to find out the quality of service provided by the network in terms of faults and performance, and to master the configuration of the network when expanding or reconfiguring it. Network-wide operations for accounting and security parameters can also be carried out from one centralized management site. For instance, a large GSM network may have thousands of base stations providing network coverage to cellular phone users. It is far more cost-efficient to manage such a network from one centralized monitoring room, rather than have thousands of operators sit at the service terminals of the network elements.

Figure 3-6 illustrates the main elements of a GSM network. The network management systems are large by nature. We define the scope of this simplified GSM Network Manager to include only fault, configuration, and performance management of GSM networks. The size of such a system could be about 1,000,000 lines of code when the code lines of third-party components are not counted.[6] It provides thus a suitable case study for illustrating our solutions for large-scale development.

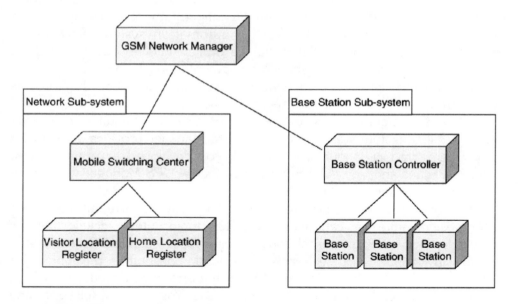

FIGURE 3-6. GSM Network Manager manages the elements of the Network Subsystem through Mobile Switching Center (that is, the switch) and the Base Station Subsystem through Base Station Controller.

Systems as Product Families

We approach the question of subsystem decomposition from top down starting from the highest level subsystems. Our proposal for carrying out the high-level decomposition aims at solving the fundamental problems caused by large size. We want to define a subsystem structure that enables effective project work and helps in developing and delivering new functionality in a shorter span of time. Meeting these goals requires that the release development projects are small enough. It must be possible to organize development, test, and delivery processes so that the small features of the system do not have to wait for the whole release to be complete. These goals are best met by decomposing the system into subsystems that each comprise a *deliverable* part of the system. That is, the system is considered as a family of small subproducts rather than one large product. Then each subsystem, comprised of a small product, can even have a release schedule of its own as long as the dependencies to other similar subsystems are managed.

We call a deliverable grouping of closely related features an *application product*. Respectively, we call a tested configuration of these application products a *system product*. An office automation system provides an example of a system product that can be broken into application products such as text processing, spreadsheet, and presentation graphics. Each can be considered a product in its own right, but when used together, they provide even more valuable solutions to a user's needs.

Different configurations of the application products for different market segments all constitute system products. GSM Manager provides an example of a system product in our case study. If you developed a variant of that system for managing, say, AMPS[7] networks, then *AMPS Manager* would constitute another system product.

More often than not, there are several alternatives to carry out the system decomposition into application products. The main criteria include that the composites have strong internal cohesion and loose couplings to other subsystems. In addition, each such subsystem should constitute a meaningful set of functionality to justify its delivery. Often, the application products differ in size, complexity, and volatility of customer needs. You can gain full-cycle time advantage only if the application products constitute physical, deliverable entities including all software, documentation, and other assets required to get the application product up and running.

To illustrate high level system decomposition, consider the GSM Network Manager case study. For one thing, you could draw the application product boundaries according to the problem domain structure. In the context of GSM network management, that would result in product structure that maps to subsystems of the network to be managed, such as the Network Subsystem and Base Station Subsystem. You could also define the application products respectively as Network Subsystem Management and Base Station Subsystem Management. After analysis of these subsystems, you might have smaller application products, such as Base Station Controller Management.

Or, you could identify products according to functional areas of network management, such as Fault Management or Performance Management. The third possible product structure could be the one that defines products according to customer's core business processes related to network management. Such business processes could be Network Construction or Network Maintenance, for example.

In this case study, we decided to decompose the system into application products according to functional areas. So, the application products of GSM Network Manager are Fault Management, Configuration Management, and Performance Management.

If the application products are independent enough, you can evolve them in their own projects, each with their own schedules, as long as you make sure each project is responsible for managing and verifying the compatibility of its result with other parts of the system. The impact of breaking up GSM Network Manager into *fully independent* application products is depicted in Figure 3-7. It shows the difference in cases in which you have either one monolithic GSM Network Manager release or a system broken up into three loosely coupled application products.

Consider a case that you can deliver new releases of *Fault Management* (FM), *Performance Management* (PM), and *Configuration Management* (CM) separately to customers. As Figure 3-7 indicates, development of Fault Management features takes a lot longer than the rest of the project in this case. If some customers are interested only in the new functionality provided by the new release of Configuration Management, they will perceive about 75 percent cut in the process cycle time because they do not need to wait for the two others be completed. This situation is typical when an existing system is enhanced with many new features, and the customers do not need them all.

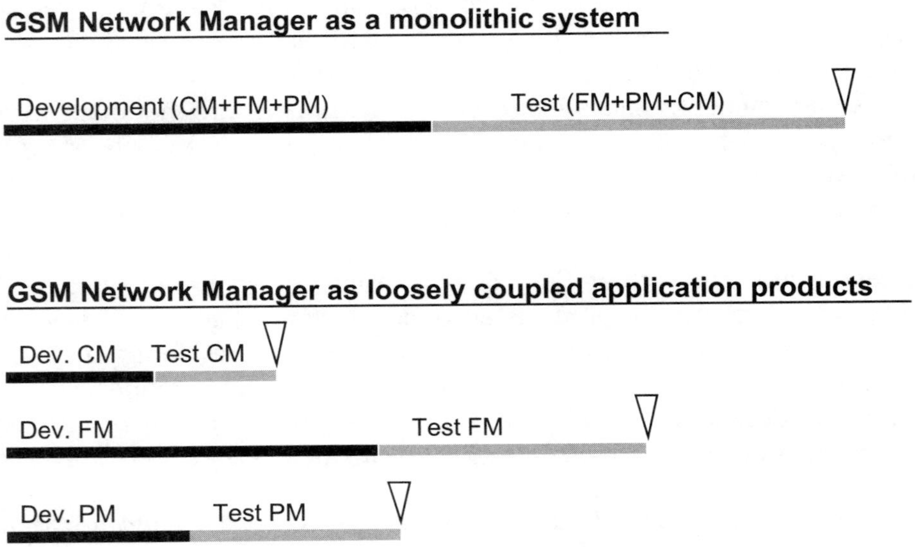

GSM Network Manager as a monolithic system

Development (CM+FM+PM)   Test (FM+PM+CM)   ▽

GSM Network Manager as loosely coupled application products

Dev. CM   Test CM   ▽

Dev. FM   Test FM   ▽

Dev. PM   Test PM   ▽

FIGURE 3-7. **Having fully independent, deliverable subsystems allows you to deliver the subsystems as soon as they are ready without waiting for other subsystems to be complete.**

The caveat of this approach is that the cost of functionality delivered in stages is higher due to higher development and delivery costs. The total effort required to build three loosely coupled subsystems tends to be higher than the effort required for one monolithic system. The extra development effort originates mainly from the fact that developing three products for the same domain independently inevitably misses several reuse opportunities. So, similar wheels are reinvented several times if the application products are kept independent. In addition, you need extra effort for managing the interfaces of application products as well as for testing their compatibility and system integrity when parts of the system are released in different times.

Increase in delivery cost is inevitable when you deliver a system as many small releases instead of one large one. The reason for this is that a great deal of delivery costs is not dependent on the amount of functionality installed. Enhancing an operational large system with new functionality requires, each time, the same kind of traveling, backing up some vital data, software installation, and so on. However, in most cases, the reduction in cycle time contributes far more to long term success of the company than the higher costs due to faster cycles.

The precondition of utilizing the described approach is that the interfaces of application products are well defined and managed. System level design practices must have quite a bit of discipline to keep the application products independent enough without loosing their compatibility and the conceptual integrity of the whole system. In the long run, a flexible, modular product architecture can provide competitive advantage toward building sophisticated applications rapidly.

You can benefit from breaking down large systems into application products even if you still plan to deliver the whole system at once. This approach can help you a lot in organizing internal responsibilities and projects into high performance application product teams. You can establish cross-functional product teams consisting of marketing representatives, analysts, designers, testers, technical writers, and QA engineers that all have the same goal of delivering the best possible application product according to schedule and budget. Such an empowered team with shared goals and incentives for success has a strong feeling of ownership, and acts like a small software house inside the company resulting in fast decision making and better overall productivity.

Application Platforms and Product Lines

A compromise between one monolithic system and fully independent application products is often the most cost-efficient solution. You can achieve both high reuse of common design solutions and existence of releasable, highly independent application products if you organize the common parts into one independent, high-level subsystem of its own. We call this subsystem an *application platform*. Application products depend on it, but not vice versa, as illustrated in Figure 3-8.

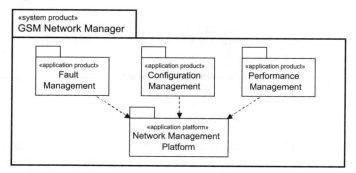

FIGURE 3-8. Application platform contains common design solutions for application products.

Whereas the application products provide applications to users, the application platform provides reusable components, frameworks, and design guidelines to software designers. The better these services of the application platform, the faster the application development. However, a separate application platform always causes some overhead, as well as some unwanted waiting in application product development. For instance, consider a case in which you, as an application developer, are using a GUI component from the application platform and find a simple bug in it. If the bug were in your own code, you could fix it immediately. Now that the bug exists in the application platform, you need to wait for the correction to be made by someone else. This sort of dependencies increase the complexity of the development process, which can decrease the short-term productivity.

In general, having a separate application platform and a project focusing to it lengthens the nominal development cycle of small applications. Sometimes a platform release can be on the critical path and the projects developing application products may need to wait for platform development, as illustrated in Figure 3-9. However, thanks to reuse, this mode of operation is more cost-efficient in the long run, and the *average* cycle time of application products may be immediately shorter. It also pays off in terms of other reuse benefits, such as reduction in maintenance costs and increased reliability of delivered systems.

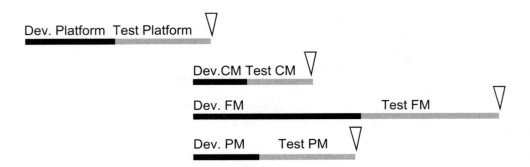

FIGURE 3-9. An application platform improves long-term productivity, but the nominal schedule for a small application product release may extend more in the short term than with completely independent application products.

An application platform is not only useful for managing the reusable assets of the current product portfolio. It enables you to have a *product line*[8] *approach* [Bass et. al., 97] to help system development in the future. The leading principle in such an approach is to release a *new* line of closely related products and product variants cost-effectively over time. The products are built on top of a common application platform that holds the common software assets.

The motivation of the product line approach to collecting the reusable software assets into an application platform is to make the future variation easy and economical. It is, naturally, tempting to reuse results of past large-scale projects when creating completely new products. For instance, if you have developed a large business support system for car resellers, why not make variants of it for other kinds of resellers if it were economically feasible?

The product line approach resembles the idea behind application frameworks to easily instantiate, modify, or generate new applications. The difference is that now we are not only talking about applications, but about new products created using the assets of the application platform, as well.

We consider this product line approach inevitable for large systems that evolve for several years, because there will be always some needs for product variation. What you need to decide on is the scope of the common part, the application platform, and the level of investments allocated for its development. Making upfront investments that are too heavy results in too long time-to-market for the first systems. In an extreme case you might allocate all resources to platform development for years and produce a great platform having components, frameworks, design patterns, and guide-lines, but no deliverable systems. At the other end could be a case in which you assign one guy to define the application platform and after a while he mails you the platform specification: "Let's use Windows NT and MFC." Maybe a compromise works best here, as well.

We like to see platforms grow with systems. When you are starting the development of a new, (eventually) large product line from the scratch, the first platform release should include primarily commercial, off-the-shelf components. If you immediately start developing domain specific components for anticipated future needs, you will most likely waste some effort. In our experience, a better way is to first implement specific solutions within system product development, and then later generalize the special solutions into common platform services if their reuse potential is high enough. This kind of incremental approach ensures that the platform components match true needs of application developers.

Design Levels

Although the class abstraction used in programming provides fine means for information hiding and modularity in small applications, you need higher level subsystems to create elements of design that enable modular design of large systems. Classes are at too low a level of abstraction if there are, say, more than 3,000 of them. You can hardly consider a system modular if it has thousands of classes and millions of dependencies between them. Therefore, you need to restrict the visibility of low-level classes and hide some of them behind subsystem interfaces. To do this, we introduce two more design levels between application products and classes. The higher one contains *applications* and *service blocks*, and the lower one *components*.[9] While applications provide some services to the end users, the service blocks are groupings of components providing services for the application developers. They exist particularly in application platforms.

The complete design level model[10] for large-scale system is illustrated in Figure 3-10. The design level model provides a structure for organizing systems into subsystems. A subsystem at a design level above classes can be decomposed into subsystems of the design level below it. Elements at each design level are also physical composites, not only logical ones, so they can be items of configuration management as well. This helps in effective implementation of software engineering and management practices as we will demonstrate later. Now that we have already introduced system products and application products, we continue the discussion with applications and service blocks.

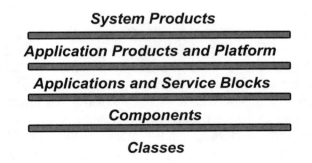

FIGURE 3-10. Design levels of large-scale systems.

Applications

An *application* is an executable piece of software that provides value and that can be perceived by the users of the system. While small software products often have only one application to be used after installing the product, the large system products may have even hundreds of applications. The role of the concept application in our design level model is to link the product planning point of view, the application products, to the design point of view, the components.

An application product is a configuration of applications. Knowing the applications belonging to one product provides a good overview over the functionality and value provided by the product. One application, in turn, may belong to several application products. A *generic application* is an application that can be used as such in several products. Most typical examples of generic applications include a wide range of commercial, off-the-shelf applications such as text editors, spreadsheet programs, and Internet browsers. It is rarely feasible to reproduce the functionality provided by such commercially available software packages, if only they can be integrated to the system.

Most of the applications are *user interface applications*. Such applications provide some interactive user interface to the users of the system. The rest of the applications are *background applications*. Such applications carry out some useful tasks without interaction with a user. For example, an application that backs up critical files on a file server each night provides an example of what we call a background application. However, note that we carry out the decomposition of application products into applications to understand the substance of application products. You should not yet be concerned with whether some application is implemented as one or more processes. Decomposition into processes takes place at the next design level, the *component level*.

To reify the notion of application, let's have a look at our GSM Network Manager case study. The functionality of the application product Configuration Management would cover management of software and hardware configuration, such as reading that information from the network into the management system, management of radio network parameters, and management of time of network elements. The applications of Configuration Management are listed in Figure 3-11.

APPLICATION	PURPOSE
Configuration Uploader	Periodically uploading of the network topology from the network.
Network Hardware Manager	Hardware management of network nodes.
Radio Network Manager	Management of configuration parameters of the radio access network.
Network Time Manager	Time management of computational resources in the network.
Base Station Software Manager	Remote software downloading and deployment to Base Station Subsystem.

FIGURE 3-11. Applications of Configuration Management.

The Configuration Uploader is a background application; the others in Figure 3-11 are user interface applications. You should break down an application product into user interface applications primarily according to use cases, so that, if possible, each use case fits in one application. Otherwise you may need to carry out some use cases using several applications and switching between them continuously to get the job done.

Application integration techniques, such as ActiveX or Java Beans, allow development of applications as separate components, and their integration at user-interface level. This kind of approach allows you to define applications that provide users with conceptual integrity while providing developers with modularity at component level. If you have built the application out of components, you can redefine the scope of applications and their support to use cases by creating user interface layers on top of applications.

Service Blocks

A *service block* is a grouping of closely related components that provide a consistent set of reusable software assets to designers using the service block. As subsystems, the service blocks belong to the same design level as the applications. Whereas the applications are subsystems of an application product, the service blocks are usually subsystems of an application platform. There is an exception to this rule, though. An application product may have some reusable but application-product- specific components used by more than one application of the application product. Such a component group constitutes a service block that is part of an application product, not part of the application platform.

Component group is not the only form for a service block. A service block can also be an *application framework*. Initially, most applications have been designed only to meet the needs of the first case for which they were originally designed. The development team is seldom able to foresee all the flexibility requirements, which in most cases appear only after the first version of the application is available. From time to time, you recognize an application that can be used for more than one purpose if you only tailor it a bit. Adaptation can be made at source code level using conditional compiling or branching facilities of a software configuration management system, for instance.

From the software designer's perspective, an application framework provides often the most productive way of creating new variants of similar kinds of applications. By an *application framework*, we mean a frame for a generic application and a number of *hooks* that can be used for specializing the applications from that frame. The specialization may take place by writing some code to be called by the framework, or by specifying the differences in some parameter file to be read by the framework. One of the most advanced framework specialization approaches used in many programming environments is to provide *wizards* that ask for the properties of applications and generate the application or a frame for it accordingly.

Creating a service block that offers a domain specific framework requires sometimes relatively high initial investment. You may still find it feasible to invest in developing an application frameworks to achieve flexibility for changes to come for established and well understood domains, if the product life cycles are long enough to ensure return on that investment.

Components

By a *component* we mean a configuration of files implementing a basic architectural building block, such as an executable program or a link library. Each component provides a set of defined services for its clients through interfaces. Hence, if you use an object-oriented programming language, a component is a self-sufficient configuration item containing the code for one or more class declarations and their implementation. The client may be another component, or a real user in the case the component implements an executable user interface program. Size of a typical component is between 500-15,000 lines of code. A component is typically implemented and maintained by one software engineer. Both applications, as well as service blocks, are configurations of components.

The executable components can be programs implementing interactive applications, demons running as background processes, or batch programs, such as report generators. You often need to use other components to create new components. The component interfaces may be specified using a programming language, such as C++, or using an interface definition language, such as IDL.

Managing the complexity of a large system is mostly carried out at component level. Dependencies between components determine the real code dependencies in an existing system. If a vital component is missing, the system can't be integrated. If a component required to build an application is broken, this bug will most likely show in the application as well. And, fixing a bug in the system requires that you first identify the broken component and fix it, and then find its dependencies to other components and test all affected parts of the system.

Managing the Dependencies

As the components are physical design composites with concrete interfaces, the dependencies between components are real implementation dependencies. Hence, the complexity of the dependency network of components correlates directly with the complexity of the whole system.

To reduce system complexity, each component should follow the strategy of information hiding by hiding the low-level classes behind higher level interfaces. For example, consider the 12,497,500 possible dependencies between 5,000 classes that we calculated earlier. Let's assume you organize this system into, say, 200 components providing about 500 classes in their interface instead of 5,000 classes organized in one flat hierarchy. Hiding the remaining 4,500 classes behind the modular structure of components would decrease the number of possible dependencies to be managed from 12,497,500 to 124,750, that is, by 99 percent!

The lesson learned: making all classes visible is not feasible in a large system, because the inherent complexity in terms of dependencies grows drastically if you do not restrict the use of the classes. Developing a large system calls for information hiding at many levels to make it possible to manage the architecture. Understanding, evolving, testing, and maintaining a system made of classes is far easier than a system made of bits and bytes using assembler. At the same time, it is far easier to manage a large system having some hundreds of components than a system having just a flat architecture of thousands of classes.

There are two dependency types between components: compile-time dependencies and run-time dependencies. As the terms suggest, the former is identified by reading the code and the latter is identified by running the code. A *compile-time dependency* is born when the code of a component refers to the code of another component during compilation or linking. Typical run-time dependencies are inter-process communication and dependencies through some shared persistent objects.

The dependencies between two classes propagate to component dependencies, if the classes belong to different components. In proportion, if there is a dependency between two components belonging to different applications, there is also a dependency between these applications, and so on. If your ultimate goal is to build large systems to consist of self-contained, independent application products that can be evolved and even released independently, you need to start managing the dependencies at component level. You need to remove all unwanted dependencies between components belonging to different application products. Especially, the *cyclic dependencies* between components tend usually need to be removed.

A *cyclic dependency* between two components, say *c1* and *c2*, is such that *c1* depends on *c2* and *c2* on *c1*. A change in either component may break the behavior of the other, and these components need to always be analyzed together. Thus, with cyclic dependencies the integration and testing is more laborious, and the amount of regression testing increases, as all the dependent components should be retested when any one of them changes. Cyclic dependencies also make the reuse of code painful. Reusing a single component may require you to take along tens of irrelevant components for your purposes due to some cyclic and transitive dependencies. An alternative to cyclic dependencies between the pieces of the system is layered trees of components organized so the components and dependencies between them can be presented as directed acyclic graphs. Simple cyclic and acyclic dependencies are presented in Figure 3-12.

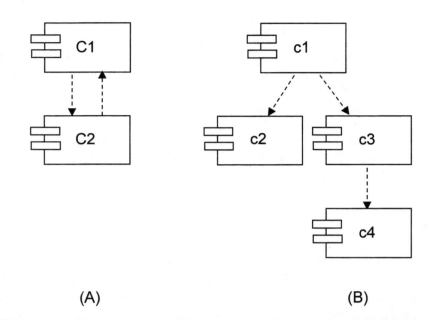

(A) (B)

FIGURE 3-12. Cyclic dependencies between C1 and C2 (fig. A) and acyclic
dependencies c1-c2, c1-c3, and c3-c4 (fig. B).

To get rid of unwanted dependencies, start by making the dependencies between components visible. Then you can consider means for limiting the absolute number of elements visible to designers, as well as eliminating the dependencies between them. Organizing the components into layers based on their expected roles and responsibilities reveals easily poor design of component dependencies. The basic rule is that a component belonging to a layer should only refer to components of one layer below, or the ones belonging to the same layer. The common components shared by many applications should be allocated to the application platform to avoid cyclic dependencies brought about sharing the same code. We discuss the views to architecture that help in carrying out this kind of reasoning in the section "3+1 Views to Architecture."

Impacts of Levelized Design

The presented approach for organizing subsystems into levels that separate the design concerns is primarily designed to manage the complexity and enable the concurrent engineering of large software systems resulting in shorter time-to-market. However, this approach can also help define the organizational responsibilities and implement effective software engineering practices.

Ownership of Subsystems

We find it beneficial to organize responsibilities so that you can assign clear ownership over the subsystems. This is important for practical reasons such as maintenance and development responsibilities, but also from the team building point of view.

Application products are large enough subsystems to be allocated for departments having about 6–20 developers. When you build cross-functional teams primarily around application products, the team is still small enough to be perceived as a team with shared objectives. It is often practical to define also the line organization according to application product boundaries if the product life cycles are long.

Each application of an application product is a suitable composite to be allocated for a small feature team of 2–5 persons. Such teams are typically formed on project basis, and they show mainly in project organization.

Components should be small enough that an owner can be assigned to each. This clarifies the development and maintenance responsibilities. However, we recommend you organize maintenance of components so designers are not doomed to maintain eternally all the components that they have once developed. Otherwise, the most experienced engineers will end up simply maintaining the old code.

Software Engineering Concerns

How a system is broken into composites has great ramifications to effectiveness of many software development and management activities. In addition to design, the process areas most affected include software configuration management, project management, maintenance, and integration. In the following list, we briefly discuss the way subsystem decomposition influences these processes:

- **Software configuration management.** To manage software configurations, you need to have items that can be isolated and identified so that you can build them. Components, in particular, are the key elements for software configuration management. You can build applications from components, application products from applications, and finally system products from application products.

- **Project management.** Useful subsystem division provides modules that can be easily allocated to individuals and teams when planning a project and tracking its progress. There should be as few dependencies between the subsystems as possible to reduce the total risk of failure when one subproject has some problem with its subsystems, and to make the estimation and follow-up easier. Independent, deliverable subsystems at all design levels help in accelerating projects by *pipelining*[11] development.

- **Maintenance.** When fixing a bug, a key concern is whether the fix will have negative effects. Such effects are sought out during maintenance. Maintenance work benefits from loosely coupled, clearly defined subsystems, because the unwanted side effects are less likely if you can localize a bug inside one subsystem.

- **Integration.** Minimal but well-defined subsystem dependencies and clear interfaces between subsystems are preconditions for cost-efficient and fast integration. We cover integration more thoroughly in the section "Evolutionary System Development Process."

The bottom line is that you need concrete, loosely coupled components to implement effective key practices for the software process.

3 + 1 Views to Architecture

You cannot manage anything that you cannot make visible. This applies particularly for software development—a process that deals with remarkably abstract and complex entities. It is therefore not surprising that most software engineering methods focus a lot on the modeling notations and techniques. This focus shows also in the names of methods, such as *Object Modeling Technique* (OMT).

In Chapter 1 we introduced the 3 + 1 views framework that utilizes UML for modeling the architecture of an application from four perspectives. UML modeling facilities provide an adequate means for modeling large-scale system architectures. However, before you start leafing through the UML notation for various boxes and arrows, you need to understand *what* you want to achieve with these figures. You should decide the useful perspectives to the architecture that help developers understand the system when developing and maintaining it. When considering large-scale development, an architecture description should answer at least the following:

- **What is the logical partitioning of the system into subsystems?** Knowing this helps you to understand the overall structure of the system and to comprehend how system functionality is allocated.

- **What is the run-time configuration of the system?** Designing what processes there are, how they relate, and how they are allocated to available computers is an essential part of architectural design. This helps in debugging the system and estimating its performance as well as in planning the development and the integration order.

- **What is the configuration of the developed system in terms of components?** This helps in organizing the development and integration work as well as in software configuration management.

- **How does the architecture implement the most important use cases?** This provides visibility to design rationale and makes it possible to validate the performance of designed system from the user's point of view.

The 3 + 1 views presented in Chapter 1 for managing the architecture of interactive systems scale up to large-scale development as well. The *logical view, run-time view, development view,* and *scenario view* answer the question as summarized in Figure 3-13. They make the architecture manageable by providing adequate visibility to it at product and application level. The elements of the lowest level in these system level models are components that are further elaborated in detailed design phases using our practices for application development (described in Chapter 1). In the following section, we explain the application of these views in large-scale development and show how UML can be used to provide these viewpoints to the architecture.

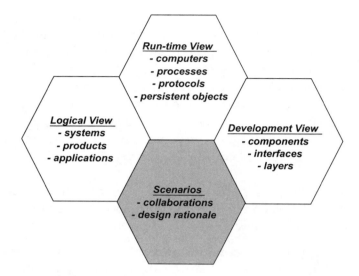

FIGURE 3-13. 3 + 1 views to architecture in nutshell.

Logical View

Logical view illustrates the high-level partitioning of the system into application products and applications. Its purpose is to view the system at the content level and to provide a structure for organizing and navigating in the architecture models.

We use the *packages* of UML to view the subsystems in a logical view. We prefer attaching the packages with stereotypes to describe the types of subsystems. Following our suggestion for design levels in section "Subsystems", we propose that you use stereotypes such as «system product», «application product» and «application» for classifying the packages in the logical view. They provide means for describing the product breakdown structure.

As you see in Figure 3-14, GSM Network Manager consists of three application products: Fault Management, Performance Management, and Configuration Management. The arrows between packages in the logical view illustrate dependencies between parts of the system. A subsystem depends on another subsystem, if the functionality of the first subsystem cannot be fully used without the other. Applying this definition means that the functionality of Performance Management application product cannot be fully used if Fault

Management or Configuration Management application products are not available. An example of such a case is a Performance Management application that asks a Fault Management application to give an alarm when the network performance is below an acceptable limit. As in this example, most of the dependencies shown in the logical view illustrate the need for integrating the application products and finally the applications themselves because some use cases involve more than one application.

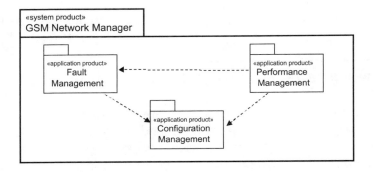

FIGURE 3-14. Top-level logical view to GSM Manager.

You need to look inside each application product to understand its contents. An application in the *logical view* is an executable program assisting users to carry out their use cases. To depict this, we have expanded the Configuration Management application product of GSM Network Manager in Figure 3-15. It illustrates the applications of Configuration Management and their dependencies. As the figure shows, the configuration management functionality is provided by five applications, which we presented already in section "Applications." Four applications depend on Configuration Uploader, which is an application that reads configuration information from the network elements and makes it available for other applications.

Often you need to break down one logical application into several processes for performance reasons. Note that the purpose of the logical view is to provide insight into the content of a large system in terms of its product structure and applications. Therefore, it is not necessary to describe all demons and scripts that could possibly be needed by the user interface applications. These implementation solutions belong to the *run-time* and *development views*.

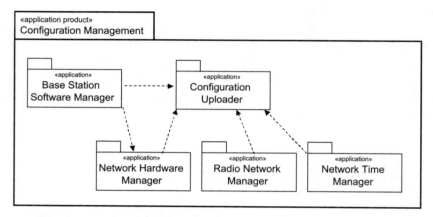

FIGURE 3-15. Applications of Configuration Management.

One way to use the logical view is to apply it for product portfolio management. Then you illustrate the products and product variants that constitute a product line. Note that the logical view is open-ended: for extremely large systems—actually, systems of systems—you can add a layer in which the system product would exist as one package.[12] You can also open each large application in the model and break it up into smaller logical pieces, if that helps you understand the system structure. In addition, you can add objects such as databases to illustrate the functionality and structure of the system. We suggest, however, that you keep the logical view at the system content level. A good test for this level is to think of it from customer's and developer's perspectives: If you were able to explain the logical view both to the customer and to your own team of software engineers, then it is probably at the right level of detail.

Run-time View

A large-scale system consists of several executables as a rule. Often it is practical to construct even one application from several executables when there are operations that take a long time to execute. One classic example is printing, which is often handled by a process or thread of its own in many applications. Other typical design goals for breaking down one logical application into several communicating executables are reliability, scalability, and plug-and-play upgradability. In addition, an executable process provides a well-defined component abstraction that helps in building modular systems having high reuse potential.

The *run-time view* provides useful means to describe the architecture in terms of executable programs. It expresses the run-time dependencies of executable components of the system as well as their allocation to the available computational resources.

We use the *deployment diagram* of UML to model the run-time view also for the large-scale systems. Let's illustrate the run-time view by looking closer to one of the applications of Configuration Management, the Base Station Software Manager. *Base Station Software Manager* is an application that takes care of upgrading and installing software from the network management system to base stations in a geographically distributed GSM network. The key concepts of this application are illustrated in Figure 3-16. Because a large GSM network may have thousands of base stations, this type of application may save a lot of time and money, because the software management can be carried out remotely rather than visiting each site.

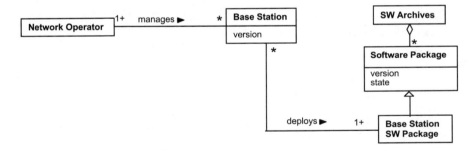

FIGURE 3-16. Analysis class diagram for Base Station Software Manager.

The use cases of such an application include:

- Storing a new base station software package into archives of network management system
- Downloading a software package from the network management system into the network
- Activating a software package in selected base stations
- Showing the software configurations of selected base stations

Many of the use cases may take a relatively long time to execute, and there are also scheduled and mass operations carried out for hundreds of objects. In addition, the application needs to handle the messages—events—sent by the network regarding the success of management operations and changes of network configuration. Obviously, it is feasible to implement such an application as a collection of several executables. By considering the design scenarios, you design a process architecture that looks like the deployment diagram in Figure 3-17.

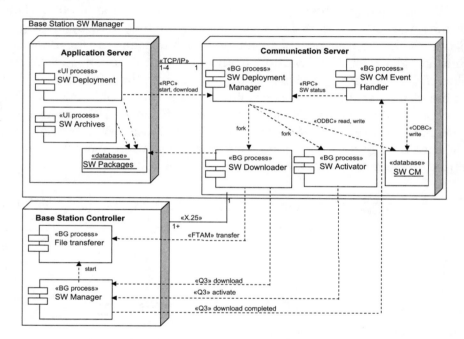

FIGURE 3-17. Run-time view for the Base Station Software Manager.

The processes of Base Station Software Manager are allocated to two servers: the *application server* and the *communication server*. Software management of base stations is handled using the operation and maintenance functionality of the base station controller, which is a special telecom equipment for managing the base station subsystem of GSM network. The associations between the computational nodes indicate communication paths between the nodes. We use stereotypes such as *«TCP/IP»* and *«x.25»* between these nodes to indicate the used communication protocols.

We have applied the extension mechanisms of UML and defined two stereotypes to categorize executable components: *«BG process»* for background processes, or demons if you like, and *«UI process»* for those executables that provide user interface. These processes, in most cases, provide adequate means for describing the executables and their dependencies. If your system conforms fully with the client-server model, then you could naturally use stereotypes such as *«client»* for the client processes and *«server»* for the server processes respectively as we showed in Chapter 1.

Only executable components and the data storages are shown in the run-time view. The nonexecutable components, such as link libraries, are not shown in the run-time view; these components belong to the development view. Run-time view makes the run-time dependencies of components visible, whereas the development view shows the static compilation dependencies between the components.

You may also draw objects that live in processes inside components. *Threads* are considered active objects that live inside processes. Threads would be modeled like any object instances using the *«thread»* stereotype. We use the stereotype *«database»* for database objects to illustrate the processes' use of database.

The dependencies between processes are expressed using dashed arrows from client to supplier. A client process depends on a supplier process if the client sends messages to supplier. However, in the case of synchronized communication, the acknowledgment messages (from supplier to client) are not considered to cause dependencies. We encourage you to indicate the communication protocol within messages by using a stereotype for that. We do not want to predefine all the possible protocols to be used. Instead, each organization developing a large system should identify the relevant protocols to be used and define stereotypes accordingly. An example of such a stereotype is *«RPC»*—which was used for modeling the use of remote procedure calls in Figure 3-17. When you have identified all allowed communication protocols, you can then provide reusable components and design patterns for implementing these protocols effectively.

Run-time view provides a compact overview over the structure of the run-time system. We recommend preparing it as one of the first tasks of architectural design after you have prepared the logical view and understood the requirements allocated to parts of the system in question. A run-time view makes the run-time dependencies visible, thus helping in assessing the performance, scalability, reliability, and modularity of the designed system. It also helps in planning a feasible order for the development and integration. After design and implementation, a current run-time view provides valuable information when debugging, as well as for planning the installation and upgrade procedures for the system. However, it does not tell the static structure of the code to be developed. This design information is provided by the development view.

Development View

The *development view* shows the partitioning of the system into components, which we discussed in the section on "Subsystems." The run-time view shows some of the components; that is, those components that are executable. The rest of the components are those entities such as link libraries that need to be developed to create the executable components.

We present the development view using the component diagrams of UML. Because you are trying to create the executables, we recommend you organize the development view according to the executables found from the run-time view. Of course, you can combine the development views of more than one executable together if they are simple enough. The point is, if you are not able to view all processes and the link libraries used by them in one picture, you can break it into parts. Packages of UML provide a clear way of showing this sort of grouping.

We suggest you organize the development view into layers. An executable component resides on top, naturally, because no component in the development view depends on it. An executable component typically uses a number of library components that are specific to the process being built. These components may use external library components, which should be either reusable platform components or components required when integrating the process with some other process.

Figure 3-18 illustrates the development view for the user interface of *SW Archives*. The configuration items that comprise the SW Archives process are shown as components that have dependencies to other components. The main program of SW Archives—in this case, the user interface—resides on top of the package. The rest of the code related to SW Archives is allocated into four libraries inside the package boundary: *DAT Handling*, *SW CM User Interface*, *SW CM Database*, and *SW CM Configuration File* libraries.

The external libraries used are presented as components outside the boundary of SW Archives. As an example, the user interface process SW Archives uses the printing services of a *printing library* (PRNLIB). This use of service should be interpreted as a compilation dependency, and it is shown using dashed arrow in the development view.

The arrows point at interfaces of the components. Interfaces are classes or other definitions of services provided by the components. We recommend you define interfaces for each component regardless of tools you use. If you are able to define clear interfaces for components, the components actually depend on the interfaces of other components, not on their implementation. This enables concurrent development of components.

We use the same stereotypes «*UI process*» and «*BG process*» used in the run-time view for the processes also in the development view. A vast majority of components in the development view are libraries as a rule. We recommend you use a stereotype such as «*library*» for classifying these components as libraries.

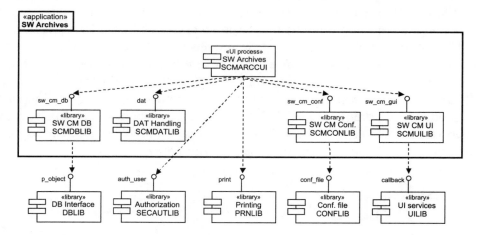

FIGURE 3-18. Development view for the user interface of SW archives.

Development view organized in layers provides useful information about the source code architecture of the system. Figure 3-18 provides an example of carefully designed, clear component structure with no cyclic dependencies. From the maintenance and evolution points of view, the process SW Archives looks good as far as its development view is concerned. If the design were poorly carried out and full of unwanted dependencies, a messy development view would have revealed these flaws in the design easily.

Looking at the used external libraries provides interesting information. A design walk-through may reveal that an external component never intended for reuse, was used. Or, a suitable framework might exist but be not used for some reason. This sort of reasoning can be made when a development view to architecture is available. Although you can provide similar kind of information in free text and partially also in makefiles, the graphical presentation has proven to be a lot more user friendly when design teams discuss and reason about the architecture.

Scenario View

Use of design scenarios expressed using the sequence diagrams of UML comprises one of our corner stones for application design. Design scenarios play an important role also in large-scale architectural design. They can be used in the same way they are used in application development, but the collaborators are different. Whereas the collaborators are normally objects in detailed design scenarios, they are components and larger subsystems in architectural design.

The rationale for using scenarios in architectural design is to illustrate how the most important use cases or operations are implemented by the architecture. A use case may involve several processes. A scenario view for a large software subsystem contains mainly executable components as participants in the sequence diagram. Figure 3-19 presents a sequence diagram for the design of one use case of Base Station Software Manager: *Downloading a base station SW package from NMS into network*.

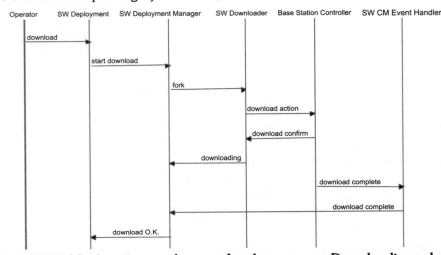

FIGURE 3-19. A sequence diagram for the use case Downloading a base station SW package from NMS into network.

It is worth noting that not all use cases are interesting from the point of view of the architecture. The interesting ones are those that touch most of the critical or new subsystems, generate a lot of database transactions or other loading, or otherwise explore the risky elements of the system. Our recommendation is that you make a design scenario for all those use cases.

Although documented scenarios provide a useful insight into the design rationale of the whole system, they are even more useful for drafting, communicating, and validating the design. You should prepare scenarios at the same time as you prepare the run-time and development views to identify the interfaces and responsibilities of subsystems. Whereas the run-time view and the development view illustrate the structure of the system, the scenarios provide a means to illustrate collaboration of the subsystems.

Like the logical view, the scenarios are open-ended. The approach depicted fits well for constructing systems and applications with more than one communicating processes. However, if you need to model collaboration of systems or systems of inter-working systems, you simply change the participants of the sequence diagram from processes to systems, or whatever object you choose. And, if you wish to illustrate the roles of library components in implementing a use case or an operation, you can put libraries and other components as participants in a sequence diagram in addition to executable components.

The 3 + 1 views to architecture provides you with the visibility required to manage even large architectures. Logical view illustrates the structure and content of the whole system in terms of products and applications. You can use it to view product configurations, such as the decomposition of application products into applications. The run-time view shows the run-time elements of the system, their dependencies, and their allocation to the available hardware. And, the development view gives you visibility over the components and their dependencies that constitute the software configuration to be developed and managed.

When you evolve a large, evolutionary system for years as consecutive releases, you need to take good care of the conceptual integrity of the system. This means the customers and designers should perceive the system as an integrated, consistent, whole. This is to say that you should manage both the internal architecture perceived by a designer as well as the external architecture perceived by an end user so that both can obtain a concise understanding about the structure and organization of an inherently complex system. The 3 + 1 framework for viewing complex systems is designed to help you to meet this goal. How it is applied in the development process is discussed next when we look closer at the process issues.

Evolutionary System Development Process

An *incremental process* is one that develops the functionality of the system piece by piece so that first the core functionality is developed and then later the rest on top of that. An *iterative process*, in turn, is one that accepts that you cannot make complete specifications when uncertainties exist; you may need to iterate requirements, design, and virtually any phase of development to get the job done.

An iterative and incremental process helps manage risks. The risks increase with the project size, and so does the probability of project failure in terms of cost, schedule, and software quality. Using an incremental approach, you can make sure you are able to deliver at least the core functionality and avoid complete project disasters. Iterating, in turn, enables you to make required adjustments to project, process, architecture, and delivery content when you learn that some of the original plans are no longer valid. Incremental development combined with iterative process can help thus in developing the best possible solutions to customers given that available time and resources are limited.

Evolutionary systems are developed incrementally by definition. Each new release introduces an increment, actually an outstanding one, on top of the existing functionality as the system evolves. Successfully developing a large system with a product life span of several years is largely determined by an organization's capability to select the content for these system increments and enable effective reuse of the legacy system assets. Finding the most valuable content for the releases requires means for identifying product ideas and studying their feasibility. Effective reuse of the existing system calls for strong system architecture. You need to apply a design practice that enforces common design patterns and provides blueprints that make the architecture visible.

In the previous sections, we set the stage for our recommended development process by describing the principles for identifying subsystems, and by illustrating 3 + 1 views for representing the architecture using this levelized subsystem structure. In the following sections, we complete the discussion of practices for large-scale development by providing process guidelines for large and evolutionary systems.

Product Line Development

By *product line development* we mean the macro process that covers both the development of deliverable products and the application platform. Figure 3-20 shows the three key processes of product line development: Product Planning, Platform Development, and System Product Development.

Product Planning is a continuous process of scanning for new product ideas and elaborating them into features allocated to platform and product releases. The role of Product Planning process is to ensure that the R & D investments are focused on right things.

System Product Development and *Platform Development* processes are executed concurrently, and translate the features selected by the Product Planning process into new system product and application platform releases. The releases are synchronized so the application platform release that provides reusable assets for system product development is available early enough for application designers. The release cycle time for the application platform should be longer than it is for deliverable products. That is, there may be several releases of system products and application products on top of a single application platform release.

In the following sections, we look inside these three core processes of product line development.

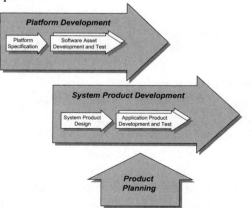

FIGURE 3-20. Core processes of product line development.

Product Planning

The most important factor affecting the productivity of any product development effort is the capability to select the right product features for the development pipeline. Even if you were able to develop, say, 100,000 lines of code in a week, your productivity would still be zero if you selected useless features out of the known product ideas. Therefore, it is of paramount importance to provide enough focus and resources for evaluating the product ideas and for selecting the best ideas for elaboration, because this may eliminate several years of wasted effort later. This important mission is part of *Product Planning*, which encapsulates all activities relating to understanding customer needs and translating these needs into product specifications. The target of Product Planning is to select features for product development so that the products provide a competitive advantage over competing products. Effective Product Planning enables you are able to focus often scarce resources on areas where they best contribute to success of your organization.

Product Planning takes place at many levels in large-scale development. At product line level it is about product portfolio management, that is, about making strategic decisions about the scope of business and the products to be developed for the product line. Product Planning at system Product level is concerned with competitiveness and the conceptual integrity of a system product as a whole. It focuses on identifying feasible product structure for the target market segment in terms of application products so that the whole system provides nicely integrated solutions to its users. At application product level, in turn, Product Planning is more concerned with the functionality of one application product and on finding valuable features for this product. Finally, the lowest level of Product Planning is classic requirements management, which is about eliciting, analyzing, and representing the requirements for a given piece of software using requirements analysis techniques.

You should think of Product Planning as a continuous process on all levels, because the development cycles of large systems are so long that you cannot foresee all requirements at the outset. When you have delivered first releases to the field, you receive feedback continuously if you organize your processes to collect it. You will recognize important product ideas once committing to a feature list during a large development project. These emerging product ideas are often so attractive that you need to iterate project plans and the release content to try to add some of the new features to an ongoing project. However, you cannot change plans purely on the basis of a gut feeling; you need some means for evaluating the product ideas, screening the less important ones, and deciding on the implementation of the most valuable ones.

We propose you organize the Product Planning process as a sort of sieve that searches for the most valuable nuggets by quickly screening the less valuable product ideas. This process is illustrated in Figure 3-21. To prioritize the true candidates for new features or products, you need to evaluate them carefully. After the evaluation, the best product ideas are fed to development projects.

We call the practice of evaluating a product idea as *feasibility study*. On the basis of feasibility studies, you perform a final screening of feature candidates and allocate the best features to upcoming or ongoing projects. We discuss the feasibility study practice that suits for evolutionary systems in the section "Feasibility Study."

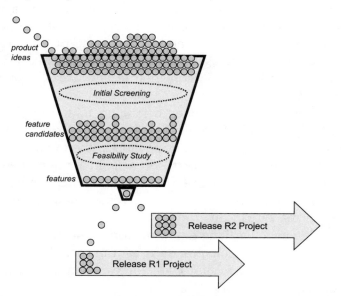

FIGURE 3-21. Product Planning is a continuous process that feeds the voice of the customer to product development.

Platform Development

The *Platform Development* process yields new, reusable software assets to System Product Development. An application platform release provides a collection of reusable components grouped into service blocks, design guide-lines, and policies for using them. The Platform Specification phase, shown in Figure 3-20, provides the *application platform architecture*[13] that specifies these software assets. In addition to specifying the reusable components, the platform architecture sets the rules for the development of application prod-ucts belonging to the product line. These constraints are needed to keep the whole product line that builds on platform consistent.

You need to test the developed software assets carefully. As the platform code is highly reusable, the reliability requirements for it need to be even higher than for ordinary applications. A severe bug in a frequently used plat-form component will show several times in the applications using it.

Although you often need to have relatively short release cycle for cus-tomer products to achieve short time-to-market, there is no such pressure for the application platform releases. On the contrary, the application platform should remain mostly stable but grow gradually, because most changes in the application platform require extra effort from some of the application devel-opers. A change in a widely used component can potentially break all appli-cations using it, so at lest some regression testing needs to be done to verify that the change was safe.

Like any components, the ones belonging to the application platform should be loosely coupled. If you are able to organize the application plat-forms into relatively independent service blocks, then you can introduce new platform services incrementally only for a limited set of new applications, while the other applications are built on previous application platform releases. This makes it easier for you to introduce new technologies fast and in a flexible, yet managed way.

The main drivers for making a new release of the application platform are developments in core technologies, such as a major release of the used data management system. The release cycle for platform development should be mainly driven by these factors.

System Product Development

System Product Development builds releases of system products, which are tested configurations of application products. Depending on the characteristics of the system you are developing, you may release only system products or also application products and even features[14] of application products separately.

Often the mode of operation used by organizations developing large systems is a combination of these alternatives.

If you have a mass product with hundreds or even thousands of customers, you surely aim at releasing your products bundled in relatively large units, such as the system products, if the competition allows. You need to try to optimize the variation and the number of new releases, especially if the system is difficult to upgrade or the delivery costs are otherwise high.

If the time-to-market is critical, you should aim at such a plug-and-play architecture that enables you to deliver features as stand-alone system increments. However, there often are dependencies between the features, and even pressures to also upgrade the application platform when introducing a new feature. In such cases, making the application products deliverable is often the best alternative. Therefore, we have tuned the System Product Development process so that it supports you to release application products in particular.

An application product release consists of a set of closely related customer features that provides valuable solutions to users' requirements. As we discussed, each application product should be such that it can be installed separately as far as the common parts of the product line have been installed. In addition to software, an application product release typically consists of customer documentation, installation instructions, and application product specific hardware, if such is needed.

When you are releasing parts of the system at different times as application products, you win in cycle time but you risk loosing in system integrity. Customers want integrated "wholes" that support their processes in a cost-effective way. If you forget this and ignore coordination among application products, you may provide customers with costly and unsatisfactory solutions.

For instance, you may deliver several racks of unnecessary computers if you provide dedicated hardware for all application products even if they can be run in same servers. You might also deliver applications that do not support natural workflows. Consider a case in which the user needs to use two applications belonging to two different application products to perform a frequent use case. These two logically related applications might run on different hardware platforms and operating systems. This would be annoying, even expensive, if the user needs to spend time changing from one workstation to another to get the job done. You need to coordinate product decisions as well as the architecture to avoid this kind of design. We look at the means to achieve conceptual integrity at architecture level in the section "Caring for the Architecture."

You can consider the System Product Development process a program that results in several coordinated releases of application products. System Product Development starts with system design, which creates the *system product architecture*[15] for the release under development. When the platform and system product architectures have set the rules for the road, each application product can be developed in their own projects concurrently.

You need to verify the compatibility of each released application product against the other configurations of application products in the field. If you have a large product line, then you have to test several configurations. You can hardly release parts of the system separately if you do not know the dependencies among the items that you are releasing over time. That is why we dedicated so many pages to the discussion of architectural design.

Now that we have shown the big picture, that is, the key processes of product line development, let's have a closer look at a couple key practices that contribute to successful evolution of large software intensive systems. We start by discussing one of the most important topics of Product Planning: the means to evaluate and select new features to a system. Then we will look at architecture-centric feature development practices that take into account the legacy system but focus on the new or changed functionality, the *delta*.

The Right Things

In the following we will have a look at the feasibility study practice that evaluates feature candidates. Then we discuss the actual decision process that decides of features.

Feasibility Study

We presented a technical feasibility study practice for application development in Chapter 1. That suits well for studying the feasibility of a new small- to medium-sized software product or customized software system. In the case of a customer project, such a feasibility study provides a good foundation for both the vendor and customer to prepare a contract on the basis of realistic expectations for the functionality to be delivered, the time schedule, the effort, the technical solutions, and the risks. A technical feasibility study enables you and your customer to understand whether it is feasible to start a software project. It also helps to balance the ambition level according to time, money, and resource constraints.

When you are developing an evolutionary system, the circumstances differ a bit from green field development regarding the role of feasibility study. If you succeed in creating a system that has a large customer base and long life span, you will receive more feasible product ideas than you can implement. It is not just about making the GO/NOGO decision for one proposal.

When you make product decisions for an evolutionary system, you need to find out what product ideas are the most valuable out of all feasible ideas recognized. That is, you need to supplement the technical feasibility study with *business perspective* to provide adequate information for prioritizing the product ideas and allocating development effort accordingly.

An extended feasibility study suitable for evolutionary system development evaluates the following five things:

- Value of a product idea
- Technical feasibility
- Costs
- Time-to-market
- Risks

The conclusions of a feasibility study provide a good rationale for evaluating how reasonable it is to make a positive investment decision to allocate resources for the development and support of a studied feature candidate. We call the statements evaluating the value of a product idea as the *business case*. The value of the product idea takes into account the value from both the customer's and the supplier's points of view. In most cases, a feature that is particularly valuable for a customer is valuable for the supplier as well. The added value provided to customers typically shows in the reduction of some operations costs or differentiation in quality of products or services as perceived by the customer's customers. You can estimate the value of the feature to your organization in terms of expected revenue, impact to market share, increase of customer satisfaction, or reduction of maintenance and further development costs. Quantitative value estimation can be difficult, but even a qualitative impact estimation using the scale of low, medium, or high is better than not explicitly considering the value at all.

Understanding a product's value requires understanding what the product idea is all about. In practice, this calls for an initial requirements analysis and specification. The very same practices we use in technical feasibility study apply for this purpose. For instance, the use cases provide excellent tools for identifying the value of a solution to a user. They reify the expected context of use for a piece of software, and provide practical means for communicating the expectations for the feature candidate to customers and to the development team.

Use cases also help to evaluate the *added value* of a planned feature. You can express the current situation as a baseline by mapping the relevant user activities and task sequences as use cases without the software support to be developed. If you then create corresponding versions of the use cases that demonstrate the use of the planned new feature, you can evaluate the benefits of the feature even quantitatively. This information is invaluable in marketing argumentation and finally in pricing.

You need to carry out requirements analysis to the level of detail that allows the feasibility study team to understand the key requirements and represent the main solution alternatives for these requirements. In complex cases, or when you are studying a new domain, this may call for a thorough requirements analysis with requirements statements, analysis class diagrams for key concepts, and so on in addition to use cases.

The scope of a feasibility study depends a lot on the novelty and complexity of the product idea being evaluated. For simple and understandable enhancements to an existing system, you need not do any formal feasibility studies; whereas a large new product idea may require even months of domain analysis and prototyping. An extreme case of this would be a feasibility study for a completely new product which would require some market research and careful preparation of business plans in addition to other feasibility study work.

Be it a large feature or a small one, there are normally a few reasonable alternatives to specifying the functionality in terms of scope, used technology, level of usability, and so on. You need to make the relevant two or three main alternatives explicit by illustrating their pros and cons and differences as we described for the technical feasibility study. Finally, you should draw conclusions providing a recommendation for the preferred alternative and the reasoning used in making the recommendation. However, you cannot make this recommendation only on the basis of expected high customer value. An alternative that would provide the highest customer value may require such a long time-to-market due to high development effort that the feature would be obsolete when finally ready for delivery. Therefore, you need to consider the alternatives for implementing the most promising specifications for the functionality of a feature. When you know the main implementation options, you can derive effort, cost, and schedule estimates for all of them. You can then iterate requirements, design, resources, and schedule when you finally see the implementation scenarios for the preferred specification of functionality and understand their schedule and budget implications.

The cost distribution of feature implementation is largely determined by the amount of development and testing effort in large software intensive systems. However, you need to consider whether the feature requires some special hardware or upgrade of existing hardware, such as more memory or disk space. If you have delivered hundreds of systems and you are responsible also for maintaining the hardware of these systems, then the cost of hardware upgrade may be even far higher than the software development cost. On the other hand, sometimes you can save some development effort by upgrading the run-time environment with more powerful equipment. Such trade-off considerations are important to the feasibility study process when you consider solution candidates and their implications to costs and overall customer satisfaction.

To estimate the effort required to implement and test a feature candidate, you need to carry out the rest of the technical feasibility study; that is, you must create first an initial design for the implementation addressing the components to be used and other main design decisions. The guidelines we gave for the technical feasibility study in Chapter 1 also apply for feature development.

When you have prepared the solution alternatives and selected the most attractive one, make a rough estimate about the required effort by preparing initial project planning for the feature. You need this estimate for considering the cost and schedule of the feature.

When you know what effort is required and what resources are available, you can allocate the feature to one of the next releases to come depending on the calendar time required. This gives you the time-to-market estimate. Then you need to make the GO or NOGO decision. The NOGO decision often seems to be harder for a manager having some engineer background to make than the GO decision. However, the whole idea of evaluating the feature candidates is to better understand on which identified needs you should focus the resources. You should be prepared for completely rejecting an idea that may have sounded great originally if the facts tell that there are even better product ideas around.

You should perform a *risk assessment* before you document your final conclusions of a feasibility study. Typical risks involved in large-scale feature development include the dependencies to other parts of the system, the availability of resources, and the volatility of requirements. Making the risks visible helps in making conscious feature decisions and in planning the preventing actions early enough. For the purposes of a feasibility study, it is often enough to understand the risk levels using a qualitative scale of low, medium, and high for each risk category. When you see, for instance, that there are high risk levels in some otherwise reasonable feature candidate, you may ask for further information about the risks and sometimes even find it feasible to reject the feature due to too high risks.

When you have completed the feasibility study, you have a compact package of information that provides a good foundation for making rational decisions about the features to be developed or rejected. The table of contents for a feasibility study is shown in Figure 3-22. Business case describes the business value of the product idea from the customer's and your organization's point of view. Marketing function should carry primary responsibility for providing the contents for the business case section.

| **1.** Introduction |
| **2.** Business case |
| **3.** Technical feasibility study |
| **4.** Costs |
| **5.** Risks |
| **6.** Conclusions |

FIGURE 3-22. Table of contents for a feasibility study.

We described the contents for a technical feasibility study in Chapter 1. In Figure 3-22, *Costs* translates the effort estimates of the technical feasibility study into money and specifies estimates for other relevant cost elements such as required hardware upgrades, investments in the development or test environment, and costs for possibly required special training or customer support. *Risks* specifies the identified risks, their severity and probability, and initial plans for preventing the risks. *Conclusions* summarizes the results of the feasibility study and makes proposals for allocating the studied feature candidate into some project or rejecting it. In the case of a GO proposal, the conclusions also proposes the scope of the feature and the design approach.

Preparing a simple feasibility study may take a day or two, but a more complicated one may require a couple months. The payback time for this investment is short. When you *reject* one product idea that originally looked attractive, you save the otherwise wasted time and money that would have been required to develop and support that "wrong" feature. In addition, the feasibility study effort for the features that are later accepted for development is not either wasted, because the results of that work can be reused as such in requirements specification, design, and project planning.

Making the Product Decisions

A feasibility study examines the feasibility of one product idea at a time. Even if the feasibility study team considered the product idea worth implementing, there may be even more valuable product ideas around. Prioritization is tough, especially when you have to decide between short-term and long-term investments, such as whether you should allocate some man-years for developing a useful customer feature now or develop software assets that will improve overall productivity significantly next year.

The starting point for effective product decision practice is to create a clear product strategy that guides the decisions. If you have a common agreement on product strategy, you can define the responsibilities for and the rights to make decisions according to product structure. We prefer empowering the product teams and facilitating the interproduct team communication over slow, hierarchic decision making, but the way to organize responsibilities depends a lot on the organization and its management style. However, you need to define the responsibilities clearly and most likely you need to establish some Product Decision Board to which cross product issues can be escalated.

All feature decisions should be based on feasibility studies. Sophisticated market research methods—conjoint analysis or calculus methods such as Quality Function Deployment, QFD, or its simple versions—can be used to support decision making work. However, no matrix or any other method can give you the right answers if you are asking the wrong questions. It is perhaps then even more important to allocate highly qualified people to Product Planning work and allow them to grow to top experts in the application domain and line of business of your customers. When it comes to decision making, the methods do not make decisions; people do.

Caring for the Architecture

A high quality architecture can provide a competitive advantage by enabling rapid application development and low maintenance costs. Unfortunately, the architecture deteriorates unless you take good care of it when you evolve a system for many years. It is like with old buildings: if you try to extend and restore an old, precious building without respecting its architecture, in the end you loose the designed architecture.

Given the fact that architecture is a significant success factor in large-scale development, you need to tune the development process so that it addresses caring for the architecture. This is best done by embedding a dedicated architectural design step into all design phases and resourcing the architectural design process.

Architects

Each major design object should have an architect responsible for it. It is often feasible to nominate even full-time architects to care for the architecture of large design composites, such as the application products. Architects design the architecture for the subsystems for which they are responsible. Thus, architects play a key role in keeping the whole product line architecture in good shape. When you have a team of architects responsible for application products, it is a lot easier for you to develop and deploy common design policies, share experiences, and implement major reengineering of architecture when necessary.

Creating an initial architecture is only one job of an architect. A professional architect should also act as a consultant who continuously guides software designers in using the architecture, who audits design work products for their conformance to architecture, and who assesses the design practice. Architects also allocate enough time for exploring new technology opportunities and threats and consider whether breakthrough improvements are required.

Making the Architecture Visible

Architects need to make something as abstract as software architecture visible, because it is hard to improve anything that you cannot see. Therefore, architects need to prepare *architecture blueprints* to manage the evolution of system architecture. Architecture blueprints need to give valuable information that is neither redundant nor self-evident. For instance, if you can generate some information from the system online using reverse engineering tools, there is no point in copying that information to a separate document. All information to be documented needs to have a clear purpose and audience to ensure that it is worth writing down.

Often the only blueprint you find is the lazily commented code. Sometimes you find descriptions about the architecture, but they are just filed and not used because they are out-of-date or otherwise useless. We prefer modular and thin specifications that have as little information as possible organized so that design decisions are documented only once, and at feasible level of abstraction. Organizing the architecture documents according to design levels in a modular fashion helps in maintaining the blueprints when design changes take place. Focusing on the particular architectural aspects of subsystems at each design level helps in separating the design concerns of each level. We recommend the following classes of architecture blueprints for large-scale systems:

- Platform architecture
- System product architecture
- Application product architecture
- Application architecture

These deliverables are created and updated as a part of Platform and System Product Development Processes and their subprocesses as illustrated in Figure 3-23.

Platform architecture is a description of reusable core software assets that can and should be used in the development of new products for the product line. It specifies the common things, such as the supported hardware, the operating systems, and the middleware for all products that are built on top of the application platform. The platform architecture blueprint plays an important role in keeping the applications belonging to the product line consistent.

System product architecture defines the system breakdown into application products and the run-time configuration for the system product such as GSM Manager that we use as a case study. In this system product architecture, the integrated set of application products that comprise a system product constitutes a whole that looks like one system from the customer's point of view. Whereas the platform architecture specifies the allowed technologies to be used in software development, the system product architecture sets constraints for the design by specifying the run-time environment. You can combine the platform architecture and system product architecture into one single architecture blueprint if you have only one system product and not yet a true product line.

Application product architecture breaks an application product into subsystems that are either applications or service blocks. It also specifies the architectural solutions that are required to make an application product an installable composite.

Application architecture focuses on breaking down an application into components and identifying their interfaces. It is prepared as we described in Chapter 1 of this book when we discussed architectural design of interactive applications.

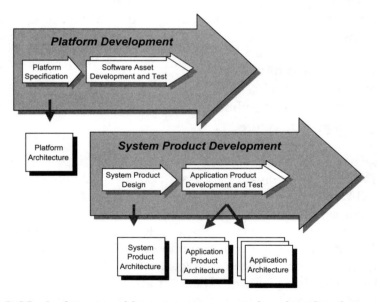

FIGURE 3-23. Architecture blueprints are created and updated as part of product line development processes.

Detailed design of a component results in a component architecture dealing with classes and their collaboration. However, we do not require that these blueprints of detailed design also be kept up to date. Because they contain detailed design information which often changes during programming, they are subject to frequent changes.

As long as the components are as small as we proposed, it is enough to make the original detailed design documents presenting the component architecture accessible by using a software configuration management system. The original design documents provide you with key design decisions, such as the use of MVC++ as the architectural style. If you need to look at the details, you need to go to code level anyway. Today you can find helpful browsers and other reverse engineering tools for most programming languages to support this task.

Applying the 3 + 1 Views

We use the 3 + 1 views discussed in section *"3 + 1 Views to Architecture"* as the main means to illustrate architecture. Figure 3-24 summarizes the use of these views in each architecture blueprint. Note that even if the same views are applied, the design concerns are different in each blueprint.

	Logical View	Run-time View	Development View	Scenario View
Platform Architecture	✓		(✓)	
System Product Architecture	✓	✓		
Application Product Architecture	✓	✓		(✓)
Application Architecture		✓	✓	✓

FIGURE 3-24. Use of the 3 + 1 views in architecture blueprints.

We use the *logical view* for presenting the groupings of subsystems. In the platform architecture, it shows the grouping of components into service blocks, and service blocks to layers as shown in Figure 3-26. The system product architecture makes use of the logical view when presenting the configuration of application products that belong to the system product, as we showed in Figure 3-14. Application product architecture, in turn, uses the logical view for presenting the applications and service blocks that constitute an application product as illustrated in Figure 3-15.

We use the *run-time view* in all blueprints except the platform architecture. To make it possible to also deliver application products and even applications independently, you need to specify the run-time environment for all these. The system product architecture specifies the run-time environment in terms of supported hardware configurations using just free text or simple deployment diagrams as illustrated in Figure 3-28. The application product architecture presents the run-time environment of an application product. You do not need this model if you do not plan to release an application product independently. And, finally, the run-time view for an application presents the allocation of executable components to computers as we showed in Figure 3-17.

The *development view* is relevant to application architecture in that it presents the components that need to be developed and managed to create an executable component. Figure 3-18 shows an example of this. You may also find it useful to apply the component diagrams for presenting the components inside the service blocks of an application platform.

Also the *scenario view* is most useful in application architecture. Figure 3-19 shows an example of the sequence diagram for the Base Station Software Manager application. However, you may find it sometimes useful to present the collaboration of other subsystems, especially of the applications, with the sequence diagrams as well. Then you would use the scenario view in application product architecture.

In the following sections we look closer at the actual architecture blueprints. We use the terms *run-time architecture* and *development architecture* in the document headings of blueprints when we refer to respective views to architecture.

Platform Architecture

The table of contents for a Platform Architecture blueprint is shown in Figure 3-25. It specifies the application platform for network management systems such as *GSM Manager*.

The first sections specify the supported run-time environments in terms of computer equipment, operating systems and middleware. All applications to be built on top of this application platform need to take these specifications into account.

1. Overview
2. Hardware
3. Operating systems
4. Middleware
5. Platform services
    5.1. General services
    5.2. Domain services
6. Application design constraints

FIGURE 3-25. Table of contents for a platform architecture.

The platform services constitute an essential part of the Platform Architecture. They are the ones that help but also restrict in making the design decisions. It is practical to organize an application platform into layers and service blocks, and view its architecture accordingly. Figure 3-26 provides an example of this.

The *general services* include components, tools and other software assets such as reusable data structures and exception handling classes, GUI components and frameworks, a database engine and its wrappers, and services for implementing inter-process communication and object distribution. The top layer of the application platform consists of domain specific service blocks, which in this case would relate to network management. They would contain reusable software assets that enable rapid development of network management applications that need to manipulate network data, communicate with managed network elements, or carry out system management operations such as checking the authorities of the operator using the system.

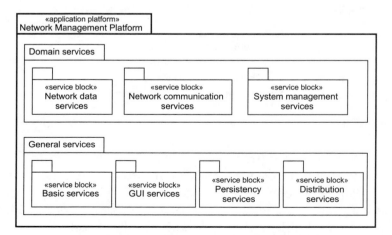

FIGURE 3-26. Platform architecture layers.

Application design constraints set the rules for the road for application developers that build products on top of the application platform. The purpose of this section is to ensure that all applications you build on top of the application platform comply with the product line requirements for applications. That is, all relevant applications are technically compatible and provide conceptually consistent view to the user. An example of such a constraint could be: "*All applications shall provide online help functionality using the HTML help component HTMLHelp.*" Usually the application design constraints address also the design strategies for implementing object persistency and distribution.

Platform Architecture, in particular, is a document that can be made much easier to read and maintain if it is maintained as Web pages. Then you can organize it so that each service can have a standard home page. You can apply this same principle to all blueprints we recommend for the architecture, because they are structured in a modular way.

If you do not truly have an application platform but only an operating system and some libraries to be used, you do not need this blueprint. You can then embed that information to the system product architecture.

System Product Architecture

The table of contents for the System Product Architecture blueprint is shown in Figure 3-27. *Product architecture* specifies the product structure of one system product in terms of a configuration of application products.

| **1.** Overview |
| **2.** Product architecture |
| **3.** Run-time architecture |

FIGURE 3-27. Table of contents for System Product Architecture.

Whereas the Platform Architecture specifies the supported hardware, operating systems and middleware, the System Product Architecture specifies the exact run-time environment for a system product. *Run-time architecture* defines the hardware parameters such as the computer models, CPU speeds, required memory and disk space, or bandwidth of network connections. You need to know these in order estimate hardware costs and explain them to customers, but also to set some limits on the use of resources in software development.

Figure 3-28 shows example of a hardware configuration for the GSM Network Manager. This simple run-time view, with only nodes and their dependencies, provides a quick overview of the possible hardware configurations. You need to supplement the diagram with detailed information of hardware attributes, but often this information is best described in written text.

If you have a product line of several closely related system product variants, you can describe the architecture of all these products in a single architecture blueprint. If there are major differences, then it is more practical to make a blueprint for each system product separately.

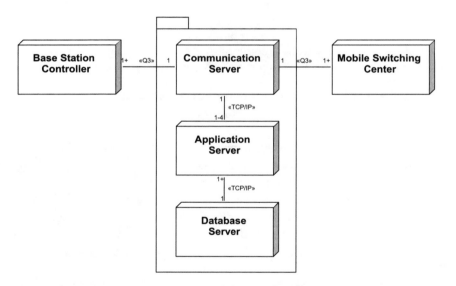

FIGURE 3-28. Hardware configuration of GSM Network Manager as described in System Product Architecture.

It is worth noting that architecting a system product differs considerably from architecting an application product and architecting an application. Breaking a system up into application products calls for good business understanding to make the breakdown so that it results in meaningful, deliverable products. It also requires an understanding of technical dependencies and of the development process to break the system down so that the cycle time goals of organization are met. In turn, specification of the run-time environment requires proper understanding of business realities, such as what hardware configurations exist in the field, what pricing and image implications might the technology selections have, and so on.

Application Product Architecture

The purpose of the Application Product Architecture is to describe the subsystems and design solutions used for constructing an application product. The table of contents for the application product architecture is depicted in Figure 3-29.

1. Overview
2. Applications
3. Service blocks
4. Run-time architecture
5. Data architecture
6. Application design constraints

FIGURE 3-29. Table of contents for an application product architecture blueprint.

Application Product Architecture breaks the application product first into *applications* as seen by the user. In the case of a large product, you may wish to group some related applications into logical subsystems.

Application products sometimes contain components and frameworks that are not part of common application platform but are specific to the application product only. It is useful for an application developer to be aware of these, so the section on *Service blocks* is there in the Application Product Architecture.

The section "Run-time Architecture" describes the run-time environment needed for running the applications of the application product. You define it in the same way you define the run-time architecture for system products using the run-time view. You do not need this section at all in the Application Product Architecture if you do not intend to release application products separately. In addition, if your application products are so loosely coupled that you release them always only as independent products, then you need to specify the run-time architecture for application products but not necessarily for the system product.

Data architecture describes the common data storages of the application product. It lists the data files and databases shared by more than one application and describes their purposes, structures, locations, and access methods.

We have included a section for *Application design constraints* also in the Application Product Architecture. It specifies the application product specific general design decisions that need to be taken into account in the design of applications for the application product in question. It does not copy the design constraints stated by the Platform Architecture but supplements them.

Application Architecture

Application Architecture is designed using the practices of architectural design presented in Chapter 1. Application Architecture describes the architecture for an application or for a group of closely related applications. It focuses on breaking up an application into components and identifying the components' interfaces. Design of the application architecture is guided by the application design constraints stated in the blueprints of platform and application product architecture. Table of contents for an application architecture blueprint is shown in Figure 3-30.

> **1.** Overview
> **2.** Run-time architecture
> **3.** Development architecture
> **4.** Scenarios
> **5.** Data architecture

FIGURE 3-30. Table of contents for an Application Architecture blueprint.

The *run-time architecture* describes the allocation of executable components to available computational resources that come from the application product architecture. The development architecture presents the components needed to develop the executables. These components are the participants in *scenarios* in addition to actors such as users and other applications.

The *data architecture* describes the specific data storages used by the application. It is worth describing the data storages to the level of detail that helps in design and in planning for the installation and upgrade of an application. You can view the data storages also in the run-time view to illustrate how processes access the data.

The proposed blueprints fit well for managing and improving the architecture of large-scale systems, but of course they need to be adapted for each system according to their individual architectural characteristics. The number of different documents is quite high because of the modular structure of blueprints. However, the documents should not be too thick and writing each document should not take much time. The tricky part is not the writing or drawing the proposed diagrams, but making a clever architecture that stands the test of time as the system evolves.

Blueprint names, section headings, and the given grouping of contents need to be adapted for each case, but we believe the proposed substance provides a good foundation for evolution of advanced product lines. If the stable structures of architecture are adequately documented, you can streamline the detailed design process so it can focus on the increments of the system. This makes the design specifications thin and saves quite a bit of time and effort. In the following sections we examine such a feature development practice that utilizes the architecture blueprints we just described.

Developing Features

The development of an evolutionary system is characterized by the fact that you build the new release on top of a legacy system, which provides reuse opportunities but also restricts the space of possible design solutions. Therefore, the software development practice needs to focus on the system increment but it also must respect the software architecture and other assets of the legacy system. By focusing on the increment, we mean you should tune the development process and its artifacts so you can focus on developing the new functionality of the release without needing to rewrite the specification for the whole existing system. At the same time, you still need to have some system level descriptions that view the whole system from needed perspectives.

We have already described a set of architecture blueprints that provide visibility to system architecture. In addition to architecture, you need to manage at least the overall functionality and also the test cases for the whole system. It goes without saying that you need to know what functionality your system offers, and you need to have at least regression test cases for the whole functionality.

We use the concept of *feature* for representing a significant system increment. The word *feature* is generally used for describing software characteristics. In the following section, we explain what we exactly mean by features.

Feature

By *feature* we mean a system improvement that brings value to customer's operations or introduces software assets that improve the productivity of the development organization. Most features fall into this first category of *customer features*. They may be completely new applications or changes to existing ones. Such a feature should be so significant that you could demonstrate its value to a customer, attach a price tag to it, and consider it in general as a sales item that can be sold to a customer.

Let us return to our GSM Manager case study to reify the concept of feature. One of the application products of GSM Manager that we have explored a bit is *Configuration Management*. One feature of it, in turn, could be named *"Remote software installation to base station subsystem."* As even the name of the feature indicates, it seems to be a valuable support system that maps to several use cases that we presented in the section "Run-time View." In general, each customer feature should provide support for at least one use case. So, when we discuss features, we do not mean just any improvements to an existing system; we mean major functional improvements having a clear purpose and value.

The second category of features represents *internal features* that are not necessarily communicated to customers. Platform and architecture improvements fall into this category. For instance, if you change the graphics toolkit to a new one, you might spend several man-months porting the existing applications on top of it. Your customers would not necessarily recognize that change when they receive the first release using the new toolkit. However, customers should recognize such a system improvement in the long run, supposing that the better graphics toolkit enables faster development and better usability of applications.

A feature is a practical concept in project management. A new feature represents requirements for a valuable system change. You can describe the outcome of a development project with a list of new features. However, you should not forget the existing functionality, so the release feature list should contain existing features as well to show the complete release contents. For instance, you need the complete feature list when you prepare test plans and customer documentation.

Use case-driven application development has gained wide acceptance, because it helps in structuring the development activities according to value adding use cases. We strongly promote use cases in object oriented software development. However, a pure use case driven-approach has some drawbacks when you try to scale it up to large-scale development. First, use cases are too low level entities for *managing* large products and projects. More often than not, a use case is neither a sales item nor a deliverable product item. When the development effort is large enough, a use case is a too small unit for product decision and project management purposes. Second, not all research and development investments can be expressed as use cases. A feature that provides an architecture improvement, such as an object cache on top of a relational database, is an example of requirements that are not best described using use cases. There is, however, still a need to describe all planned system changes to make the release contents manageable. Therefore, we recommend the concept of feature for managing large-scale development projects and releases.

Feature Development Process

The software engineering process for one feature is illustrated in Figure 3-31. The Application Product Development and Test process illustrated in Figure 3-20 consists of this sort of feature development processes that run concurrently for all features of an application product. Although the process is described as a linear sequence, we strongly recommend using one of the incremental development approaches described in Chapter 1.

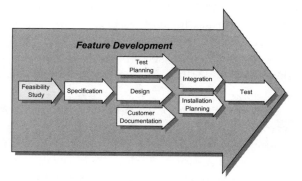

FIGURE 3-31. Software engineering process for feature development.

Feasibility study evaluates how feasible a feature is, as we discussed earlier. It results in an information package to be used in deciding whether to invest in developing and supporting a feature. The valuable by-products of a feasibility study for the software engineering process are the initial versions of specification sections such as requirement statements and use cases. It is practical to use compatible document templates in feasibility study and in feature specification and design documents to minimize unnecessary rework. This is best achieved by structuring the results of a feasibility study so you can attach these reusable document sections to the feasibility study as first versions of the feature documents.

If the feasibility study results show that it is feasible to invest in the feature, then the software engineering process for the feature continues with activities of specification, design, test planing, customer documentation, installation planning, integration, and testing. Let's have a closer look at these activities.

Feature Specification

The specification phase elaborates the analysis prepared in the feasibility study. Specification results in *feature specification*, the table of contents shown in Figure 3-32. It combines the analysis document and user interface specification, but you can prepare them as two separate documents as shown in Chapter 1. When you are making a feature that is an enhancement to some existing application, it is practical to specify only the new functionality in one feature specification.

---

1. Overview
2. Requirements
3. Use cases
4. Analysis class diagram
5. Operations
6. Operations with the user interface
7. Structure of the user interface
8. GUI operations

FIGURE 3-32. Table of contents for a feature specification.

Of course, not all sections are relevant to all features, and sometimes you need to add new sections, depending on the feature. Often the internal features that focus on developing architecture are especially unique, and it is close to impossible to define a generic document template that suits for all cases. Our standard templates for analysis documents suit best for developing new customer features. You need to modify this template for features that introduce new reusable software assets with sections that describe interfaces of components, purpose of patterns, changes in architecture, and so on.

Feature Design

The objective for the feature design is to find out the required changes to existing components and the needs to create new components to implement the feature. We call the result of design as the *feature design*. It documents both the architectural design as well as the detailed design solutions required to implement a feature. Its contents are shown in Figure 3-33.

```
1. Overview
2. Architectural design
    2.1. Run-time architecture
    2.2. Development architecture
    2.3. Scenarios
    2.4. Data architecture
3. Detailed design
    3.1. Component 1
    3.2. Component 2
```

FIGURE 3-33. Table of contents for a feature design document.

Detailed design is carried out for each major component to be developed following the practices we presented in Chapter 1. It is practical to make the detailed design sections as documents of their own for large features for which you need to create *several* new components.

Note that the feature design specifies the needed *changes* to the existing system. Therefore, it describes the changes to architecture, not the whole architecture, and the design scenarios for changed functionality, not for all use cases and operations. For instance, the run-time architecture describes only the computational resources and executable components needed for the feature under development. The development architecture, correspondingly, illustrates the relationships of components needed in developing the new functionality, and same goes for the data architecture.

When you are making a feature that is essentially a completely new application, you need to design the architecture for the whole application. Naturally, you would then create a maintainable blueprint of its own for the application architecture as we described in the section "Application Architecture." In such a case, the architectural design section of the feature design document would simply refer to that document.

When the feature design has been approved and changes implemented, architecture changes are updated to affected architecture blueprints. To make sure this really happens, you can make it an acceptance criterion for a feature to enter integration testing. You should also make the updating of architecture blueprints as easy as possible, by at least using compatible document templates. If you have advanced CASE tools, you can automate this information transfer from feature design to architecture blueprints largely if you follow our levelized design approaches.

It requires a lot of discipline to implement a software process that develops software for a large system so you focus on the increment but still maintain the conceptual integrity of the whole system. It is not only a question of specification and design. In the following sections, we look at some implications of evolutionary development to customer documentation, testing, and installation planning.

Customer Documentation

A set of customer documentation is an important result of software process. Sometimes a well-documented procedure of using several applications of a large system together can replace or at least postpone the need to develop a dedicated application for a use case. Development of customer documentation for evolutionary systems calls for similar modular solutions that we proposed for the software to manage the documentation as a whole but also to enable its incremental evolution.

Customer documentation can be harnessed to also serve as a functional description for the whole system. When you specify a system as features like we proposed, you do not have any functional specification for the whole system product, not even for its application products. We recommend you do not prepare any huge system specifications, but instead use customer documentation for the purpose of describing the whole system and its applications.

It depends a lot on the system and user characteristics which documents best meet customer expectations. In general, the following classes of customer documents seem to be useful for most large systems:

- Feature descriptions
- User's guides for applications
- Use case descriptions

You can prepare a *feature description* on the basis of feature specification. A feature description illustrates the concept, the purpose, and the use of a new customer feature. Feature descriptions are useful for a customers who want to familiarize themselves with new features of the system. They are also valuable for the development organization, because they describe functionality of developed features as a whole. Note that the customer features do evolve. A feature description provides an overview to the functionality of a customer feature with all its enhancements introduced so far by development projects. A feature description provides a good overview to a feature in case you need to enhance an existing feature further or prepare test cases for a feature.

User's guides for applications provide adequate functional descriptions for the functionality of existing applications. Like feature descriptions, they are also prepared using the feature specifications, and of course, by studying the developed application. A user guide is a document that describes the menus, the windows, and the other functions that an application performs. Whereas a feature description gives an overview to a feature that may address several applications, a user's guide describes the complete functionality of one application. More and more systems provide the user's guide in electronic form as a sort of extension to online help.

Use case descriptions are particularly valuable customer documents because they illustrate the most important ways to use the system. They rarely follow any use case template used by software designers for specifying the use cases, and they are often called as operating procedures, workflow descriptions, or something of that sort.

We have had very positive experiences preparing customer documentation that essentially describes the use cases. Although the use case descriptions are based on the use cases of feature specifications, they should not be restricted to application, feature, or even application product boundaries. Instead, they should describe the most important tasks the user of the system needs to carry out to achieve his objectives with a system. This documentation is particularly valuable for getting an integrated view to the functionality of the system as perceived by its users. This view is particularly necessary in system testing.

In addition to these user documents, you may need also several other kinds of manuals such as the ones that describe the installation and upgrade procedures and the administration of the system after installation. Requirements for these documents depend a lot on the mission criticality and complexity of the system. Information for these documents should come as a result from the development process. In the following section, we look at the integration and installation planning activities that play a major role in providing that information.

Integration

Integration is the step in which the results of feature development activities are integrated with each other and with the existing system. It is practical to organize the feature development environment so that each feature development activity can progress concurrently without disturbing the others. However, there are often dependencies between the components needed for implementing the features. The features often share some resources, such as the computational resources or a common database. Sometimes two or more features have explicit dependencies so that one cannot exist without another in place. Therefore, the features can be only partially tested until they are integrated with the rest of the system.

One widely used integration strategy is the so-called *big bang integration*. With this strategy, you develop the new features until you have most of the software to be integrated ready for the integration. Then you start testing the system as a whole to see if it works. You do not need to worry much about the architecture in that approach, but you will face some hard problems when trying to integrate the system. We claim that the big bang integration of large systems results in long cycle times, extensive and costly regression testing, and still lower confidence on the quality of delivered systems.

When you start integrating a large system, you find several integration faults inevitably. Usually, you find some serious faults that force you to stop testing until you have fixed them. Then you fix the faults you find and test the corrections. If you are lucky, the faults no longer appear, but you may have caused new bugs while fixing the found ones. So, you need to run regression tests before you continue testing new functionality. This makes the integration period long. After the last bug corrections, you cannot be sure whether they broke some other part of the system if you do not have good understanding of the side effect of the system.

We recommend an incremental, architecture-centric integration process in which you start integrating the features as early as possible.[16] If you have a well-documented architecture, you are able to analyze the dependencies between the software of features, and plan the order of integration accordingly. This approach is about scaling up the incremental development practices for applications discussed in Chapter 1 for large-scale development.

We propose a process in which the features are developed incrementally in cycles that each deliver a significant part of feature functionality to the integration process as depicted in Figure 3-34. The integration activity starts as soon as there is a feature increment that can be integrated. In Figure 3-34 there are four features: two of which are developed as three increments and two of which are developed in two increments. The integration process is designed so it integrates the four features in three phases in this case. The first integration integrates the results of first evolution cycles of features 1 and 2. Development of features 3 and 4 requires longer first cycles, so it continues until they enter the second integration of the integration process. That integration takes also the results from the second evolution cycle of features 1 and 2.

It is important to select the increments that enter integration so they both comprise meaningful sets of functionality from the features' point of view, and so they also constitute such architectural wholes that once you test them, you do not need to modify that part of the architecture much any more. That is to say that you should aim first at integrating such parts of applications that enable you to test the most important use cases, but are implemented by subsystems which are fairly ready.

Managing an incremental integration process, which is illustrated in Figure 3-34, may get too complicated if the system being integrated is very large. Embedded systems, for instance, often require a test laboratory that needs to be configured according to software to be tested. Therefore, it is often practical to define clusters of features that are integrated together. Such a cluster should comprise a meaningful, loosely coupled entity from the architectural point of view. The *application products* should be installable

groupings of features that constitute such entities. We recommend you organize the incremental integration process according to application products.

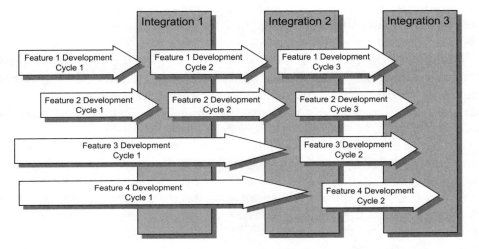

FIGURE 3-34. Evolutionary delivery applied to feature driven development.

This kind of approach enables early detection of integration defects, such
as incompatible interfaces or uncoordinated changes in database structure.
Even more important is the reduction in the amount of needed testing. When
you integrate the system piece by piece so that you start from the independent parts and proceed to those having most dependencies, you do not need
to run so many regression test cases. You can test one corner of the system
thoroughly and then consider it ready. Then you can integrate another chunk
of code and test it, and so on until the whole system is integrated. This is
often the most cost effective way to integrate a system, and this results in
shortest possible integration periods.

Planning this sort of order of integration requires you to have a thorough
understanding of the architecture of the evolved system, and to know well the
changes to be introduced by new features. It is possible to achieve this if you
allocate enough resources for planning the integration, and if you have visibility to the architecture and to the expected changes to it. The practices we
described earlier for caring for the architecture and for organizing the development process will give you a good foundation to implement this.

Installation Planning

Installation of a simple application is not an issue usually. However, installation of a large and evolutionary system is often such a complex process that you need to make installation planning an integral part of the software process.

Installation planning refers to the required preparations to make a piece of software installable. The results of this planning may include installation instructions but also scripts that automate the installation procedure. Note that there are two kinds of installations: the *first time installations* and the *upgrades* of existing systems. The former is easier, because you do not need to care about any legacy system. The latter requires often that you convert or replace some data, and add only changed parts. For mission critical systems any upgrade is a risky business, and you must prepare for it.

You can find the installation information by mining it from the code and developers, or you can produce it as a part of the design practice. We recommend the latter alternative. A typical installation procedure carries out many of the following tasks:

- Creating directories to hold program and data files of the system
- Copying files from the delivery media to the disks of the run-time environment
- Patching configuration files according to required system settings
- Configuring the database
- Carrying out possible data conversions
- Starting the required applications of the system

The design practice needs to be such that the specifications related to installation information are easily accessible. The proposed architecture blueprints and design documents of features support producing this information. If you have advanced CASE tools or a documentation environment that support structured documentation, you can pick up most of the the information relevant for preparing installation from the architecture blueprints.

We propose that you prepare an installation procedure for each feature so that the features can be installed on top of an existing system. The best form for such a procedure is a documented, executable installation script that automatically carries out all possible installation steps. The more installations there are, the more automated should the procedure be.

The installation procedure should be available before you start the final test of the feature. Otherwise, you cannot test the feature under the same circumstances as it will be in the field, when the system is installed using the installation procedure. Also this advocates the approach in which you prepare the installation instructions and the installation programs along with the actual software and its artifacts.

Testing

The focus and approach to testing should be different in different phases of testing. Low-level testing, that is, unit testing of components, should be architecture driven and aim at covering all accessible paths of execution. Functional testing that verifies the specified functionality should be based on feature specifications primarily, because the specifications cover detailed functional requirements. Product-level testing should be use case-driven to validate the products from user's point of view. Our recommendation for testing phases and their main inputs are shown in Figure 3-35.

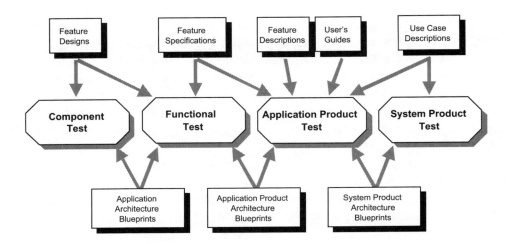

FIGURE 3-35. Test phases and their use of development artifacts for test planning.

We call unit testing *component testing* to describe the scope of this testing activity. It is practical to carry out component test planning and actual testing concurrently with component development to find programming and design bugs as early as possible. You should prepare component test cases and test drivers for each increment that you design, and manage them as carefully as the code using configuration management practices.

The black box test cases should be based on the requirements of the component, that is, its specified interfaces. The design scenarios and design class diagrams for components allow you to develop the glass box test cases on the basis of the implementation.

Functional testing is often combined with the integration, which we discussed in the section "Integration." The objective of functional testing is to verify that all specified functionality exists and works as specified. In functional testing you explore each feature and learn whether it meets its requirements. Obviously, the main inputs for testing a feature come from feature's specification and design. You should also use all relevant customer documents such as user's guides and feature descriptions in testing as early as possible. However, note that they are not specifications but developed results like the software, so you should also consider draft customer documents as objects of testing.

The architecture blueprints provide the required information to plan the order of integration. In addition, they specify design constraints, such as mandatory policies, to use certain components always for some particular purpose. You should also test these requirements to verify that tested software is compliant to requirements stated for the product line applications.

Product-level testing aims at revealing integrity defects at feature and product level. The emphasis on testing the functionality of a system should reside in functional testing to detect faults early enough. The role of product-level testing is more on verifying that core functionality still works when features are first integrated to application products and they in turn to system products.

Application product test checks an integrated application product as a whole to analyze whether the features of an application product constitute an integrated whole that meets customer expectations. In addition to testing the usability of features working together against use cases, this test phase addresses technical attributes such as capacity, responsiveness, and reliability. Application product test should be thorough enough to convince you about the quality of the product so that you were able to deliver the application product after the last fault corrections.

System product test is often needed for testing the interoperability of application products when there are dependencies between the products. It aims at verifying that all members of the product line work together. System product test cases should resemble the real use cases as much as possible and focus on cross application product use cases. Therefore, the use case descriptions of customer documentation provide valuable inputs to these test cases.

Evolutionary nature of development also affects system testing. Test cases become valuable assets, when you develop a product line for several years. Like with the code and customer documentation, you need to manage and maintain the existing assets and develop new ones for the new system increment; that is, you need to maintain at least a set of regression test cases for the existing system and develop a set of new test cases for the new features. Therefore, also the test plans and test cases need to have a modular architecture that maps to product architecture and the design level model.

Putting It All Together

We presented a development practice designed to manage the evolution and inherent complexity of large systems with even millions of lines of code. Breaking down systems into lines of products and then breaking them down further into applications, service blocks and components provides a structure that helps in managing the architecture, assigning the responsibilities, and implementing the mature software engineering processes.

A product line approach to development calls for an application platform that provides common software assets. Organizing the common components into an application platform is one of the best reuse strategies, because it makes the implementation of software assets and their reuse as planned and managed as the actual application development. We are positive that reuse does not just happen; you need to get organized for it.

We have also shown how the 3 + 1 views to architecture scaled up to large systems. These views are valuable tools for describing the architecture of any nontrivial software system. To show how they are applied to large-scale systems, we introduced a set of architecture blueprints that make use of these views.

Last, we introduced the concept of a feature and of a feature-driven, incremental process model that focuses on the increments of an evolutionary system but also cares for the architectural perspective. We also emphasized the need for considering customer documentation and installation design as essential elements of software process. Figure 3-36 summarizes the main artifacts and main information flows in our approach to object-oriented development of large-scale systems.

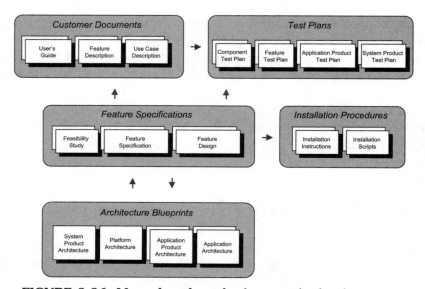

FIGURE 3-36. Map of artifacts for large-scale development.

We know by experience that there is a long way to go from an idea to implementation as far as fundamental software engineering practices are concerned. You need to adapt all described practices to meet your particular circumstances, which as such requires quite a bit of mental exercising. The hardest part of any change is its implementation—changing the organization, processes, technologies, and practices. Although we know that these practices are in use—adapted, of course—and work in successful large projects, it is still impossible for us to tell which of our practices work in each organization. We hope, though, that this discussion of large systems stimulates your thinking. A clear trend is that software systems are growing, so there will be more and more systems that cannot be managed with small scale development practices any longer. We hope these documented experiences from our large-scale projects help you if you are some day involved in large-scale software development.

Notes

1. Note that the macro process is *like* a perpetuum mobile that never stops. As you know from physics, it is not possible to build a perpetuum mobile. Same goes for software systems: it is not likely that any system is developed for ever. So even evolutionary system development process stops some day when the system becomes obsolete and it is time for phase-out.

2. By defect density we mean the number of faults/1000 lines of code.

3. Exceptions to this rule may be some teams developing computer games and other shrink-wrap software. Even large software products can be developed by a relatively small team having a strong vision and software design skills, if the problem domain is well known and there are no explicit customer requirements. You can then select the most suitable tools and technologies and design the system to your selected tools. For most business oriented systems the circumstances are not as favorable.

4. We are not alone here. John Lakos, in particular, has stressed the importance of managing physical dependencies [Lakos 96].

5. GSM stands for Global System for Mobile communications.

6. Real Nokia NMS/2000 for managing GSM networks had more than 2,000,000 LOC C++ in its ninth release 1997.

7. AMPS stands for Advanced Mobile Phone Service. AMPS networks are analog cellular networks.

8. Software Engineering Institute defines a *product line* as a group of products sharing a common, managed set of features that satisfy specific needs of a selected market or mission [Bass et al 97]. They use the term *product family* for a group of systems built from a common set of assets. A product family need not always constitute a product line, because you can use the same assets for designing individual systems without any clearly coordinated role for a single market. And, a product line need not be built from a product family, because the members of the product line may be developed independently. However, most product lines are also product families.

9. Note that we present in Chapter 1 of this book how to construct applications from components and classes.

10. Usefulness of separating the design concerns according to architectural levels has been recognized also by Thomas J. Mowbray [Mowbrau and Malveau 97] and Ivar Jacobson with his coauthors [Jacobson et al 97].

11. Pipelining means a strategy for accelerating projects by breaking up single large tasks into smaller ones whose results can be passed along as soon as they are completed [Ulrich and Eppinger 95]. Following the proposed guidelines for physical, deliverable subsystems, you could pass the results of subsystem development along as soon as they are available without waiting for the other subsystems unnecessarily. For instance, if you have a well defined component, you can develop the test it independently of other subsystems as long as you know the required interfaces of possibly related components.

12. In the case you wish to model the whole GSM network, for instance, you should do it like this. All major elements of a telecommunication network can be considered as system products from the point of view of presented design level model.

13. Please refer to section "Platform Architecture" for further details.
14. Please refer to section "Feature" for further discussion about features.
15. Please refer to section "System Product Architecture" for further details.
16. This is actually one application of the evolutionary delivery approach presented by Tom Gilb [Gilb 88] scaled up to large-scale development.

CHAPTER 4

Small-Scale Development

We have noticed that object-oriented software development methods tend to be too big and complex for small software projects. Large and complicated systems require that processes and tools scale up. However, not all projects need such massive arsenals, and therefore, practices must also scale down.

Need for a Streamlined Approach

Instead of detailed and complex modeling notations, many companies simply need a practical process, clear notation, and "how-to" guidelines. We argue that it does not really matter if the selected practices do not cover all details of object paradigm. Instead, the approach should first concentrate on covering the most important aspects of software development. Only after that can the details be handled.

To help you meet these requirements, we present a simplified process tailored especially for small teams implementing their first or second object-oriented application [Jaaksi 98a]. It is a streamlined version of our standard process model presented in Chapter 1.

263

The simplified process uses UML. It also uses our standard two-path approach, enabling developers to view systems as collaborative entities. The process is tailored especially for small companies with little knowledge on object-oriented software development. The use of the process requires that the architecture of the developed system is fairly simple, and consists of only a few separate run-time components. It suits especially well for the applications consisting of only one executable program implemented in an object-oriented language.

Overview of the Approach

Our simplified process supports three aspects of the system to be developed. First, the process models the external functionality of the system; that is, what the system provides to the end user. Second, the process models the objects that constitute the system; that is, what the objects are and how they relate to each other. The approach helps software designers to discover the objects based on the analysis of the problem domain. The approach also refines and transforms domain objects into a form that can be implemented in a programming language. Finally, the process models how objects collaborate to provide desired functionality.

The simplified process uses *natural language* and two main notational elements of UML: *class diagrams* and *sequence diagrams*. Natural language is the main tool used to capture requirements, and it is typically used whenever there is a need to communicate with the end users. Natural language is also used if there is a need to emphasize something related to diagrams. Class diagrams provide a static view to the classes related to the system in various phases of system development. Sequence diagrams provide a dynamic view to the objects by illustrating the co-operation between the objects.

All produced figures should be clear and readable, and not all details of UML are necessary. In class diagrams, it is typically enough to depict one-to-one associations, one-to-many associations, many-to-many associations, aggregation, and inheritance. Also the associations that are not inheritance or aggregation need descriptive names. Figure 4-1 depicts all the main elements that we use in class diagrams. A car, either a sedan or a station wagon, includes one engine, and an owner may own many such cars.

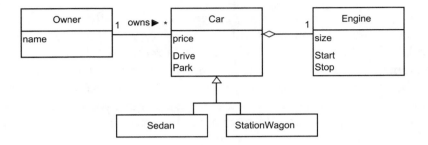

FIGURE 4-1. Basic elements of the UML class diagram notation.

Sequence diagrams illustrate how instances of various classes communicate with each other. Each sequence diagram illustrates a sequential flow of events. The flow may be set in motion by the end user's actions, such as pressing a button or moving a slider; or by internal incidents, such as calls from a timer. Thus, sequence diagrams depict how a set of objects communicates to provide desired functionality. Figure 4-2 illustrates the basic elements of the sequence diagram notation. Time runs from top to bottom. The names of objects are written at the top of the sequence diagram figure. Arrows are messages from an object to another. An arrow starts from a caller object and points to an object that is being called. The name of each message is written above the arrow, and the message can include parameters. Comments and actions that refer to a single object can also be added as notes.

Operation: The owner starts to drive his car.

Preconditions: The car is parked.

Sequence Diagram:

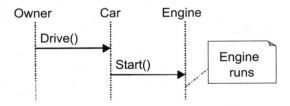

Exceptions: Cannot start the engine.

Postconditions: The owner is driving his car.

FIGURE 4-2. The notation of sequence diagrams.

Figure 4-3 illustrates the five phases of the simplified process: *Requirements Capture, Analysis, Design, Programming,* and *Testing.* Although the phases are listed sequentially, iterative approach can be adopted, and is presented later. Requirements capture collects all requirements that there are for the system to be developed. The analysis phase aims at modeling the concepts, that is, the classes of the problem domain, as well as analyzing the operations of the system. In the design phase, the products of the analysis phase are transformed into a form that can be programmed. Design illustrates how the objects form structures, what their interfaces are, and how they collaborate. The programming phase produces the code and typically concentrates on one class at a time. Finally, the test phase tests the system against the requirements.

The simplified process has very similar structure with our standard process model presented in Chapter 1. Both approaches use two parallel paths in the process of system development. The *static path* uses class diagrams to illustrate the static properties of the system, and the *functional path* uses operation descriptions and sequence diagrams to illustrate the functional properties of the system. These two paths are related to each other, and they both aim at a code that has been tested, as illustrated in Figure 4-3.

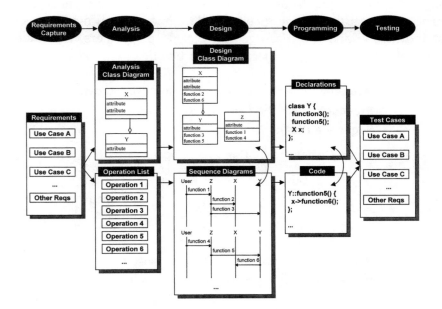

FIGURE 4-3. Static and functional paths of the simplified process model.

Process Phases

The simplified process has five phases each performing a closely related set of activities. The outcome of these activities is stored into documents. Thus, each phase of the simplified process produces a document that can be reviewed and accepted.

Requirements Capture

The process of developing a system starts with *requirements capture*. The purpose of the phase is to communicate with end users and document the requirements. The requirements are divided into *functional* and *nonfunctional requirements*. Functional requirements can be modeled in the form of use cases, which are concrete stories describing the use of the future system.[1] Other requirements are documented simply as a numbered list. All requirements should be so exact and measurable that they can be used as test cases.

Take the following simple example to illustrate the phases of the simplified process. Let us suppose that you are about to implement an application that allows elementary school pupils to compose simple musical tunes. The application is called Elementary Composer. Figure 4-4 describes the use cases of the application, and Figure 4-5 illustrates all the nonfunctional requirements.

Use Case #1: Composing a tune
  The application shows an empty staff and a selection of possible note types. The pupil selects a quarter note. Then he or she places the quarter note on the staff. After this, the pupil selects a half note and places it on the staff after the quarter note. By selecting note types and placing them on the staff, the pupil constructs a tune. Then, he or she asks the computer to play the constructed tune. Finally, the pupil saves the tune on a disk.

Use Case #2: Listening to a previously composed tune
  The pupil loads a tune that he wants to hear from a disk. All notes of the selected tune appear on the staff. After that the pupil asks the computer to play the tune, which it does.

FIGURE. 4-4. Use Cases, that is, functional requirements of the example application.

Nonfunctional requirement #1:
  The application supports the C major scale and eight, quarter, and half notes, and eight rests.
Nonfunctional requirement #2:
  The maximum length of a tune is 20 notes.
Nonfunctional requirement #3:
  Tunes are stored as ASCII files.

FIGURE 4-5. Nonfunctional requirements of the example application.

You should discuss the requirements with the end user. If possible, the end users should participate in the writing of the use cases. Typically, the software designer writes the first versions of the use cases. The designer then reviews these use cases with the end users. This means use cases are written so that the users can understand them and make comments. Sketches of the user interface can make the use cases more concrete.

After the use cases and other requirements have been documented and agreed on with end users, they form the basis for the following phases of the system development. In each step, phase products must be checked against the use cases and nonfunctional requirements. Finally, the use cases form the basic test case set for system testing.

Analysis

The purpose of analysis is to understand the problem domain and the system to be implemented. The analysis phase uses the collected requirements and use cases, and the phase includes two tasks: namely object analysis and behavior analysis. *Object analysis* aims at specifying all key concepts related to the system to be developed. It produces an *analysis class diagram* that documents the concepts of the problem domain. Behavior analysis defines the operations that the user performs with the system. *Behavior analysis* models the system as a black box. It models only the external functionality of the system and produces an *operation list*. The final system must support the performance of all the operations in the list.

Although the operation list and the analysis class diagram are separate models, operations utilize the concepts and terms defined by the class diagram. Still, you should not try to push operations back into the analysis class diagram by guessing member functions for the classes. Thus, the analysis class diagram includes few operations; typically, only classes and their attributes are presented. Also, the diagram does not include software-related classes, such as user interface or data structure classes.

Object analysis uses collected requirements, use cases, problem descriptions, and discussions with the end users. You identify concrete real world objects from these sources and illustrate their relationship using the class diagram notation of UML. Figure 4-6 illustrates the analysis class diagram of the Elementary Composer application. The composed tune is written on staves. Each staff consists of notes and the duration and pitch of each note is specified. The notes can be of various types, such as quarter notes, half notes, or quarter rests.

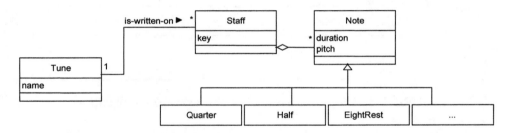

FIGURE 4-6. The analysis class diagram of the Elementary Composer application.

Behavior analysis produces the operation list, which is constructed on the basis of use cases. Figure 4-7 lists all the operations performed with the Elementary Composer application. Operations 1 through 4 are found from the first use case and operations 3 and 5 are found from the second use case.

> **1.** Selecting a note type.
> **2.** Placing a note on the staff.
> **3.** Playing a tune.
> **4.** Saving a tune.
> **5.** Loading a tune.

FIGURE 4-7. Operations performed with the Elementary Composer application.

This simplified process does not include a separate phase for the specification of user interfaces. Simple user interfaces, such as presented in Figure 4- can typically be designed by drawing them with one of the various graphical user interface builders or application development environments.[2] User interface prototypes can also be built with the help of real end users.

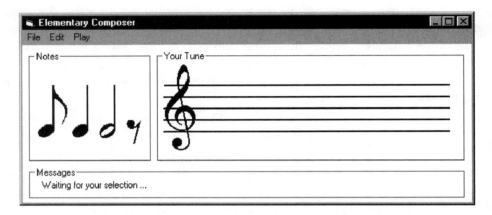

FIGURE 4-8. The main window of the example application.

Design

The purpose of design is to transform the products of the analysis phase into a form that can be implemented in a programming language. While analysis concentrates on objects and functionality, which are relevant to the end user, design deals with objects and functions that will be programmed.

The design phase includes two paths, as illustrated in Figure 4-3. The analysis class diagram is transformed into the design class diagram, and the operations in the operation list are modeled as design sequence diagrams. Domain classes discovered in analysis are modified so they can be implemented with a selected programming language. Modification means, for example, adding implementation specific classes, modifying class structures, and identifying operations and attributes. In the analysis phase, the static and functional paths were separate from each other, but in the design phase these two paths meet. The sequence diagrams modify the design class diagram, and the design class diagram provides objects and attributes for the sequence diagrams.

The creation of the design class diagram is a controlled process. You must select or develop an appropriate *application architecture*, an application framework, if you will, to form the basis of design decisions. For example, Model-View-Controller approach could be selected for Smalltalk [Krasner and Pope 88], Document-View architecture could be user with Microsoft's Visual C++, and the MVC++ approach [Jaaksi 95a] could be selected for large C++ and Java applications. Most of the modern programming environments, such as Borland's Delphi, Microsoft's Visual C++, Microsoft's Visual Basic, for example, provide simple frameworks upon which the design decisions can be built. Thus, successful design requires good knowledge of the selected programming language, operating system, hardware, and other issues, which will affect the final coding.

You should use simple and understandable application architectures. Such architecture should, among other things, promote modularity and separate the user interface from the rest of the application and allow the effective use of modern programming tools. Such architecture can consist of two major types of classes: the user interface classes and application classes.

The selected tools typically dictate basic design rules, such as rules on how to manage user interfaces and how to handle databases. Let us assume that you are going to implement the Elementary Composer application in Object Pascal by using Borland's Delphi programming environment. In the Delphi environment, the user interface is implemented within the user interface classes. Typically, each window or dialogue box is an object. Push buttons, menus, and other controls are objects, too, and they are object members of windows and dialogs. Other objects of the application work together with the user interface objects, thus enabling the communication with the end user and providing the functionality of the application.

You start the design by constructing the *first version* of the design class diagram, shown in Figure 4-9. In the very first version, the analysis class diagrams forms the basis of the design class diagram and the classes representing the windows of the user interface are added at the top of the model. The user interface classes and their attributes can be found from the user interface figures.

The first version of the design class diagram needs a lot of refining and tuning. Refining is done by using sequence diagrams systematically. You analyze every operation in the operation list and draw sequence diagrams for each operation by using the design class diagram. By doing so, you refine connections between the classes and add operations, attributes, and new classes.

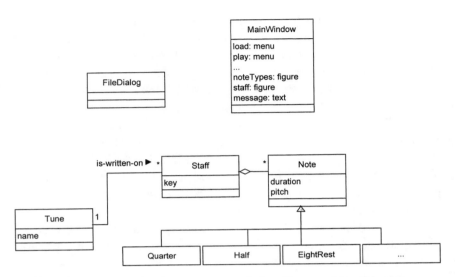

FIGURE 4-9. The first version of the design class diagram.

When drawing sequence diagrams, you specify what responsibilities the design objects have and how they function in practice. An arrow starts from an object that calls the member function of another object, and points to this other object. The name of the function is written above the arrow. Function calls are written with the needed parameters in parenthesis, and the return values of the function calls are written without parenthesis.

As a first step to refine the design class diagram, draw a sequence diagram to illustrate how objects communicate with each other and thus allow the end user to place a note on the staff. Figure 4-10 depicts the *"Placing a note on the staff"* operation as it will be programmed. Before the operation can start, the user has to select a note type, and the type information is stored within the MainWindow object. The sequence diagram for depicting the selection operation is not illustrated here. The first action of the user is to click the staff on the screen. This clicking launches the StaffMouseDown(x,y) member function of the MainWindow. At first the function determines the pitch, that is, the height of the note to be added, by calculating the position of the mouse relative to the staff. Then the MainWindow object calls the AddNote(selected-Type,pitch) member function of the Staff object, which creates the note object. In this case, the type of the note is QuarterNote. The AddNote(selectedType,pitch) member function returns the OK message if the creation of the new note has succeeded. Finally, the MainWindow asks for the entire set of notes to redraw the tune on the staff. For this the MainWindow calls its own ReDraw(notes) method.

Operation: Placing a note on the staff (The note object can be of any type, and the sequence diagram illustrates the quarter note case.)

Preconditions: The type of the note is selected.

Sequence Diagram:

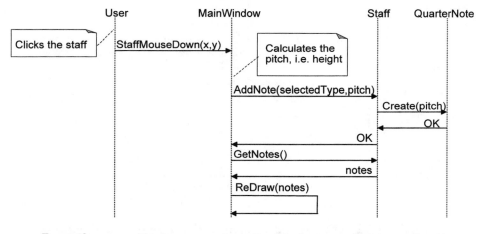

Exceptions: Maximum number of notes is exceeded, cannot add a new one: Error message is shown in the message field.

Postconditions: New note is added on the staff.

FIGURE 4-10. A sequence diagram illustrating the co-operation between objects when the user places a note on the staff.

Each sequence diagram specifies a set of member functions, attributes, and associations and adds them to the design class diagram. For example, an arrow pointing to an object adds a member function to the class in question. Correspondingly, an arrow between two objects adds a connection between the classes in question to the design class diagram. Still, the sequence diagrams do not illustrate object communication in every detail. Instead, the sequence diagrams should be readable and simple. They should only depict the threads of execution as they are normally performed. Therefore, pre- and postconditions are written above the sequence diagram and exceptions to the normal sequence of events are written below the sequence diagram.

Figure 4-11 illustrates the *second version* of the design class diagram. The operations and connections suggested by the sequence diagram illustrated in Figure 4-10 are added into the model. Based on the sequence diagram, member functions have been added to various classes and a new connection between the MainWindow and the Staff has been established.

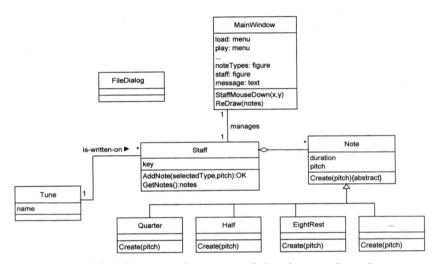

FIGURE 4-11. The second version of the design class diagram.

Figure 4-12 shows how the objects of the design class diagram communicate with each other when the user wants to hear a tune. Thus, the figure specifies the "Playing a tune" operation. Figure 4-13 presents the *third version* of the design class diagram with the modifications suggested by the second sequence diagram.

You must specify all the operations in the operation list as sequence diagrams, and refine the design class diagram accordingly. When you draw the sequence diagrams, think about the final implementation, that is, how the software will function in practice. When drawing sequence diagrams you often need to add new design-specific classes into the design class diagram. You may also decide to alter the object structure specified in the analysis phase, and remove classes that are not involved in any sequence diagram. In any event, all changes should be justified and minimized, and unnecessary changes to the analysis class diagram should be avoided. The goal is to design classes that resemble objects of the real world and are at the same time suitable for implementation.

Operation: Playing a tune.
Preconditions: There is a tune on the staff.
Sequence Diagram:

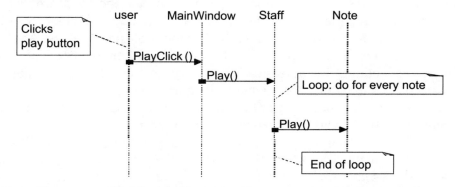

Exceptions: Problems with music drivers, cannot play the tune: Error message is shown in the message field.
Postconditions: The tune is played.

FIGURE 4-12. Cooperation between objects when playing the tune on the staff.

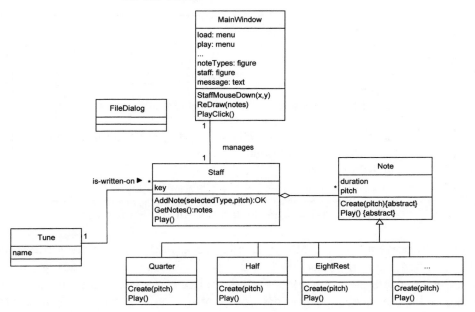

FIGURE 4-13. The third version of the design class diagram.

Programming

Programming transforms the design class diagram and the sequence diagrams into a programming language. Design has already modeled all classes of the system and communication between the instances of these classes. According to our simplified process, you do not model the inner functionality of individual objects during design. Instead, the programming of classes is based on the design class diagrams and sequence diagrams. Thus, while design concentrates on object structures, object interfaces, and cooperation between objects, programming deals with the inner functionality of individual objects.

The class declarations are based the design class diagrams, and the code of individual member functions is based on the sequence diagrams. Figure 4-14 illustrates the declaration of the Staff class. The declaration is based on the class diagram presented in Figure 4-13. Figure 4-15 illustrates the code of the StaffMouseDown member function of the MainWindow class. It is written in Object Pascal on the basis of the sequence diagram illustrated in Figure 4-10.

```
NoteStructure = array[0..20] of ^Note;

Staff = class
private
        key: integer;
        notes: NoteStructure;
public
        function AddNote(selectedType: Integer; pitch: Integer):Boolean;
        function GetNotes: PChar;
        procedure Play;
end;
```

FIGURE. 4-14. The declaration of the Staff class.

It is important that classes, their interfaces, and the cooperation between objects have been modeled during design. Based on such a design, a programmer can concentrate on one class and one member function at a time. This is why our simplified process does not use any notation for the internal functionality of a single object. In most cases, there is no need to assist the implementation of a single class with any additional graphical notations.

```
procedure TMainWindow.StaffMouseDown(...X, Y: Integer);
        var
                pitch : Integer;
                ok : Boolean;
                notes : PChar;
begin
        {Calculate the pitch based on the Y parameter}
        ...
        ok := MyStaff.AddNote(selectedType, pitch);
        if (ok = false) then
                MessageText.Caption:='Cannot add more notes, sorry.';
        notes := MyStaff.GetNotes;
        ReDraw(notes);
end;
```

FIGURE 4-15. The StaffMouseDown procedure of the MainWindow.

Testing

The purpose of testing is to find errors and ensure that the software functions as planned. Therefore, testing is performed against the requirements. According to our simplified process, each use case is run with the implemented system, and every nonfunctional requirement is checked. Various testing tools can improve the quality of testing by providing views into the implemented code. Still, the most important job in testing is to run each use case and compare the results against the initial use cases. Such blackbox testing can spot at least the most severe errors.

Incremental Software Development

Incremental software development constructs applications piece by piece. Systems are implemented in sequential cycles, and each cycle implements only a slice of the required functionality. Each new phase builds on the previous phases and each phase can learn from experiences gained during the previous cycles. After each cycle, you can also validate requirements by testing the implemented part of the system and even by delivering it to the end users.

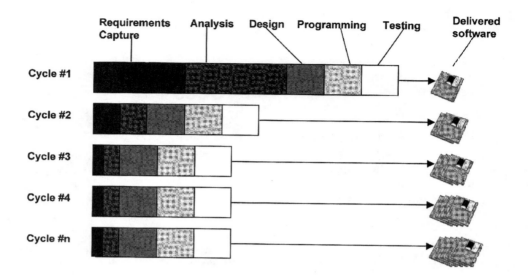

FIGURE 4-16. Phases of iterative and incremental software development.

Figure 4-16 illustrates the phases of incremental and iterative software development. The length of each slot illustrates the amount of work and time required. You should perform requirements capture and analysis thoroughly and carefully already during the first cycle. This is how you ensure that you have the right goals for the cycles that follow. You should collect all requirements that are available before you start the analysis phase. You should therefore write all the use cases that can be specified.

Analysis should be as complete as possible during the first cycle. Without thorough analysis, you could easily end up with design solutions that cannot be extended beyond the first iteration cycle. In addition to the analysis phase already presented, you should identify the subset of operations that needs to be implemented during the first cycle. The implementation of these operations forms the first version of the system. This version, capable of performing only a few operations, should then be given to the end users for comments. Typically, the operations of one single use case form a good set to start with. The use case selected for the first iteration should be the most important use case from the end users' points of view.

Only the selected operations are transformed into sequence diagrams during the design and programmed. Some objects and operations that may have been discovered already in the analysis phase are not implemented at all. The cycles that follow take care of the rest of the operations.

Using the Simplified Process

When a company starts to develop software in an object-oriented way, in needs a pilot project. During the pilot project the company can learn the new technology and adopt new ways of working. To get the most out of the pilot project, the company needs a simple but powerful method for developing the software. Without a systematic approach, the company cannot maximize its learning. Ad hoc hacking during the pilot project does not provide real knowledge for the future projects, although some details may be tackled. Thus, a simple and practical process with usable notations and how-to guidelines is needed to form the basis for the development of object-oriented practices of the company. This approach should be used starting from the very first pilot project.

The presented simplified process is such an approach. It supports the development of reasonable small stand-alone application. It consists of five clear steps and a simple notation. Although the method is simple, it covers all phases from collecting end user requirements to testing the code. It includes notations and process descriptions and specifies phase products. It is a complete method that can be extended and modified. Although the method itself is described in a waterfall form, iterative software development has also been discussed.

The software process must be visible. All the phases of the process must produce visual phase products that can be discussed. There are plenty of CASE tools available that support the modeling notations used in the development of the Elementary Composer application. Still, the tools should not dictate the process. Especially during the first object-oriented projects, it is better to keep tools simple and use, for example, whiteboards and stick-on labels.

Regular office applications can be used for drawing diagrams and writing textual descriptions. For example, a word processor with predefined document templates is a good tool. Document templates make all documents look similar and, therefore, them easier to read. The template should define the table of contents and the places where various figures and other models can be attached.

The software process should produce concrete phase products that can be organized as documents. The Requirements Document should include use cases and all nonfunctional requirements. The Analysis Document should contain the analysis class diagram and the operation list. The Analysis Document can also include windows and dialogs of the user interface, although a prototype alone may be sufficient. The Design Document should include the design class diagram and all sequence diagrams. The Design Document should also include all other design decisions, such as database solutions. The code itself is also a document. It is read both by the compiler and the maintainer of the application.

The presented simplified process does not address reuse as its main goal. Before any reuse can take place, the company needs to follow a systematic and repeatable method. Activities to support reuse, such as identification of reusable components and modifications in class inheritance hierarchies, should be added to the method once it is in operational use. Also, the simplified process presumes that the system is built from scratch. Reusing the components of the system in other projects or building on the current software is not discussed at all.

This simple approach does not support large development teams. The project using the method must be small. You should have, say, no more than three persons in the project team. One could take the user interface part and the other could take care of the domain specific classes. The third person could manage the project, collect feedback from the others in the project, modify the process based on the feedback, arrange integration sessions in the end of each iteration, perform testing of the implemented software and commercial components used in development, and do other such supportive work. In any event, no more than a few person should work in the first object oriented project of a company.

There are risks in adopting a simple approach for software development. A method that is too simple may fail in specifying the key properties of object systems. Still, we feel the real problem with the methods available lies in their complexity. A method needs to be simple and intuitive enough so that it is easy to identify the value added by following it. If the process is too complicated or the produced artifacts too laborious, the engineers will not commit themselves to working with it and a repeatable process cannot be achieved. Therefore, instead of trying to cover full details of software development, the method should first support only the most important phases. Only after they are applied in practice can the process be extended.

Notes

1. For us, the object orientation of the use cases in not an issue at all. Use cases are simply stories that are written in the language of the end user. Actually, we thus use "instances of use cases."
2. For more about user interface specification, see Chapter 1 of this book.

SUMMARY OF OUR STANDARD PROCESS

The following pages summarize our process model for the development of interactive software systems. We provide an overview of the phases and document templates for the phase products. Chapter 1 of this book presents the process model in detail. Chapters 3 and 4 show how the model scales up and down.

Phases

Our process model consists of four main phases, namely *object-oriented analysis, object-oriented design, object-oriented programming,* and *testing*. There are two parallel paths through the process: the upper *static path* and the lower *functional path*, as illustrated in Figure 1.

The analysis phase consists of subphases called requirements capture and requirements specification. This phase collects, analyses, and refines the requirements, produces the requirement statements, the use cases, the analysis class diagram, and the operation specifications, and specifies the user interfaces.

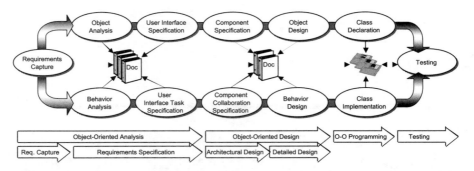

FIGURE 1. The main phases and the two paths of our process model.

The next phase is the design phase, which consists of architectural design and detailed design. Architectural design produces specifications that model the executable processes, libraries, data storage, devices, and other such components of the system. Detailed design produces an inside view to these architectural elements in the form of design class diagrams and sequence diagrams.

The programming phase includes coding as well as compiling, linking, and debugging.

Finally, the test phase tests the system to find errors in design and programming and to verify that the system meets the requirements. The testing phase also includes the integration of the entire system into a form that can be delivered to the customer.

We use two paths, called *static* and *functional*, throughout the system development. These paths provide different views to the developed system. In each phase, first we model the static entities of the system. During the analysis phase these entities are the system itself, concepts dealt with by the system, external devices, and end users. During the design phase the static entities are, first, subsystems, and then components such as processes, libraries, and devices, and finally classes that will be programmed. During the programming phase, the static entities are C++ or other such classes that constitute the system in question. In each phase, the functional path illustrates how instances of these static entities collaborate in the context of system functionality. Thus, during the detailed design phase, for example, the functional path concentrates on how instances of C++ classes collaborate.

Although two separate paths exist, the paths are closely related. The static path uses packages and class, component, and deployment diagrams to illustrate the static properties of the system, and the functional path uses use cases and sequence diagrams to illustrate the functional and dynamic behavior of the system. These two paths complement each other, and they both aim at a complete, tested system.

Phase Products

Software projects must produce visible phase products for several reasons. Project managers use phase products to steer the project; your colleagues use them to study your ideas and specifications; quality assurance uses them to look after the quality standards; and future projects will build on them. Above all, by drawing, writing, programming, and discussing, you dig into the problem domain and cultivate your ideas into a functioning software system. Let us now look at the phase products in the form of conventional paper documents illustrated in Figure 2. In real life, they also can be stored within CASE tools. However, all the needed information must be found.

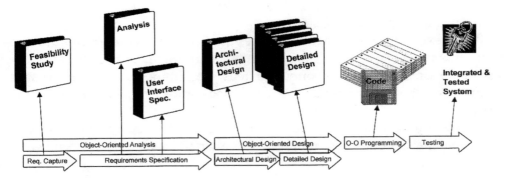

FIGURE 2. The main phases and the phase products.

The ultimate purpose of a software development project is not to produce documents. Only the final software matters; documents merely are a visible storage medium for the information that is created, analyzed, and organized during software projects. For example, to produce a high-quality user interface specification document requires a great deal of work that does not appear in the document itself. You need to organize brainstorming sessions, draw user interface sketches on whiteboards, demonstrate your ideas with prototypes, and make compromises between competing ideas. Only the final outcome of these various activities is documented. However, for those who study the documents later, such as quality engineers or other software designers, the documents are their main source for information. Also, in order to create a document of good quality, you are forced to think things over and organize ideas properly. Thus, writing documents should be a value-adding task of every software project.

Object-Oriented Analysis

Analysis is the first phase of software development activities. The objective of analysis is to collect requirements and analyze the problem at hand. In addition, the analysis phase constructs a high-level solution to the problem from the user's point of view. The analysis phase answers two fundamental questions: "What is the problem?" and "What kind of a solution solves the problem?" Thus, we have a problem-oriented approach for the analysis phase, and the analysis already aims at a system to solve the problems. Analysis uses only concepts that are meaningful to the end user and it does not answer questions such as "How does one technically implement the solution?" or "What kind of software components are needed to construct a solution?"

The analysis phase has two subphases, namely *requirements capture* and *requirements specification*. Requirements capture aims at eliciting and representing requirements from various sources. Requirements specification aims at analyzing the requirements and producing various models to depict the problem and the initial solution to it.

The analysis phase produces three documents, namely, the feasibility study, the analysis document, and the user-interface specification document.

The Feasibility Study Document

The first document that is written describes the requirements and use cases related to a planned piece of software. Thus, this document could also be called the "early requirements document." However, it is called the feasibility study document because it also includes preliminary solution suggestion and work estimations. These are used as a basis for project decision-making and planning. Write the feasibility study document from a feature's or an enhancement's point of view. The document includes the following sections.

- **Overview:** This section includes the summary of the current situation, that is, the problem description, the summary of the most important requirements, and the summary of the suggested solution with effort estimates.

- **Requirements:** This section lists all requirements in two major groups: functional requirements and other requirements. A source of each requirement is documented.
- **Use Cases:** This section documents the use cases. Use cases illustrate the use of the system from the end user's point of view.
- **Solution Suggestions:** Ttypically, many possible solutions to the problem at hand are available. This section describes the most viable possibilities. It documents general principles, requirements that are not met, and how influences to other parties and software modules relate to each solution suggestion. Also, this section typically presents some discussion about the positive and negative sides of the presented solutions.
- **Effort Estimates:** This section includes the estimations of how much work is required for each solution alternative. Thus, each solution alternative produces its own estimation. Estimation is based on our standard work breakdown structure, and estimates for each phase are documented.
- **Appendices:** All information, drawings, models, text, and so on, that have been produced during the feasibility study phase are stored here to be used later in the project.

The Analysis Document

The analysis document is produced during requirements specification. It includes a more detailed analysis of the requirements, the use cases, and the solution suggestions of the feasibility study document. It is written from one application's point of view. One feasibility study document may start the implementation of multiple applications. Thus, you can write many analysis documents based on one feasibility study document. However, in most cases the requirement chapters of the feasibility study document are copied to form the basis of the analysis document. The document includes the following sections:

- **Overview:** This section gives an overview of the application in question. It also explains which features are affected and/or provided by this application.
- **Requirements:** This section contains the requirements of the feasibility study documents allocated for the application under development. This

section enhances, improves, and documents the requirements found from the feasibility study document. In addition, other relevant sources are studied for new or changed requirements.

- **Use Cases:** This section contains the use cases of the feasibility study documents that affect the application. This section enhances, improves, and documents the use cases found from the feasibility study document.
- **Analysis Class Diagram:** This section contains the analysis class diagram and the data dictionary that explains the classes and their relations. Conceptually, only one analysis class diagram exists. However, this section may spread to many pages.
- **Operations:** This section lists all operations. It includes the operation specifications of each operation provided by the application. Operation specifications use sequence diagrams if significant communication exists between the system and its external agents. This section also includes the layout specifications of all reports if such are produced by the application.

The User Interface Specification Document

The *user interface specification document* together with user interface prototypes specify how to present the objects of the analysis class diagram and the specified operations to the end user. In simple cases, the user interface specification can be a part of the analysis document. The document includes the following sections:

- **Overview:** This section summarizes the purpose and characteristics of the user interface.
- **Operations with the User Interface:** This section lists the operations that the end user can perform with the user interface. In most cases, the list
- **Structure of the User Interface:** This section includes the dialog diagram of the user interface. The dialog diagram places the operations of the preceding section into the dialog boxes of the user interface. After that, a subsection is added for each dialog box of the dialog diagram. These subsections include the list and short explanations of the user interface components of the dialog in question. These sections also include screen shots of the final layout as well as exact wordings and bitmaps.

- **GUI Operations:** This section provides the detailed specification of each user interface operation. How to perform the operations is explained in natural language. This section is the basis of the user's guide and online help.

Object-Oriented Design

The objective of the design phase is to specify how one should construct the solution to meet the requirements analyzed in the analysis phase. Design answers two fundamental questions: "What kind of objects comprise the system?" and "How do these objects collaborate to provide the needed services?" Our process model provides static and functional paths for the designer to find answers to these questions. Whereas the analysis phase uses the concepts meaningful to end users, design concentrates on the concepts meaningful to programmers. Design deals with concepts that can be implemented by using the chosen hardware, operating system, programming language, and other such technical elements.

The Architectural Design Document

We produce two kinds of documents during the design phase: architectural design and detailed design documents. The architectural design document describes the components of the application, their collaboration with each other and with external devices and agents, and the database and distribution solutions. The document includes the following sections:

- **Overview:** This section gives an overview of the application from a technical point of view. For a large software system, this section contains the logical view that illustrates the product structure in terms of logical subsystems, such as applications.
- **Run-Time Architecture:** This section lists the executable components and devices of the application in question. It gives a short explanation of each component. This section also provides an explanation about how the components of this application relate to each other, as well as to the components of other relevant applications. Also, relations with external devices, such as printers, databases, and networks are

explained. Run-time architecture is illustrated by using deployment diagrams accompanied with proper explanations.

- **Development Architecture:** This section lists the components that will be implemented independently and that are the elements of software-configuration management. These are the components that constitute the executable components specified in the run-time architecture. The section gives a short explanation of each component. It also provides an explanation about how the components of this application relate to each other, as well as to the components of other relevant applications. Development architecture is illustrated by using the component diagrams accompanied with proper explanations.
- **Data Architecture:** This section illustrates the database solutions of the application and explains the tables and fields of the database.
- **Design Scenarios:** This section provides a functional view to the collaboration between the components and external elements related to the application in question. Sequence diagrams are used for this purpose. In most cases, the collaborating components are those of the development view.

The Detailed Design Document

The detailed design document includes the output of the detailed design phase. We produce a detailed design document for each major component of the application, but small and simple components can naturally be merged into one document. The document includes the following sections:

- **Interfaces:** This section documents the interfaces implemented by this component. For large interfaces, a separate document can be written.
- **Design Class Diagram:** This section illustrates the design class diagram of the component in question. The class structure follows the MVC++ architectural pattern. Classes and associations presented in the model are also briefly explained.
- **Scenarios:** This section shows how the instances of the classes presented in the design class diagram collaborate. This collaboration is illustrated as sequence diagrams. For objects with complex, dynamic behavior, you can construct a state diagram to exemplify the states of an object during its lifetime.

- **Design Decisions:** This section justifies the design decisions taken. It also documents all hints and tips that may help somebody else to maintain the component in question.
- **Components Test Plan:** This section lists the classes that will be tested by using a test driver. It also presents the name of the test drivers.
- **Headers:** If the implementation language is C++, this section provides the class declarations of the component in question. These declarations need not need be complete or final. Because the first versions of the declarations are often produced during design, they may help the reader to understand the design in the review situation, for example.

Programming

During the programming phase, software designers perform the most detailed design and transform the design class diagram and the sequence diagrams into the programming language. The transformation is not trivial. The graphical notation does not depict all the details of the programming language. Therefore, designers need to make important decisions on how to implement the software based on the graphical design specifications.

Integration and Testing

Software developers unit test their own components. This ensures that the components arriving to integration are of good quality. As a matter of fact, such low-level unit testing typically is considered a part of the programming phase; programming is not over until the programmed classes have been tested.

The integration phase integrates unit-tested software modules. Software designers work in a laboratory environment, which means that all equipment, operating system versions, component versions, and other such elements are carefully controlled. The version of each software component is known, and the same integrated software system, that is, a build, can be constructed later if necessary. Also, the integration happens in a separate environment that doesn't have online connections to the development environment. This separation ensures that the integrated system is a self-sufficient stand-alone package and has no references to designers' own work spaces, for example.

Integration testing tests the integrated software build. It concentrates on the communication between the software modules and devices of the system. Similar to unit testing, integration testing aims at finding flaws in design and programming. If a project has dedicated integration testers, integration testing can happen as an independent project thread concurrently with the development of the next build.

Finally, system testers test the final software package. These testers use the view of the end user. They try to find flaws in usability and overall system functionality. They evaluate finally how the implemented system fits into its purpose.

All phases of testing must be planned. In simplest form, this planning means that test sessions are designed beforehand in a form of test case sets. These test cases are then run with the software, and their success or failures are documented. However, especially during system testing, experienced testers can find errors just by browsing around with the software. Thus, during the testing sessions, the number of faults discovered per day is a good indicator of how well testing is performing.

Project Example

Let us now take an example from a real software project. We ask that you not take this section literally; it should only give you some rough guidelines about the granularity and number of various artifacts produced during a software development project. We take the example from a subproject developing one application for NOKIA NMS/2000 Network Management System. The application consists of three components implemented by three software designers within a project lasting eight months.

The contents of the document produced during the project is as follows:

The Feasibility Study Document
- 30 functional requirement statements.
- 15 other requirements.
- 6 use cases.
- 3 different solution suggestions.

The Analysis Document
- A list of 35 operations.

- One analysis class diagram drawn on two pages.
- Specifications of 20 operations.

The User Interface Specification Document
- 25 GUI operations.
- One dialog diagram with seven dialogs.
- Four GUI components, such as graphical presenters and list components, from external sources.

The Architectural Design Document
- Three components.
- According to the development view: two library-type components, one client process-type component.
- According to the run-time view: one client process-type component, that is, only one executable process.
- Seven scenarios.

The Detailed Design Document
(Three documents, one for each component.)
- Design class diagram consisting of 35 classes.
- 15 design scenarios.
- Test plan with 45 test cases.

Code
- 250 classes in three components (some of them generated).

Integration Test Plan
- 45 test cases.

System Test Plan
- 6 use cases.
- 15 additional test cases.

EPILOGUE

This book has presented our process model as a collection of phases, notations, models, documents, tips, and rules of thumb. The bigger the development team and the more complicated the system, the more we must place emphasis on how to:

- Gather and understand requirements.
- Divide the problem and the system into manageable pieces.
- Communicate about these pieces.
- Make these pieces work together to meet the requirements of our customers.

For gathering and understanding, we use use cases, object analysis, and frequent communication with the customers. For successful management, we use concepts such as system products, application products, applications, components, and classes. These entities divide the problems and the systems into manageable pieces. For communication, we use documents, executable software increments, and face-to-face meetings. The Unified Modeling Language (UML) provides the common notation that can illustrate the different views of problems and systems. Finally, we use frequent builds and incremental software development arranged around prioritized use cases to ensure that we create a beneficial software system in time.

We use many activities and tools during software development that are not included in the process framework. These issues are equally important and they are required to make the use of the process model successful.

Typically, we use a lot of group work and brainstorming during software development projects. For example, we may call a meeting to analyze requirements and use cases, to create analysis class diagrams, to construct preliminary user interface sketches, or to give feedback from a user interface prototype. A process model, though, cannot give much to these sessions. It can give notations, concepts, and phases for these sessions, but the final quality of the meetings depends on the atmosphere and management of the session and the skills of session members.

We produce models, such as class, component, sequence, and dialog diagrams in a pre-defined form. However, we are also free to use Post-It notes, whiteboard sketches, role games, or any other means to handle information related to the problems and solutions at hand. Sometimes at meetings the worst possible white-board drawing with just some messy lines is most expressive, when accompanied with proper explanations. These random sketches must then be transformed into the proper notations after the brainstorming meeting. Otherwise, when you forget the explanations and the meeting itself, you also forget the essential parts of the information. The purpose of proper notations is not to restrain a creative mind but to document things clearly and with a suitable level of nuance and necessary details.

Almost any activity that is performed in teams and that aims at good quality outputs within a limited time frame requires guidelines, phases, and a means for communication. Phases, such as composing, arranging, rehearsing, recording, and making corrections, are used to make a musical recording. Phases, such as analysis, design, programming, and testing, can be used in the development of software systems. Whereas musicians use chords and notes, software designers draw class and sequence diagrams. However, nothing can be accomplished without skilled people, and phases and notations together with proper guidelines make it possible for them to construct outputs in manageable pieces.

A recording of a musical tune cannot succeed in chaos. Let us imagine a situation in which musicians have gathered together in a recording session: They have tuned the recording equipment and instruments, and everything seems to be ready for recording—except that nobody has composed and arranged the songs to be played. There are rare exceptions, true, when such an arbitrary, chaotic method has produced high-quality output, and talented individuals have managed to create a record in a recording studio nearly from scratch. In most cases, the bigger the orchestra, and the more demanding the musical tunes, the more a successful recording session requires discipline, phases, and a means for communication.

Based on our experiences, the same applies to software development.

REFERENCES

[Aalto and Jaaksi 94]   Aalto, J.-M. and A. Jaaksi. "Object-Oriented Development of Interactive Systems with OMT++." In *TOOLS 14, Technology of Object-Oriented Languages & Systems*, edited by Ege R., Singh M., Meyer B., 205-218. Prentice Hall, 1994.

[ANSI 98]   SQL3 Standard Working Draft (ANSI X3H2-93-091/YOK-003) ftp://jerry.ece.umassd.edu/isowg3/dbl/BASE-docs.

[Atkinson et al. 89]   Atkinson, M., F. Bancilhon, D. DeWitt, K. Dittrich, D. Maier, and S. Zdonik. *The Object-Oriented Database System Manifesto*. Proceedings of the International Conference in Deductive and Object-Oriented Databases, Kyoto, Japan, 1989.

[Bass et al. 97]   Bass, Len, Paul Clements, Shalom Cohen, and Linda Northrop. "Product Line Practice Workshop Report." (CMU/SEI-97-TR-003) Carnagie Mellon University, 1997.

299

[Boehm 88]   Boehm, B. W. "A spiral model of software
                     development and enhancement." *IEEE
                     Computer* 21, 5 (1988): 61-72.

[Brooks 95]   Brooks, Frederick P. Jr. *The Mythical Man-
                     Month : Essays on Software Engineering.*
                     Addison-Wesley, 1995.

[Cattell 94]   Cattell, R. G. G. *Object Data Management.*
                     (ISBN: 0-201-53092-9) Addison-Wesley, 1992.

[Coleman et. al 94] Coleman, D., P. Arnold, S. Bodoff, C. Dollin,
                     H. Gilchrist, F. Hayes, and P. Jeremaes.
                     *Object-Oriented Development. The Fusion
                     Method.* Prentice Hall. 1994.

[Committee 90]   Committee for Advanced DBMS Function.
                     "Third-Generation Database System
                     Manifesto." ACM Press Sigmod Record,
                     volume 19, no. 3 (September 1990).

[Coutaz 87]   Coutaz, J. "PAC, an Object Oriented Model
                     for Dialog Design." In *Human-Computer
                     Interaction: INTERACT Ô87*, edited by
                     H. J. Bullinger and B. Shackel, 431-436.
                     Elsevier Science Publishers, 1987.

[Fowler 97]   Fowler, M. and K. Scott. *Uml Distilled :
                     Applying the Standard Object Modeling
                     Language.* Addison-Wesley, 1997.

[Gamma et al. 95]   Gamma, E., R. Helm, R. Johnson, and
                     J. Vlissides. *Design Patterns: Elements of
                     Reusable Object-Oriented Software.* Addison-
                     Wesley, 1995.

[Gartner 97]   Gartner Group. "1996 DBMS Market
                     Shakeout: The Big Four DBMS Vendors."
                     Burton, Research Note (1997).

[Gilb 88]   Gilb, Tom. *Principles of Software Engineering
                     Management.* Addison-Wesley, 1988.

[Jaaksi 95]   Jaaksi, A. "Implementing Interactive
                     Applications in C++." *Software Practice &
                     Experience*, volume 25, no. 3 (March 1995):
                     271-289.

[Jaaksi 97]   Jaaksi, A. "Object-Oriented Development of
                     Interactive Systems." Doctoral Thesis, Tamper
                     University of Technology, Finland, 1997.

[Jaaksi 98a]   Jaaksi, A. "A Method for Your Object-Oriented
                     Project." *Journal of Object-Oriented
                     Programming*, volume 10, no. 8 (January
                     1998): 17-25.

[Jaaksi 98b]   Jaaksi, A. "Our Cases with Use Cases,"
                     Journal of Object-Oriented Programming,
                     volume 10, No. 9 (February 1998): 58-65.

[Jacobson et al. 92] Jacobson, I., M. Christerson, P. Jonsson, and
                     G. Övergaard. *Object-Oriented Software
                     Engineering: A Use Case Driven Approach*.
                     Addison-Wesley, 1992.

[Jacobson et al. 97] Jacobson, Ivar, Martin Griss, and Patrik
                     Jonsson. *Software Reuse: Architecture,
                     Process and Organization for Business
                     Success*. Addison-Wesley, 1997.

[Krasner and Pope 88] Krasner, G. E. and S. T. Pope. "A Cookbook
                     for Using the Model-View-Controller User
                     Interface Paradigm in Smalltalk-80." *Journal
                     of Object-Oriented Programming*,
                     (August/September, 1988): 26-49.

[Kruchten 95]   Kruchten, P. B. "The 4+1 View Model of
                     Architecture." *IEEE Software* , (November
                     1995): 42-50.

[Lakos 96]   Lakos, John. *Large-scale C++ Software
                     Design*. Addison-Wesley, 1996.

[Maher et al. 96]   Maher, A., J. Kuusela, and J. Zieger. *Object-
                     Oriented Technology for Teal-Time Systems:
                     A Practical Approach using OMT and
                     Fusion*. Prentice Hall, 1996.

[Mowbrau/Malveau 97] Mowbrau, Thomas J. and Raphael C.
                     Malveau. *CORBA Design Patterns*. John
                     Wiley & Sons, 1997.

[ODMG 97]   *The Object Database Standard: ODMG 2.0*.
                     Morgan Kaufmann Publishers (ISBN: 1-55860-
                     463-4).

[Rumbaugh et al. 91]	Rumbaugh, J., M. Blaha, W. Premerlani, F. Eddy, and W. Lorensen. *Object-Oriented Modeling and Design*. Prentice Hall, 1991.
[Ulrich and Eppinger 95]	Ulrich, Karl T. and Steven D. Eppinger. *Product Design and Development*. McGraw-Hill, 1995.
[UML 98]	Unified Modeling Language version 1.1 at http://www.rational.com/uml/index.shtml.
[Wills 96]	Wills, A. "Abstract Realism: Beginning with a model and refining toward a design." *Object Expert*, volume 1(2) (1996): 29-33.

INDEX

303